Python for the Life Sciences

A Gentle Introduction to Python for Life Scientists

Alexander Lancaster
Gordon Webster

Apress®

Python for the Life Sciences: A Gentle Introduction to Python for Life Scientists

Alexander Lancaster
Amber Biology, Cambridge, MA, USA

Gordon Webster
Amber Biology, Cambridge, MA, USA

ISBN-13 (pbk): 978-1-4842-4522-4
https://doi.org/10.1007/978-1-4842-4523-1

ISBN-13 (electronic): 978-1-4842-4523-1

Managing Director, Apress Media LLC: Welmoed Spahr
Acquisitions Editor: Celestin Suresh John
Development Editor: James Markham
Coordinating Editor: Aditee Mirashi

Cover designed by eStudioCalamar

Cover image designed by Freepik (www.freepik.com)

Distributed to the book trade worldwide by Springer Science+Business Media New York, 233 Spring Street, 6th Floor, New York, NY 10013. Phone 1-800-SPRINGER, fax (201) 348-4505, e-mail orders-ny@springer-sbm.com, or visit www.springeronline.com. Apress Media, LLC is a California LLC and the sole member (owner) is Springer Science + Business Media Finance Inc (SSBM Finance Inc). SSBM Finance Inc is a **Delaware** corporation.

For information on translations, please e-mail rights@apress.com, or visit http://www.apress.com/rights-permissions.

Apress titles may be purchased in bulk for academic, corporate, or promotional use. eBook versions and licenses are also available for most titles. For more information, reference our Print and eBook Bulk Sales web page at http://www.apress.com/bulk-sales.

Any source code or other supplementary material referenced by the author in this book is available to readers on GitHub via the book's product page, located at www.apress.com/978-1-4842-4522-4. For more detailed information, please visit http://www.apress.com/source-code.

Printed on acid-free paper

To our families

Table of Contents

TABLE OF CONTENTS

About the Authors

Alexander Lancaster is a Research Scholar at the Ronin Institute, a visiting scholar at the University of Sydney, and a Partner at Amber Biology, a digital biology research firm in Cambridge, Massachusetts. Alex holds a PhD in evolutionary biology at the University of California, Berkeley, and also holds degrees in physics and electrical engineering. He has worked in research and development in both Australia and the United States with a major focus on evolutionary and systems biology. He has also worked extensively in the fields of artificial life, complex adaptive systems, computational biology, and genomics. He has held research and faculty positions in academia as well as R&D positions in the broadcasting and IT industries.

Alex has published many peer-reviewed papers and is interested in solving problems in biology using evolutionary and complex systems approaches. He has done pioneering work in this area as a co-developer of the open-source agent-based modeling toolkit, Swarm, one of the first tools for large-scale modeling of collective behavior in biology and beyond.

Gordon Webster is a Research Scholar at the Ronin Institute and a Partner at Amber Biology. After completing a PhD in biophysics and structural biology at the University of London, Gordon has worked in life science R&D in both Europe and the United States, with a particular emphasis on molecular engineering and computational biology. In academic and commercial environments ranging from universities and medical schools to small venture capital-funded startups and global pharmaceutical companies, he has served in a diversity of roles from research faculty to company vice president.

Gordon is the author of numerous original scientific articles and patents and has created and managed some very successful research partnerships with industrial, academic, and government organizations. He initiated and managed the first translational oncology clinical trial at a multinational pharmaceutical company and has coached and led research project teams in large matrix organizations, as well as large, distributed teams of scientists, software developers, and technical specialists, working together across multiple time zones.

About the Technical Reviewers

Sanika Bhide is a life science data expert with rich experience in big data analytics for disease genetics, genomics, microarray, and next-generation sequencing data. She has worked on data science initiatives for pharmacogenomics and clinical decision support systems like IBM Watson leveraging NLP, ML, and AI approaches. She loves to solve complex data science problems in biology leveraging R and Python.

Sanika has a PhD in health sciences from the University of Pune, India. She is an active member of the Stanford initiative for Women in data science (WiDS) and has contributed to many local meetups and national conferences in data science.

Apurva Naik has been working as a data scientist for the past 3 years, solving problems in the real estate, life sciences, and financial services domains. Python has been her tool of choice for most tasks since it is versatile, powerful, and easy to implement so that she has enough bandwidth left to focus on the business use case.

Apurva holds a PhD in chemical engineering from the University of Mumbai. This gym rat and coffee addict lives in Pune with her husband and daughter.

Acknowledgments

Gordon would like to acknowledge his lovely (and patient) wife Jennifer and his two wonderful boys Benji and Toby, all of whom have supported him tirelessly and with good cheer while he was writing this book.

Alex would like to thank his family Jessica and William for supporting him during the longer-than-expected gestation of this book. Alex would also like to thank Barismo in Arlington for excellent pour-overs and Chez Gordon in Cambridge for excellent Americanos. He also thanks Bill Tozier for making him and Gordon aware of Leanpub where they published the first edition of their book.

Alex and Gordon would finally like to acknowledge the amazing, international Python community that has developed and nurtured their favorite programming language and made it into the awesome and versatile computational tool that it is – and of course, you the reader – for joining us on our adventures in Python-land. We hope you enjoy the ride!

Praise for *Python for the Life Sciences*

Fun, entertaining, witty, and darn useful. A magical portal to the big data revolution.

**—Sandro Santagata, Assistant Professor in Pathology,
Harvard Medical School**

With *Python for the Life Sciences*, Lancaster and Webster have provided a comprehensive introduction to using Python for computational biology. Biologists use Python for data wrangling, statistical inference, and developing mathematical models, and *PftLS* provide guidance on all three of these application areas. Notably, Lancaster and Webster bring the sage advice of experienced software developers to the table – they share bits of trivia and historical context that make programming fun and make the occasional quirks of Python/Unix more understandable. This is not a superficial introduction, and careful readers will emerge with a deep understanding of Python, rather than as simple users. It is a lovely book with humor and perspective.

**—John Novembre, Associate Professor of Human Genetics,
University of Chicago and MacArthur Fellow**

Alex and Gordon's enthusiasm for Python is contagious. Their book is specifically written for those who understand they could greatly benefit from some training in computer programming. This addition to their academic research will be invaluable. The various chapters take you through a combined tour of Python and the multitude of biological issues it is relevant to. This is not just a "recipe" book for how to use Python nor a how to book on advanced tools but a way to jumpstart your imagination.

**—Glenys Thomson, Professor of Integrative Biology,
University of California, Berkeley**

Informatics is a key component of modern biological science, and programming skills are essential for the modern life sciences researcher. Even if one does not write programs, the ability to read and understand code is becoming as important as being able to read a published paper. Webster and Lancaster's *Python for the Life Sciences* is an excellent tutorial for both programming novices and experienced coders who wish to learn Python.

—Steven J. Mack, Assistant Scientist, Children's Hospital Oakland Research Institute

Down the Rabbit Hole

"Begin at the beginning," the King said, very gravely,

"and go on till you come to the end: then stop."

Our aim in this book is to teach you the basics of Python using examples familiar to life scientists from the very first chapters. Are you ready to find out how to use Python to *automate* lab calculations, *search* for *gene promoter sequences*, *rotate* a *molecular bond*, *drive* a 96-well plate *robot*, *build* a cellular toggle *switch*, *model* animal coat *pattern formation*, *grow* a virtual *plant*, *simulate* a flu *epidemic*, or *evolve* populations? If so, you've come to the right place. Ready to go down the rabbit hole? Let's begin…

Prologue

Welcome to the Kingdom of Nerdia

"But I want to write code," declared Alice. "Being able to write code could help me enormously with my research. There's only so much you can do with a hand calculator and a spreadsheet."

"Pahh!" exclaimed the Mad Hatter. "You're a biologist and everyone knows that real biologists don't write code."

Amid the uneasy silence that settled around the table, Alice appeared both angry and unconvinced.

"Python!" she uttered suddenly. "I'm going to learn Python and there's nothing you can say to talk me out of it!"

Who are you?

You are probably a life scientist working in an academic or commercial research environment, and your best friends in the lab (apart from your real friends, your iPhone, and the bobble-head Charles Darwin action figure that hangs above your bench) are probably your calculator and your Excel spreadsheets.[1] You've likely never written much if any computer code but you have wished on many occasions that you knew how to, since you know that it could help you enormously in your work.

Alas, computer programming was not a core component of the life science curriculum in your college and graduate school experience, and now that you're already

---

[1]Excel is a trademark of Microsoft Inc., and just for the record, we have nothing against spreadsheets – they're great for many things. They're just not always the optimal tool for lots of the kind of stuff you might want to do as a biologist.

committed to your deep dive down the research rabbit hole, it's hard to imagine having the time or the energy to learn computer programming at this point in your career (especially since all those pending grants, presentations, and research reports are just not going to write themselves). This at least is who we hope you are, since that's the kind of person who's most likely to put their hand in their pocket and fork over some cash to buy our book.

Who are you not?

You are probably not already an experienced bioinformatician, computational biologist, computer scientist, or experienced programmer. If you are, then your needs are likely already being met by the ton of great books that exist for duly anointed code gurus such as yourself. Our humble book is very unlikely to teach you anything you don't already know about programming or Python for that matter.

You are also probably *not* a computer scientist or programmer looking to learn some biology through the avenue of the computer programming paradigm that you are already so familiar with. If you were hoping for this, then we're afraid you're looking in the wrong place. This book assumes that you pretty much already know the biology and just need some help and encouragement to learn how to be able to get going writing code to help you with your life science research.

So in summary then

- If you're already an experienced computer head, coder type looking to enhance your computer skills or learn some biology, move along, nothing to see here.

- If you're an experienced life scientist with little or no exposure to computer programming who wants a really fast and intuitive introduction to writing code so that you can get up and running and using it in your research as soon as possible, well pull up a seat my friend because you've come to the right place!

Why Python?

Python[2] is one of the most popular and rapidly growing computer programming languages. You can use it for everything from the tiniest tasks such as a simple script of a few lines of code for reading and processing a data file from a lab instrument to large-scale research projects such as the development of Monte Carlo simulations for exploring protein folding.[3]

Did we mention that Python is free!

Yes, for zero down and zero payments of zero dollars, you can get the same official Python distribution that is used at NASA, and at Industrial Light & Magic, Google, and a host of other major organizations, the mere mention of whose names should leave you awestruck, breathless, and wondering how come you waited so long to jump on the Python bandwagon.

Not only is Python free, but the good news is that if your computer is an Apple Mac or Linux machine, there's probably already a Python distribution installed on your machine. If you're on Windows or some other operating system that we haven't mentioned already, fear not – there's very likely a simple, self-installing Python distribution for your computer that you can download from the Internet and install in next to no time.

Python code can be run as is, as soon as you have written it. Unlike some other programming languages, there's no need for the programmer to compile the code into an executable format that your computer can run. All of this is taken care of for you, under the hood as it were. This makes writing, testing, and tweaking your code much easier, since traditional, compiled languages require that the code be recompiled every time it is changed.

In contrast with some other programming languages that enforce more advanced and harder-to-learn code-writing styles such as object-oriented programming (OOP), Python also allows you (for code projects where it's more appropriate) to write the kind of simple, procedural code that you're probably used to seeing if you've ever

---

[2]www.python.org/

[3]https://conference.scipy.org/scipy2010/slides/jan_meinke_protein_folding.pdf

played around with programming languages like BASIC or C. All of this makes Python incredibly versatile, since it allows you to write and test your code very quickly and to use it even for very small, simple tasks that would be rather onerous to implement in some other programming languages.

Stuff Gordon Says …

Python is such a useful and versatile programming language, capable of helping you out in so many situations, that I like to refer to it as "The Swiss Army Knife of Programming Languages".

How to Use This Book

The chapters in this book will take you on a kind of guided tour both of the Python programming language and of the biology that we implement with it, with beginning chapters on scales of space and time at the very small and fast (e.g., the nanometer and nanosecond scales of protein dynamics) and ending chapters on the large and slow (e.g., the vast swath of a natural ecosystem and the generational timescales of its evolution).

As far as possible in this book, we endeavor to always be teaching Python programming in the context of biology, rather than introducing you to the programming language and only later following up with biological examples of its usage. Sometimes of course, we will, of necessity, have to stray from the path of pure biology (may the gods of biology have mercy upon our souls), but it will be restricted to those occasions where a little dash of something else is essential in order that you the biologist can get the most out of your Python programming.

It is our aim to get you excited about using computation in your research and where possible to jumpstart your imagination with respect to how you might use it. We want to convey a sense of how computation can aid you in your research, how versatile the

Python language can be in biology, and how wide is the spectrum of quantitative biology research problems that can be tackled using this wonderful programming language.

There is, as we have already said, a plethora of more comprehensive books on using Python in areas like bioinformatics and computational biology, whose discussions are generally focused on more advanced tools and libraries specific to these areas, **but this is not that kind of book**. We do discuss some of these areas, but this book is really designed to give the biologists with no coding experience the tools, confidence, and inspiration to start crafting their own Python solutions for the challenges that they face in their research. If you consider one of those more specialized books to be the equivalent of a full-blown meal in one specific area of biology, this book is more like a tasting menu or a life science tapas if you will.

So if you want to find out how to use Python to automate your basic lab calculations, search a genome for gene promoter sequences, perform a rotation of a molecular bond, build a data processing pipeline for next-generation sequencing, drive a robot or lab instrument to handle 96-well plates, simulate a noisy cellular toggle switch, or to try your hand at modeling animal coat pattern formation, plant growth, a flu pandemic, or the evolution of a population of organisms, then this just might be the book for you!

In order to give the reader a little preview of what's to come, at the beginning of each chapter, you will see a table that summarizes the coverage of Python topics and biology topics in the chapter you are about to read, like this:

	Declaring variables, print, comments, indented code and code blocks, numerical variables, integers, floating points, exponentials, strings, types, duck typing, conditionals, functions
	Biochemistry, buffers, molarity, molecular weight, molar volume

If you ever need to refer back to a chapter, you can use this brief summary as a reminder of the topics covered in any given chapter and also as a set of searchable keywords to help you find stuff you're looking for in the book.

You will notice that **the early chapters in the book are heavier in Python and lighter in biology**, since these chapters handle a lot of the up-front Python learning that is necessary to get the reader familiar and capable with the language. In the later chapters of the book, you will see a lot of Python that you may already have seen earlier, but being used in a new context. In a sense then, the chapters broadly run the spectrum of emphasizing Python education early on to emphasizing Python inspiration later in the book. Remember that our goal here is not only to give the life scientist reader a solid foundation in Python but also to inspire the reader to use Python in their own work, by demonstrating some of the many ways that it can be used in life science research. Like we said already – Python is truly the Swiss Army knife of programming languages!

This is not Your Grandmother's Scientific Programming Textbook

We aim to present the computational representation of biological data and biological systems in a lively and dynamic way that makes it easy to follow the text and to learn from the examples. We know that you're not a computer scientist (because if you were, you wouldn't need this book) and your goal in reading this book is to learn enough to use computation in your research, not to become a computer scientist yourself. We also understand that you're busy and that you're probably not ready to put your research on hold for a semester while you complete a course on programming. We aim to get you to where you want to be as quickly and efficiently as possible.

The examples in this book each represent a biological application or principle, but they are also brief and simple enough not get in the way of teaching you the major elements of the Python programming language and how you might apply them to your own research. In the chapters on agent-based models, for example, even if you've never had any prior exposure to agent-based models, the examples are simple enough that they don't eclipse the reader's efforts to understand their implementation in Python.

Why we Wrote This Book

Despite the great value and utility that computer programming can bring to life science research, it is, alas, still not a core component of the life science curriculum in college, unless you're taking more specialized courses in bioinformatics or in computational or systems biology. Across the span of our collective decades of experience in academic and commercial life science research, we have seen a lot of biologists trying to squeeze the square pegs of calculators and Excel spreadsheets into the round holes of research problems that would be much more effectively addressed with coded scripts, algorithms, or software applications.

Our Philosophy and Approach to Writing This Book

All Python, all the time: With just a few exceptions, we stick to just one language, Python, throughout. Yes, we are aware that there are tools or languages that might arguably be considered "better" or more efficient for some computational biology tasks than Python. We also have nothing against any of the other great languages used in computational biology such as R, Java, Perl, or Ruby: we use many of them regularly ourselves. So if you disagree with us and you'd like to start a flame war about this on some Internet coding forum, by all means have at it. Just be aware that we probably won't hear about it unless it makes the nightly news, because *we won't be there* :-)

Eclectic, not comprehensive: Our choice of examples is unapologetically eclectic – a reflection of our own backgrounds in structural and computational biology (GW) and evolutionary biology and complex systems (AL). This breadth has enabled us to cover the gamut of life science: from molecular modeling and next-generation sequencing to agent-based models and evolutionary genetics. The examples also range from the very practical (NGS pipelines and lab automation) to the more theoretical and conceptual (Turing patterns and L-systems). But even in the more abstract models of the later chapters, we try to keep a *practical approach to theory* by focusing on the code itself. This is rather different to much published research and texts that often start with high-level theory and written descriptions of algorithms, but relegate code to appendixes. Given our aim to provide the biologist with enough of a foundation in Python to be able to use it in their own research, we have skipped over some of the more arcane and advanced features of Python in order to keep the book focused and constrained to a more readable length. Once you have the basic foundation of Python under your belt, we would encourage you to venture further afield and dive into other cool Python features like decorators and object introspection. For the purposes of this book however, we will mostly limit our discussion to the kind of nuts-and-bolts, everyday Python that will probably end up being the great majority of the code that you write – at least in the beginning.

Practical, iterative, and bottom-up: In our experience, biologists are great at iterating based upon past experience and extrapolating from simple cases. In most of our examples, we jump straight in, introduce the biology, and show you the code as quickly as possible. Starting with a simple code examples to which we progressively add more complications mirrors the thought process of most scientists. *Think of this as the "back-of-the-envelope" approach*: once you've mastered simple examples, it's much easier to be motivated to build on it, to then tackle bigger problems. Our approach assumes that we're all at the bottom of a mountain, learning to climb it together, rather than us standing on the top and barking orders on where and how to climb.

A simulation-rich approach: While we cover the kind of practical and mathematical aspects of parsing and analyzing data that you would expect in a book like this, we also have a major focus on generative simulation-based models. It is our belief that in some knowledge domains, simulation builds intuition much faster than mathematical explanations, and this is often left out of introductory books in computational biology, especially those that also teach programming. In addition, especially in biology, code representations used in simulations are generally much closer conceptually to the phenomena being modeled, facilitating that all-important cognitive leap between the biology and its conceptual representation in code. Furthermore, simulation encourages one to "play" around with the model to see what happens: we believe *that play is essential to learning*!

Living with noise: Studying and working with biological systems requires some degree of familiarity and comfort with their innate noise, heterogeneity, and just downright "messiness." Breaking from the traditional approaches of most introductory texts therefore, in this book you will find that we devote a fair amount of space to the use of Python to explore stochastic models and noisy data at different levels of biology.

Writing code is part of doing quantitative biology: We sometimes encounter biologists who like building models or even developing algorithms as part of their research, but profess no love for actually writing code. This often sounds something like "I'm not a programmer, but I do design algorithms," with the not-so-subtle implication somewhere in all of this, that writing the code is some kind of lowly mechanical task akin to laying bricks according to an architect's blueprint. We believe that this is a meaningless distinction: *the code is the algorithm and vice versa*. Writing code forces you to make all your implicit assumptions explicit. The computer admits no ambiguity, and in a real sense, writing the code forces you to understand the system you are describing at a very intimate and granular level.

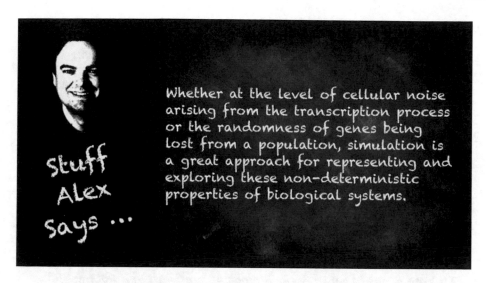

Whether at the level of cellular noise arising from the transcription process or the randomness of genes being lost from a population, simulation is a great approach for representing and exploring these non-deterministic properties of biological systems.

Stuff Alex Says ...

Biology is not all "Big Data": data science and Big Data are now all the rage in the life sciences, and we introduce some of the building blocks of these data science approaches in biology (e.g., in Chapter 4 on Bayes' theorem and in Chapter 8 on next-generation sequencing). Data is not knowledge, however, and it is our belief that models are essential frameworks with which to organize data, to reason about it, and thereby to transform it into knowledge. The lackluster returns on investment in Big Data approaches within the life science sector stand in inverse proportion to the burgeoning levels of investment in these approaches. It is our belief that the way to generate more real knowledge and biological insight is by emphasizing mechanistic and conceptual modeling over the more traditional (and universally popular) data analytics approaches. It is also for this reason that we have devoted more space to modeling approaches than is typically found in introductory books on programming for biology.

Come for the Biology, Stay for the Code

Well, you're still here which means that you're probably still interested, so why don't we take a sneak peek at the chapter outline of the book. Although we have written the book to be read linearly, most of the *core Python concepts are covered in the first seven chapters*. So it's possible to start with those seven chapters and then sample the others tapas style.

Prologue: *Welcome to the kingdom of Nerdia*

1. **Getting started with Python:** *Setting yourself up to use Python*

   We get you started on your journey, all the fun details on getting your very own Python environment set up.

2. **Python at the lab bench:** *The fundamentals of the Python language*

   We introduce some Python fundamentals and show you how to ditch those calculators and spreadsheets and let Python relieve the drudgery of basic lab calculations (freeing up more valuable time to drink coffee and play *Minecraft*).

3. **Making sense of sequences:** *Biological sequences and Python data structures*

   We introduce basic Python string and character handling and demonstrate Python's innate awesomeness for handling nucleic acid and protein sequences.

4. **A statistical interlude:** *Of Bayes' theorem and biomarkers*

   Here we discuss Bayes' theorem and implement it in Python, illustrating in the process why even your doctor might not always estimate your risk of cancer correctly.

5. **Open doors to your data:** *Reading, parsing, and handling biological data files*

   Did we already mention how great Python is for handling biological sequence data? In this chapter we expand our discussion to sequence file formats like FASTA.

6. **Finding needles in haystacks:** *Regular expressions for genomic and sequences*

   In this chapter we show how to search even the largest of biological sequences quickly and efficiently using Python regular expressions – and in the process, blow the lid off the myth that Python has to be slow because it is an interpreted language.

19. **Retracing life's footsteps:** *Evolutionary dynamics with the Wright-Fisher model*

    In which we use the Wright-Fisher model to demonstrate natural selection in action and show how being the "fittest" doesn't always mean that you will "win." Think Homer Simpson winning a game of musical chairs.

    Epilogue: *Because breaking up is hard to do*

FAQ

I have never written a line of code in my life. Will I be able to follow this book and the examples contained in it?

This book assumes **zero** knowledge of writing code. It was written with people like you in mind. Aside from having some advanced training in biology itself, the only prerequisite knowledge needed to use this book is the level of high school math that is needed to matriculate to a bachelor's degree program in biology at a college.

I'm a life scientist with a lot of experience writing code in other programming languages like Java and C. Would this book be useful for somebody like me?

You would probably find that the book spends a lot of time explaining concepts that you already understand, like the differences between integer and floating point arithmetic, for example, or object-oriented programming. If you've never used Python however and you're willing to skip over the stuff you already know, you might find this book to be a decent Python primer for a life scientist with coding experience in other languages.

I'm a computer scientist looking to learn some biology. Would this book be useful for somebody like me?

No. The basic programming concepts presented in this introductory text would all be material that you already know, and this book is not intended to be a biology textbook. In fact, almost the only assumption that we make about our readers is that they already have some training and experience in the life sciences. Because the book covers such a wide range of biological examples, we do briefly recap some relevant biology needed in each chapter to help orient the reader, but we don't spend time explaining basic biological concepts that are typically covered in college-level biology textbooks.

They say that Python is too slow and inefficient to use for large computational tasks. Is this true?

Is this the same "they" that say you can develop extraordinary night vision by eating lots of carrots?[4] Both authors of this book have used Python for computationally intensive research problems, for example, simulating the use of a novel next-generation sequencing laboratory protocol on the human genome. Yes, the standard Python distribution is not as fast under some circumstances as some other languages that are compiled (like C), but there are many approaches to using Python in ways that can raise its performance to a level that is at least in the same ballpark as these faster languages, if not equal to them. One metric that is often ignored in these kind of "who's fastest" discussions is the time that it takes to actually write the code. Python is a way more productive coding platform than many other languages (like C) in terms of how quickly you can get your code written, tested, and debugged. So even ignoring any attempts to optimize the performance of your Python code, let's say that Bob spends a month writing the code in C and it runs in a day, whereas Alice spends a day writing the code in Python and it runs in a month (completely hypothetical figures by the way, used just to illustrate a point). Who is better off? We would personally give Alice the nod since she now has a month in which she can do a load more work, or maybe even just hit the beach while Bob is still stuck at his computer writing code! For multiple calculations of course, Bob would be better off, and in this scenario, it would behoove Alice to spend some time optimizing her code (e.g., by compiling the most CPU-intensive parts of her code to C using a tool like Cython[5]) and/or her processing approach (e.g., by exploring some form of processing parallelism[6]) to increase her computational efficiency. We actually take some time to address this fallacy about Python always being slow in Chapter 6 on using Python regular expressions for next-generation sequencing – a chapter by the way with origins in a real-world research project that one of us (GW) undertook using Python.

---

[4]http://gizmodo.com/youve-been-lied-to-about-carrots-your-whole-life-becau-1124868510/1126108142

[5]http://cython.org/

[6]https://docs.python.org/2/library/multiprocessing.html

Some of the examples in this book appear to be reinventing the wheel, writing code that already exists in the many great code libraries that the Python community has created for doing biology with Python. Wouldn't you encourage your readers to just use these code libraries instead?

For their actual projects, of course. But the goal of this book is to teach life scientists how to write code. Along with writing code comes the ability to understand code. A big part of being a programmer is the ability to work with other people's code as well, modifying it, extending it, and so on. There are already plenty of books that teach the use of these libraries, and many of them are also extremely well documented. But at some point in your career working with all this code, you need to be able to understand what it means or it's all a black box. So sure, in Chapter 11, for example, we show you how to implement the kind of simple linear algebra needed to rotate a group of atoms around a covalent bond, but in practice you would almost certainly use one of the excellent math libraries like NumPy[7] or SciPy[8] to do this.

References and Further Exploration

At the end of each chapter, we have a section containing any references we make within the text and pointers for exploring further. We kick it off in this Prologue with some general pointers that have inspired us to explore the worlds of both biology and code. Most of them are not specific to any chapter. They are generally fun reads that will help prime your mind for computational approaches to biology.

For playful introductions to the worlds of ***computation, biology, and music***, the works of Douglas Hofstadter[9] can't be beaten. *Gödel, Escher, Bach: an Eternal Golden Braid* (Basic Books, 1979) and *Metamagical Themas* (Basic Books, 1985) are two standouts. Another good, although more technical, book in the same spirit of *GEB* is Gary Flake's *The Computational Beauty of Nature*[10] (MIT Press, 1998) covering nonlinear dynamics, complex systems, and other topics like game theory and cellular automata.

---

[7]www.numpy.org/
[8]www.scipy.org/
[9]http://cogs.indiana.edu/people/profile.php?u=dughof
[10]https://mitpress.mit.edu/books/computational-beauty-nature

Bioinformatics and genomics are obviously very rapidly changing fields, and much of the latest stuff is covered online rather than in texts. Two places have emerged as being standout places to share advice and answers to vexing computational biology questions: BioStar[11] (focusing on bioinformatics with an evolutionary slant) and SEQanswers[12] (which tends to focus more specifically on tools for next-generation sequencing).

Modeling, especially mathematical modeling, has a long pedigree, although most of the classic texts generally omit stochastic models. John Casti's *Alternate Realities* (Wiley & Sons, 1989) and it's two-volume follow-up *Reality Rules*[13] (Wiley & Sons, 1997) both have a free-wheeling approach to modeling across many domains (not just biology) written in an engaging style. For a good, relatively recent introduction to biological modeling that includes more stochastic approaches is Russell Schwartz's *Biological Modeling and Simulation*[14] (MIT Press, 2008).

The book that inspired many people to get interested in **evolutionary biology** is Richard Dawkins' classic, *The Blind Watchmaker* (Penguin, 1986). Whatever you think of Dawkins' politics, his exploration of morphological evolution through the program Biomorphs[15] is still a great and inspiring read.

And finally, as a scientist, researcher, or philosopher of any stripe, if you're looking for some really off-the-beaten-track meta-inspiration, look no further than Robert Pirsig's wonderful *Zen and the Art of Motorcycle Maintenance* (William Morrow, 1974).[16] It's a great read for anybody interested in the **philosophy behind the scientific method** and the ways in which we construct models of the physical world that we experience through our senses.

---

[11]www.biostars.org/
[12]seqanswers.com/
[13]www.wiley.com/WileyCDA/WileyTitle/productCd-0471184365.html
[14]mitpress.mit.edu/books/biological-modeling-and-simulation
[15]watchmakersuite.sourceforge.net/
[16]www.amazon.com/Zen-Art-Motorcycle-Maintenance-Inquiry/dp/0060589469

CHAPTER 1

Getting Started with Python

Setting Yourself Up to Use Python

Attached to the small bottle was a label bearing a set of instructions that said simply "DRINK ME."

"Hmmm. A self-installing executable that's also self-documenting," muttered Alice to herself as she examined the bottle. "Once I open this, who knows exactly how it will change things, and there's probably no easy way to go back to the way things were beforehand," she thought.

Torn between her anxiety about the consequences of opening the little bottle and her excitement about all of the wonderful places that it might take her, Alice paused just long enough to close all of her open applications and to try to remember how long ago it was that she did her last filesystem backup.

Then she opened the little bottle and drank deeply.

*The Python web site; Python versions; downloading Python; installing Python on macOS, Linux, and Windows; idle; installing **pip**; additional Python libraries, **numpy**; python editors*

Not a whole lot of biology going on in this chapter

© Alexander Lancaster and Gordon Webster 2019
A. Lancaster and G. Webster, *Python for the Life Sciences*, https://doi.org/10.1007/978-1-4842-4523-1_1

Getting Python on Your Computer

This is obviously the first step for the reader of this book, in order to be able to run your Python code. As far as editing your code goes, there are numerous options including using the kind of plain text editor that you probably already have on your computer. This is not an optimal solution by any means, but we'll talk more about what tools you might want to use to edit and manage your Python code, after we've dealt with the primary issue of actually getting a Python distribution on your computer.

For the purposes of our discussion, we're going to assume that your computer is an Apple Mac running Apple's macOS operating system, a platform with PC architecture running Microsoft's Windows operating system, or a machine running one of the many flavors of the GNU/Linux operating system. As of the time of writing of this book, this currently accounts for approximately 95% of all the desktop and laptop computers being used in the world.

For the purposes of this book, we are not specifically including any mobile platforms like smartphones and tablets in our discussion. There are some distributions of Python for these computing platforms as well, but most of them are still relatively immature, and in any case, mobile computing platforms come with a variety of additional features such as touch screens, accelerometers, and GPS that any mobile programming language must address and are beyond the scope of this book. Pretty much all of the basic Python covered in this book however is equally applicable to Python distributions on these platforms as well. If you are interested in mobile computing using Python, you might want to take a look at the very interesting Kivy[1] Python platform.

Wait – there's more than one Python?

At this point, it is worth inserting a little note about the different versions of Python that are out there. Just to be clear, we're not talking here about all of the flavors and implementations of Python that are alternatives to the official distribution. We're only talking about the official Python distribution that can be found at the Python web site.[2]

Back in 2008, a new major version of Python, Version 3.0, was launched. It included some (largely subtle) changes to the language that had the unfortunate effect of breaking Python's compatibility with a number of the most popular code libraries that many people were using in their code. This particularly impacted the scientific and technical community because

---

[1]https://kivy.org/#home
[2]www.python.org/

some of these libraries (like NumPy[3]) were core components of a great deal of the scientific and technical Python code being used around the world by the Python community.

For this reason, a very large proportion of the Python community was originally slow to adopt any of the 3.x versions of the official Python distribution, preferring to remain instead with the last official Python 2.x release which was Python 2.7. However, with Python 2.7.x being phased out in 2020, most of the holdouts have either converted or plan to convert before the phase out date (in the first edition, we were among those holdouts – no longer – this should make Guido happy).

What this all boils down to is that the Python code in this book has now been ported to using Python 3. With the looming discontinuation of Python 2.7, readers should download and use Python 3 to write and run the code presented in the book. (Moving from Python 3.x if you happen to have already learned Python 2.x is an incremental process that involves for the most part, just learning some subtle syntactical and behavioral differences between the two major versions.)

If you're curious enough to want to know more about this branching of Python versions, there's even a special page dedicated to this issue, at the official Python web site. The official view that is reflected on that page is that everybody should now be using Python 3.x, especially since many of the most important and widely used, third-party code libraries have now been updated to support it. There is however acknowledgment that not all of these issues have been resolved at the time of writing this book and that there are still legitimate reasons for some people to continue using Python 2.x.

Downloading a Python Distribution for Your Computer

Don't do this yet!

We mean it – really – **don't** do it!

Chances are that your machine already has a Python distribution on it, especially if you're using a Mac or a Linux machine. So **before** forging ahead and downloading Python from the official Python web site, be sure to check out the following sections that describe the best route to having a working Python distribution on your computer.

---

[3]`www.numpy.org/`

If after reading the section that applies to your type of computer (or if your computer is a different platform from the three major desktop/laptop platforms described here), you decide that you do need to download and install a Python distribution – you can find downloads and installation instructions for the official Python distribution on the Downloads[4] page at the Python web site. Remember also when you're choosing a version to download, we recommend using Python version 3.x.

Getting Python on a macOS Computer

If you're working on an Apple Mac, the good news is that you already have a Python distribution on your machine. Unfortunately, the default version is Python 2.7, so you will need install Python 3 separately alongside the existing Python distribution. So you will first need visit the Python site and download[5] the latest macOSX version and run the installer, which should install like any other standard macOS package. After this is complete, go to your *Applications* folder and open the *Utilities* subfolder. Inside that folder, you should find the *Terminal* application that opens a command line window on your desktop.

If you type python3 at the command line, you should see a welcome message in your terminal window, followed by the Python prompt indicating that the Python interpreter is ready to accept some input – something like this:

```
Python 3.7.2 (v3.7.2:9a3ffc0492, Dec 24 2018, 02:44:43)
[Clang 6.0 (clang-600.0.57)] on darwin
Type "help", "copyright", "credits" or "license" for more information.
>>>
```

If you want to quickly do a further check just to satisfy yourself that your Python distribution is working, try entering these two lines of code at the Python prompt (>>>) and hit return after each one.

```
>>> a = 4
>>> print(a)
```

---

[4]www.python.org/downloads/
[5]www.python.org/downloads/mac-osx/

You should see something like this:

```
4
>>>
```

One quick word of warning for macOS users – the Python distribution on your Mac is actually used by the macOS operating system for various housekeeping tasks, and it would be unwise to replace it with a different version of Python. Another elegant way to install Python 3.x is to create a virtual environment in which to run your new Python distribution in a way that will not impact any existing Python distributions or libraries on your machine. Creating virtual environments for Python is beyond the scope of this book, but if you're curious about how to do this, check out the documentation for the Python virtualenv[6] tool.

Getting Python on a Linux Computer

If you run any of the mainstream Linux distributions (e.g., Ubuntu,[7] Fedora,[8] Debian[9]), Python 2.7.x will almost certainly already be pre-installed, but you may need to install Python 3 separately (normally this is in a separate package called **python3** that can be installed in parallel with Python 2.7 – just as with macOSX). Since most of the users of Linux tend to be already a little familiar with the Unix command line, these instructions are a little less step-by-step than for other operating systems. Also, the exact way that different Linux distributions package and install software is so varied that a comprehensive guide is almost impossible. Suffice to say that to get the most of out of this book, you should use your Linux package manager to install the additional packages for **matplotlib** (for plotting), **NumPy** (Numeric Python), and **pip** (for installing packages from the PyPI repository, see the following section). For example, in Fedora the relevant packages are `python3-matplotlib`, `python3-numpy`, and `python3-pip`. Each of these distributions has graphical package management tools, a search on these packages should quickly reveal the particular package in question. Installing them from the command line is usually also fairly simple. For example, in Fedora you would run

```
$ sudo dnf install python3-matplotlib python3-numpy python3-pip
```

---

[6]https://pypi.python.org/pypi/virtualenv
[7]www.ubuntu.com/
[8]https://getfedora.org/
[9]www.debian.org/

For Ubuntu and Debian, `apt-get` is the equivalent tool, although the package names may be slightly different.

Getting Python on a Windows Computer

Unfortunately, Microsoft Windows does not come pre-packaged with a Python distribution in the way that Mac and Linux platforms do. Fortunately however, the good folks at python.org offer a set of easy-to-use Windows installers for pretty much any existing version of Python you could ever want. Just as there is more than one version of Python currently in current use, there is also more than one version of Windows in current use. For the purposes of this book, we are going to assume that you are not stranded in *Jurassic Park*, using a 400 MHz PC with 64MB RAM, running Windows 98. The instructions we provide will be based upon an installation under the current version of Windows at the time of writing this book, which is Windows 10.[10]

Our first stop to get Python on your Windows platform is obviously the Python web site.[2] The Python web site has a very large menu bar front and center on the home page, which contains a convenient link to the **Downloads** page. Clicking this link should display a pop-up menu in your browser offering you the option to download the current version of Python 3.x. Select the Python 3.x option and the download should begin automatically. Depending upon how you have your Windows system configured, the file (called something like *python-3.x.y.exe*) will normally be saved in your Downloads folder, should you need to find it again.

Once the file has finished downloading, you can run it to start the install. If you have admin privileges for your Windows machine, you should allow the default option of installing Python for all users, and it is recommended that you also check the box to add Python 3.x to your default PATH. Once you have selected these options, click "Install now" in the installer menu and answer yes to the question that asks if you wish to grant permission for the Python install to proceed. While Python is installing, you will see a "Setup Progress" with a green bar that shows you how the installation is progressing, and

---

[10]`www.microsoft.com/en-us/windows-10`

if all goes well, you will see a "Setup was successful" message. Once setup is complete, click the small "Close" button in the message window to exit the installer.

To make sure your Python 3.x installation worked correctly, use the Windows start menu to pull up the **Command Prompt** application and just type python at the prompt. If the install worked properly, you should find yourself in a Python shell and see a Python startup message that looks something like this:

```
Python 3.7.3 (v3.7.3:ef4ec6ed12, Mar 25 2019, 21:26:53) [MSC v.1916 32 bit
(Intel)] on win32
Type "help", "copyright", "credits" or "license" for more information.
>>>
```

To get out of the Python shell and back to the Windows command prompt, just type quit().

One word of caution for Windows users – you will have to separately install the excellent Python plotting library matplotlib[11] that we use in several chapters of the book. You can take a look at the subsequent section in this chapter on how to install additional Python modules using tools like the Python package manager pip, for instructions on how to do this, but if you are looking for a real "batteries-included" Python distribution that comes with a load of this useful, additional stuff bundled with it already, you might want to check out WinPython[12] (but you will probably want to make sure you download and install WinPython 3.x if you wish to stay completely in sync with the code examples in this book).

Using the IDLE Python Shell

IDLE[13] is a Python graphical user interface (GUI) that runs Python code in much the same kind of way that a terminal windows on Linux or a Mac, or the Windows command line tool, allows you to run shell commands that you type into it. IDLE even allows you to save your Python code in files and also to load and run those files. Among other things, most versions of IDLE will also color-code your Python code to highlight things like

---

[11]http://matplotlib.org/
[12]https://winpython.github.io/
[13]https://docs.python.org/2/library/idle.html

Python keywords, strings, method names, and so on, making your code easier to read and understand.

In its own way then, IDLE is in itself a very simple and bare-bones kind of integrated development environment (IDE). There are a number of really excellent IDEs available for Python, some of which are even free (like Python itself). If you start to embark on larger and more ambitious code projects, these more advanced IDEs can help you manage your code by handling issues like version control and packaging your code for distribution. Even beyond these advanced issues, they can provide a very comfortable and convenient framework in which to manage your code, by highlighting syntax and other errors in real time and helping you to manage dependencies between modules and, of course, the testing of your code. There are also lots of really nice code editors that aren't really IDEs in and of themselves, but which can be configured to function much like an IDE. In the next section, we will briefly mention some of these alternatives to using IDLE. We will also give you some recommendations of our own, but at the end of the day, the development environment that you will find most comfortable and convenient for you will probably depend as much as anything on your own personality and style of working.

To start IDLE on a Mac, open a Mac terminal window (if you don't already have it on your desktop dock, you can find **Terminal** in the **Utilities** folder in **Applications**) and type `idle`.

To start IDLE on a Linux computer, open a terminal window and type idle. On some popular Linux distributions (like Ubuntu), IDLE is included with the Python distribution, but is not installed by default. If this is the case, when you type idle, you get an error message or a nice informative message like this:

```
The program 'idle' is currently not installed. You can install it by
typing: sudo apt install idle
```

If you get a message like this, just do a `sudo apt install idle` (or `sudo dnf install python3-tools` if you're on Fedora) and enter the admin password to do the very quick installation of IDLE. If you get a message saying IDLE is not found at all, you will probably need to do the installation as we just described.

Once you have IDLE installed, you can retry typing idle in a terminal window and everything should work.

To get IDLE started on a Windows computer, just type **idle** in the Start menu search box, and if you have installed Python by following the instructions in the previous section, you should be able to click **IDLE (Python GUI)** in the search results.

As always, we recommend that you check out the extensive documentation at the official Python web site, which includes a detailed section on IDLE.[14]

Python Development Environments

There are numerous alternatives to IDLE if you're looking for a different development environment for Python, ranging from code editors like vim,[15] and the iconic emacs[16] editor (that is actually also a code interpreter in its own right), to full-featured IDEs replete with bells and whistles, such as the Eclipse IDE (with PyDev extensions)[17] and PyCharm[18] and GitHub's Atom.[19] Some of these like the emacs editor, beloved of computer geeks everywhere, have a fairly steep learning curve if you've never used them before. Some are overly heavy and feel a little like using a sledgehammer to crack a nut.

Your choice of Python development environment will depend very much on your personality, your tastes, and your own particular style of working. We would say *to each his own* when it comes to Python development environments, but if you would like a little guidance, we really like the PyCharm development environment[18] which, as well as being easy to install and use, is even free so long as you're okay using the free Community Edition.[20] There are a few more advanced professional software development features that the Community Edition lacks, but you would not need any of them in order to work through all of the Python projects that are described in this book. Best of all, the PyCharm Community Edition is available for Mac, Linux, and Windows. That's just our 10 cents worth on the subject, and please feel free to ignore us and find your own happy place from which to develop your Python code. To help you out, there's also a link to a list of IDEs for Python, hosted at the Python wiki, in the resources section at the end of the chapter.

---

[14]https://docs.python.org/2/library/idle.html

[15]www.vim.org/

[16]www.gnu.org/software/emacs/

[17]www.pydev.org/

[18]www.jetbrains.com/pycharm/

[19]https://ide.atom.io/

[20]www.jetbrains.com/pycharm/features/editions_comparison_matrix.html

Installing the Python Package Manager: pip

In this section we describe the steps to set up the nifty Python package manager: pip. Once you are able to access a command-line prompt via a terminal, these steps should be the same whether you are running on macOS, Linux, or Windows. pip is your gateway to the greater universe of Python packages outside the core libraries available from the Python Package Index (PyPI[21]). Although our book is largely focused on examples that use only the core Python and standard library, there are few places where some of these external packages are used. Firstly, you may already have pip installed (notably if you are running Linux, you should have already installed a package called something like python3-pip). *Since we are using Python 3, you'll want to be sure that you're using Python 3 version of pip, not the Python 2 version, which is specified by using the pip3 command.* To check, run the following from the command line:

```
$ pip3 -V
```

(On some systems you may need to use python3-pip pip as the command.) If you see something like this

pip 18.1 from /usr/lib/python3.7/site-packages/pip (python 3.7)

congratulations! you already have pip installed, and you need go no further. If not, you can use easy_install (which is part of the Python tools) to install pip:

```
$ easy_install-3.7 --user pip
```

Note that we use the option --user, this is important because it will install pip in the *user's* account, rather than the system Python installation, which the user will typically not be able to access unless they are an administrator. Installing packages using pip is very straightforward, for example:

```
$ pip3 install --user <package-name>
```

This will make the package available within the user's Python programs (again, note the use of the --user option). For more details on pip and installing packages than you can poke a stick at, see the *Python Packaging User Guide.*[22] Examples of pip in action are documented within the chapters in which individual packages first used (e.g., Chapter 8),

---

[21]pypi.python.org/
[22]packaging.python.org/installing/#installing-from-pypi

but if you want to get started right away, here is a one-liner that will install the two most heavily used external packages, NumPy and matplot in one hit:

```
$ pip3 install --user numpy matplotlib
```

Getting the Example Code

All of the code shown in the books is available in our handy-dandy GitHub repository[23]:

```
https://amberbiology.github.io/py4lifesci/
```

The preceding site has links to all the current code samples in both `.zip` and `tar.gz` formats. If you select the `.zip` file, the download will uncompress all the code examples into a location of your choosing. macOS should do this automatically, Windows users may need to download an archive manager like WinZip.[24] Linux users may be more comfortable using the `.tar.gz.` format.

You can also preview all the code samples here (also linked from the preceding site):

```
http://github.com/amberbiology/py4lifesci
```

For more advanced users already familiar with the `git` command-line tool,[25] you can keep to up to date with the code by *cloning* the repository directly into a directory of your choosing:

```
$ git clone https://github.com/amberbiology/py4lifesci.git
```

(You can also install and use GitHub Desktop[26] to clone the repository.)

The filename for each chapter has the following format:

```
PFTLS_Chapter_<Chapter_number>.py
```

---

[23]GitHub is the place where a good chunk of all open source software development (and a good chunk of open source scientific software) is done. It is a web site, a set of code repositories, and a development community.

[24]www.winzip.com/

[25]git-scm.com/book/en/v2/Getting-Started-The-Command-Line

[26]desktop.github.com/

Some chapters have more than one Python file, in those cases we append a subchapter number like so:

```
PFTLS_Chapter_<Chapter_number>_<Subchapter_number>.py
```

So it should be easy to locate the relevant example, for example, the code for the second chapter is

```
PFTLS_Chapter_02.py
```

To run this code, simply open the terminal of your choosing, change directories to wherever you unzipped the preceding code, and run the example:

```
cd <place-you-unzipped-code>
./PFTLS_Chapter_02.py
```

In the preceding text, we described how to install packages using "pip," but you can also download and install all the packages from PyPI needed for running all the examples by running the following command, after you "cloned" the repository:

```
cd <place-you-unzipped-code>
./setup.py develop
```

This has the additional benefit that it sets up the environment so you can run all the unit tests:

```
./setup.py test
```

References and Further Exploration

- The General Python FAQ[27]

- The Python on Windows FAQ[28]

- A list of the currently available Python integrated development environments,[29] hosted at the Python wiki

---

[27]docs.python.org/2.7/faq/general.html

[28]docs.python.org/2.7/faq/windows.html#how-do-i-run-a-python-program-under-windows

[29]wiki.python.org/moin/IntegratedDevelopmentEnvironments

CHAPTER 2

Python at the Lab Bench

The Fundamentals of the Python Language

"I am Professor Dodo, nice to meet you," said the dodo, his voice and the manner in which he leaned upon his cane, betraying his frailty and exhaustion.

"Nice to meet you too," said Alice. "Is it true that you still do all of your numerical work using a calculator and spreadsheets?" she asked.

"Oh my sweet child, why else do you think I'm always so weary?" the dodo replied. "I have experiments to run, grants to write, and presentations to give. Where amid all of that do you imagine that I might find the time to analyze the vast swaths of data that I generate daily in my research lab?"

"At the risk of sounding impertinent," said Alice with some degree of trepidation, "Are you at all familiar with the concept of extinction?"

*Declaring variables, **print**; comments; indented code and code blocks; numerical variables; integers; floating points; exponentials; strings; types; duck typing; conditionals; functions; integer and decimal arithmetic; Boolean variables; **True**, **False**, **if**, **elif**, **else**; comparison operators*

Biochemistry, buffers, molarity, molecular weight, molar volume

© Alexander Lancaster and Gordon Webster 2019
A. Lancaster and G. Webster, *Python for the Life Sciences*, https://doi.org/10.1007/978-1-4842-4523-1_2

Python is definitely your friend in the lab, so we're going to start off with that simple, daily lab stuff for which you would once have whipped out your electronic calculator with its tiny buttons seemingly designed for the fingers of children too young to even care about arithmetic. These days, it's more likely to be your smartphone you reach for, but you can put that away as well (that paused game of *Clash Of Empires III* will still be there at your next coffee break).

Declaring Variables in Python

Let's jump into Python by seeing how we declare the variables we want to use. To get things going, here's a bunch of simple numerical variable declarations that illustrate Python's variable declaration syntax and the basic Python number formats. They also illustrate the kind of variable names that are acceptable in Python – for example, you would soon discover the hard way that Python variable names cannot start with numbers.[1]

```
# Declaring numerical variables
h2oOxygens = 1
h2oHydrogens = 2
h2o_density_in_grams_per_liter = 1000
oxygenMass = 15.9994
hydrogenMass = 1.00794
avogadro = 6.023e23
```

A few points worth noting here:

Any text on a line in Python that follows #, the hash (or "pound") symbol, is treated as a comment and ignored by the Python interpreter, even if that text contains syntactically correct and sensible code that Python could actually run if the hash symbol weren't there. This is not only useful for documenting your code but also for temporarily preventing lines of code from being executed in your program – for example, when you're testing your code. You can use the hash symbol at the beginning of the line to make the entire line a comment, or after any piece of Python code on a line, to document that code.

---

[1] docs.python.org/2/reference/lexical_analysis.html#identifiers

Throughout this book, we will use the following scheme for any stuff that's going in your Python editor or development environment, so that it is easy to distinguish Python comments, Python code, Python output, and Python error messages, like this:

Python comments:

```
# oxygenMass = 15.9994
```

Python code:

```
print(oxygenMass)
```

Python output:

15.9994

Python error messages:

```
NameError: name 'oxygenMars' is not defined
```

It should be noted that if your particular choice of editor or IDE has a feature that automatically color-codes your Python input and output, it will not necessarily use this particular color scheme.

Our example shows the three basic formats that Python uses for real numbers:

- **integers**: h2oOxygens = 1

- **floating point numbers**: hydrogenMass = 1.00794

- **exponentials**: avogadro = 6.023e23

Python variable names can contain letters and numbers and the underscore character as in h2o_density_in_grams_per_liter. They cannot start with a number however and they cannot contain spaces.

Python variable names are also **case sensitive** so the following are all different variables:

```
myvariable = 1
MyVariable = 3.172
MYVARIABLE = 'Undefined'
```

In other words, subsequently specifying myvariable = 2 will not affect the values of MyVariable or MYVARIABLE.

Similarly, we can declare string variables in Python by enclosing the declared value in single or double quotes. Single and double quotes are interchangeable in Python, but they must always be used in pairs – you can't start a string with a single quote and end it with a double quote. This does however allow you to use single and double quotes inside strings (as in the following jfk example).

```
# Declaring string variables
buffer = 'Tris'
buffer = "MES"
jfk = "I'm proud to say 'Ich bin ein Berliner'"
carbonMass = "12.0107"
```

Consider the last of these examples: carbonMass = "12.0107".

Do you think it's a number or a string?

It's actually a string because it has quotes around it, and if you tried to do any math with it (like multiplying it by another number), the results would not be what you expect. More about that later, but before we put all these variables to work in some actual Python code (yes that's coming in just a moment), let's just consider a related and important issue for Python variables.

There's one more way to declare string variables in Python that allows you to even include line breaks in the string. It's useful, for example, for declaring paragraphs of text as strings. To use it, you have to enclose the string itself in **triple quotes**, like this:

```
limerick = """ Said a young researcher named Spode
          Having reached the end of his road
          'I have far too much data
          For this hand calculator
          If only I knew how to code!' """
```

You can see from this example that not only can a triple-quoted string contain line breaks, but it can also contain single (and double) string quotes as well. By the way, using triple quotes is also a very useful way of commenting out a whole section of your Python code if needs be – for testing purposes, for example.

Python Handles all Types

Those of you who have used other programming languages like Java or C might be used to seeing a syntax for the declaration of variables that includes a **type** for the variable. In C, for example, you have to declare a variable's type *before* you can even use it in your code – like this: `int myvariable;` this sets up `myvariable` as an integer, so that it can be handled appropriately in the code.

Python does not require its variables to be **explicitly typed**, as we say in computer geek speak. Python uses instead a dynamic typing approach called duck typing, based upon the idea that **if it walks like a duck and talks like a duck, then it's a duck**! So, for example, when Python sees quotes around a variable's value, as in `buffer = 'Tris'` it will treat that variable as a string, even if the contents of the string look like a number as in `carbonMass = "12.0107"`. Similarly with numerical variables, if a variable's value conforms to the syntax of one of Python's numerical formats, it will treat that variable as a number.

This duck typing approach makes Python extremely flexible, since variables can be introduced on the fly as needed and can even change types in the course of the code's execution.

For example, declaring `a = 11` (an integer) in your Python code and later `a = "One greater than 10"` (a string) is perfectly okay. Be warned though – this flexibility can also lead to problems in understanding and debugging your code later on if it's not carefully managed. For example, if you have a block of code where you do some arithmetic with `a`, it's probably not going to work out too well for you if you've redeclared `a` as a string before that code is executed.

At this point there are probably some of you that want to leap into writing some Python code that actually does something more than just assigning values to variables, while others will still have questions about Python variable declaration syntax. How long can a variable name be? Can I use other characters in variable names? What is Python best practice for the use of upper- and lowercase characters in variable names? and so on and so forth.

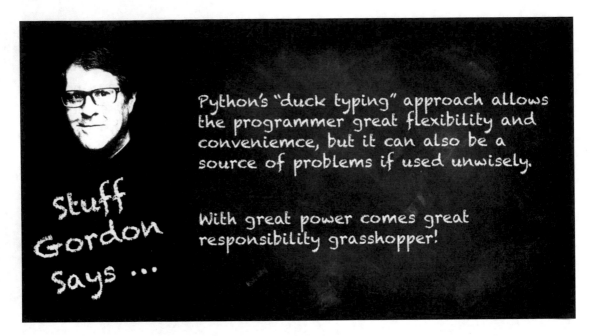

Fear not oh meticulous ones! The Python web site includes a rich documentation library that consists of a Python Language Reference[2] and even a Python Style Guide.[3] The bulk of these two documents will not mean that much to you at this point, since we have only just started our Python journey, but they are a great reference to return to as you work through the chapters in this book. Our aim here is to give you enough background to get you started using Python, and the online documentation at the official Python web site[4] is a great resource for supplementing what you learn in this book.

So without any further ado ...

---

[2]docs.python.org/2/reference
[3]www.python.org/dev/peps/pep-0008/
[4]www.python.org

Our First Piece of Real Python Code

Listing 2-1. Our first piece of Python code

```python
# Calculate mass of water molecule and output it to console
h2oOxygens = 1
h2oHydrogens = 2
oxygenMass = 15.9994
hydrogenMass = 1.00794
h2oMass = h2oOxygens * oxygenMass + h2oHydrogens * hydrogenMass
print('Molecular weight of H2O = ',h2oMass)
```

To paraphrase a certain 1980s hip hop artist with big, baggy pants – "let's break it down."

The first line in Listing 2-1 is a Python comment. As a quick reminder, any characters in Python code that appear after the hash (#) symbol are treated as a comment and will not be executed as code, and comments can even be appended to the end of lines of executable code, like this:

```python
oxygenMass = 15.9994        # standard atomic weight
```

You can use comments to annotate your code to remind yourself or to inform others what a particular piece of code is doing, how it works, what problems it has, or any other information that you would like to include with that section of code.

The second line is just a calculation of the mass of a water molecule, using the variables we declared earlier, and its assignment to the variable h2oMass.

The third line introduces output to the Python console which is the default stream for any output from the code including the contents of print function calls and any Python error messages. When you run the preceding code, the print function on line 3 will produce this output in the Python console:

Molecular weight of H2O = 18.01528

If you entered this code into your Python editor, ran it, and saw this output in the Python console, give yourself a pat on the back. You just ran your first, small Python program!

Python Functions

As with almost all programming languages, you will probably want to organize your code into nice, tidy blocks that make it easy to maintain and to understand. So let's jump straight into defining functions in Python, since functions will be a fairly ubiquitous feature in the code we will be writing in the course of this book. Later on we will start to refer to functions as **methods**, in keeping with Python's support for object-oriented code, but much (much) more to come on that later.

For now, the best way to understand Python functions is to see them in action, here's one in Listing 2-2.

Listing 2-2. Simple function

```
# A simple function to calculate molar volumes
def calculateMolarVolume(mass,density):
    volume = mass/density
    return volume
```

If you have ever written code in any of the popular programming languages like BASIC or Java, this code snippet will look very familiar. There is however one particularly distinctive feature of Python that is worth noting here:

The indent in Python code is syntactically meaningful and not just for show.

In many programming languages, the programmer is encouraged to indent code blocks to make the code more readable, but this is an aesthetic choice that the programmer is free to ignore without any impact on the execution of the code itself.

Not so in Python...

In Python, the indent is used to show where a particular block of code begins and ends. As shown in the preceding example, all of the code inside a Python function must be indented to define it as belonging to the function. To make this clearer, look at the code in Listing 2-3.

Listing 2-3. Example of indented code

```
def explainIndentedCode():
    print('This indented line is part of the function')
    print('So is this one')
print('This unindented line is not a part of the function')
```

If you call the function `explainIndentedCode` in your code, all of the indented `print` function calls underneath the function declaration will be executed, but the function call itself will not execute the unindented `print` function that follows. There are all kinds of places in Python in which blocks of code can be executed, and these can even appear inside other (already indented) blocks of code (such as functions). We will see this in action in a few minutes when we get to the Python `if` statement.

But let's get back to our `calculateMolarVolume` function.

We can see that the function definition includes two arguments, `mass` and `density`, which are used within the function to calculate `volume`, the molar volume. The `return` statement at the end of the function specifies what (if anything) the function returns when it ends. A function with no `return` statement is the same as a function with an empty `return` statement, that is, it returns nothing. Python actually has a special value for nothing called None, and we will see more of this later. For now however, you might wonder why Python bothers to have a special value for nothing. One of the reasons is that it allows you to test within the code, whether a variable is assigned to something or to nothing. But don't fret too much about this just yet – all will become clear in subsequent chapters.

Let's do a little test and run our `calculateMolarVolume` function to see what we get by running the code in Listing 2-4.

Listing 2-4. Simple function in action

```
def calculateMolarVolume(mass,density):
    volume = mass/density
    return volume
h2oMolarVolume = calculateMolarVolume(h2oMass,h2o_density_in_grams_per_liter)
print('Volume of 1 mole of H2O = ',h2oMolarVolume,'L')
```

Making sure beforehand that you have included the variable declarations we listed earlier, if you run these two lines of code, you should see the following:

Volume of 1 mole of H2O =   0.01801528 L

As the biochemistry textbooks tell us, the volume of 1 mole of water is indeed about 18 mL.

Now we're on a roll, let's create another function to calculate the number of molecules of a substance in a volume of 1 liter. To do this, we will again need to do the calculation of molar volume that we just saw, but now we will reuse the function we already wrote by referring to it inside of our new function, as we show in Listing 2-5.

Listing 2-5. Calling a function from a function

```python
# A function to calculate molecules per liter
def moleculesPerLiter(mass,density):
  molarVolume = calculateMolarVolume(mass,density)
  numberOfMolarVolumes = 1.0/molarVolume
  numberOfMolecules = avogadro * numberOfMolarVolumes
  return numberOfMolecules
```

Again note that we pass the same two arguments, `mass` and `density`, to our new function, and in the very first line of the function, we use our previous function and assign the returned result to the variable `molarVolume`.

As before, we're going to pass the mass and density of water to the function. This time however, instead of the molar volume of water, we'll be calculating the number of molecules in 1 liter of water, so let's now run our new function (again being sure to include those previously assigned variable declarations, we're assuming that you've already included them in your Python session) and see what we get.

```python
h2oMoleculesPerLiter = moleculesPerLiter(h2oMass,h2o_density_in_grams_per_
liter)
print('Number of molecules of H2O in 1L = ',h2oMoleculesPerLiter)
Number of molecules of H2O in 1L =  3.343273043771731e+25
```

Our second function has very similar features to the first – a function definition that requires two arguments, a little bit of math, and a returned result. It does show how functions can be reused in Python code, even inside other functions. Our first function is admittedly a rather trivial example that could itself be easily reduced to single line of code, but you get the idea. A real function in Python could be tens, hundreds, or even thousands of lines of code.

Using Integers and Decimals in Python

We're going to create one more function before we finish this chapter, but before we get to that, let's take a few moments to look at some of the arithmetical pitfalls that have ensnared many a Python newbie.

The first one concerns integer arithmetic.

Try running the code in Listing 2-6 in your Python editor and see what you get.

Listing 2-6. Integer arithmetic

```
a = 3
b = 6
print('a/b = ',a/b)
```

When you run this, you should get:

a/b =   0.5

It's important to realize that Python 2.7 had completely different behavior to this. In Python 2.7 the result would have been zero. This is because the preceding code, both a and b, are defined as integers, so when we do the a/b operation, Python 2.7 returned an integer result. Since the real result of 3/6 is 0.5, Python 2.7 did not return this decimal number as an integer – it just returned the integer portion of the result, which is zero. This got Python newbies into trouble. For example, you know that a piece of your code is going to have to deal with floating point numbers, so you assign floating point values to the relevant variables initially. In some other part of the code however, these get reassigned as integers and bingo – you've got a calculation that delivers a zero instead of the decimal fraction that you expected.

In Python 3 this quirk has been eliminated and code now works as you might expect – automatically converting the result to a floating point, regardless of whether the input variables were integers or not. This is important to be aware of, especially if you are converting code from Python 2 to Python 3.

So, for example, these examples now work as expected:

```
print('b/a = ',b/a)
```
b/a =   2.0
```
print('12/5 = ',12/5)
```
12/5 =   2.4

You can still do your arithmetic by manually specifying them as floating point numbers, as in the following example, but it is no longer necessary.

```
a = 3.0
b = 6.0
print('a/b = ',a/b)
```
a/b = 0.5

As a little exercise for the reader, try exploring what happens when you mix integer and floating point numbers in your code's arithmetic.

Just one more little Python gotcha to cover before we get to our final (and most useful) function of the chapter...

Try the code in Listing 2-7.

Listing 2-7. Mixing floating point numbers and integers

```
a = 6.0
b = 3.0
c = 5.0
print('a/b+c = ',a/b+c)
print('a/(b+c) = ',a/(b+c))
```

You should get this result:

a/b+c = 7.0
a/(b+c) = 0.75

This is just a friendly reminder not to forget what computer geeks refer to as operator precedence, which is just a fancy way of saying the order in which your arithmetic operators will be executed if you don't specify this yourself, for example, by using parentheses to force the addition operator in the example to be executed *before* the division operator (which would normally take precedence).

With arithmetic operators as with any other Python features, if you ever need more details about the way Python works, the online documentation library at python.org is your friend – specifically a section dedicated to operator precedence.[5]

---

[5]docs.python.org/2/reference/expressions.html

Conditional Statements

Alright – now we're ready to round out this chapter with our last function which will calculate simple stock solution recipes for some common lab buffers. In this last function, we will introduce Python **conditionals**. Conditional statements are at the heart of computer programming, and they take the broad form

> **if**: *condition is true*
>
> *do something*

Let's look at the code for our last function and see this in action in Listing 2-8.

Listing 2-8. Using conditionals

```
# Function for calculating buffer recipes that uses conditionals
def bufferRecipe(buffer,molarity):
    if buffer == 'Tris':
        grams = 121.14
    elif buffer == 'MES':
        grams = 217.22
    elif buffer == 'HEPES':
        grams = 238.30
    else:
        return 'Huh???'
    gramsPerLiter = grams * molarity
    return gramsPerLiter
```

The function bufferRecipe takes two arguments: buffer – the name of the buffer – and molarity – the molar concentration of the stock solution you want to make. Based upon the buffer name that you supply, it then applies the appropriate value to the variable grams and returns the required weight of buffer (in grams) to make up a 1L solution.

We can see the conditional statements at work in this function.

```
if buffer == 'Tris':
        grams = 121.14
```

Python conditionals take the form

```
if <condition>:
    <do something>
elif <condition>:
    <do something else>
elif
.
.
else:
    <do something completely else>
```

The first condition in our example is that the supplied buffer name is equal to the string 'Tris', as expressed by the Python equality operator ==. **Note the difference between the equality operator and the equals sign used to assign variables.**

```
buffer == 'Tris'
```

tests whether the value of the variable buffer is equal to the string 'Tris', whereas

```
buffer = 'Tris'
```

sets the value of the variable buffer to the string 'Tris'.

The Python equality operator may not look like it, but it is actually a kind of function that returns "true" or "false," represented by the special Python values True and False. The if statement then executes an indented code block or not, depending upon the true or false value it receives.

Code block?

Yes. Conditional statements in Python also use the indenting syntax to determine what should be done if the condition is satisfied. This is best illustrated by the example in Listing 2-9.

Listing 2-9. Conditional statements and code blocks

```
something = 6
anotherThing = 6
if something == anotherThing:
    print('This statement will be printed')
    print('So will this one')
print('This statement gets printed either way')
```

Let's see it in action. When you run the preceding code, we get

This statement will be printed
So will this one
This statement gets printed either way

But if we change the following variable in the preceding code

```
anotherThing = 4
```

we get

```
This statement gets printed either way
```

The elif clauses and the else clause in a Python if block are optional, but they allow for more options, including an option to do something even if all of the conditional clauses fail to be satisfied. For example, see the code and output in Listing 2-10.

Listing 2-10. Elif and else clauses

```
something = 10
if something == 6:
    print('something is 6')
elif something == 4:
    print('something is 4')
else:
    print('something is something else entirely')
```
something is something else entirely

If you just have a single statement to execute based upon the conditional statement being True, you can also use a shorthand syntax with no indented blocks, like this:

```
if something == 11: print('It is 1 greater than 10')
```

As with other programming languages, the equality operator in Python is just one of a bunch of **comparison operators** and here they are:

> **==** equals

> **!=** not equals

> **>** greater than

> **<** less than

> **<>** greater OR less than (i.e. not equals)

> **>=** greater than OR equals

> **<=** less than OR equals

In addition to these comparison operators, any conditional statement can be negated by prepending the not statement. For example:

```
not (something == anotherThing)
```

is logically equivalent to

```
something != anotherThing
```

Conditional statements in Python can also be chained together to create more complex conditions using **and** and **or** clauses, but we'll save those for another chapter.

So armed with a knowledge of Python conditional statements, we can now understand how our latest function works. If it is passed one of the three recognized buffers in the buffer argument, it returns the appropriate recipe, otherwise it returns 'Huh???'.

```
print('Recipe for 0.1M Tris = ',bufferRecipe('Tris',0.1),'g/L')
Recipe for 0.1M Tris =  12.114 g/L
print('Recipe for 0.5M MES = ',bufferRecipe('MES',0.5),'g/L')
Recipe for 0.5M MES =  108.61 g/L
print('Recipe for 1mM HEPES = ',bufferRecipe('HEPES',1.0e-3),'g/L')
Recipe for 1mM HEPES =  0.2383 g/L
print('Recipe for 1.0M Goop = ',bufferRecipe('Goop',1.0),'g/L')
Recipe for 1.0M Goop =  Huh??? g/L
```

Notice how we are now calling the bufferRecipe function directly in the print function instead of assigning and printing the variable as separate steps. Sometimes in this book, we will code newly introduced Python features in a more long-winded and un-pythonic way just to make them clearer in the beginning.

On a related note, there is actually a much better way to code the bufferRecipe function that involves the use of Python dictionaries which we will introduce in Chapter 3. Dictionaries are one of the awesomest features of Python, and as we shall see later, they can provide us a much more elegant way of implementing the bufferRecipe function.

References and Further Exploration

- Python Language Reference[6]: everything you ever wanted to know about the Python language, but were afraid to ask

- Python Style Guide[7]: making your code more readable and maintainable – remember that the person trying to decipher your code in the future may be you!

---

[6]docs.python.org/2/reference

[7]www.python.org/dev/peps/pep-0008/

CHAPTER 3

Making Sense of Sequences

Biological Sequences and Python Data Structures

"You are indeed most odd," said Alice to the bird. "You're all length and no width, and one end of you looks so much like the other that it's hard to know which end to talk to."

"In common with all other birds, I start from my head and run down to my feet," said the bird. "Just stretch me out alongside any other bird and you'll see that we're all made the same way."

Alice looked puzzled, and from her expression the bird could tell that some additional clarification would be required.

"Look, just write HEAD-BODY-FEET on a piece of paper and voila! You have a ready-made template for identifying any bird," the bird snapped.

Alice seemed momentarily lost in thought, "But that pattern would also match other little girls," she said finally.

"Okay, okay," said the bird testily. "I didn't really want to get into isomorphisms right now, but since you've raised the issue...."

String variables; lists; **len()***; iterators; code blocks; slice notation for strings and lists; objects; methods; string searching; list methods; dictionaries; key-value pairs; boolean values,* **in***,* **True***,* **False***; substrings; tuples,* **while***; mutable and immutable objects*

DNA sequences, restriction enzymes, restriction digests, molecular weight

---

© Alexander Lancaster and Gordon Webster 2019
A. Lancaster and G. Webster, *Python for the Life Sciences*, https://doi.org/10.1007/978-1-4842-4523-1_3

Sequences are a key part of biology, and by the end of this chapter, you will wonder why you ever *didn't* use Python to manage them. Python has some really fantastic features that make it a wonderful tool for storing, searching, and analyzing protein and nucleic sequences. If Python's facility for handling sequences was its only appeal to life scientists, that alone would make it worthy of its place in the biologist's toolbox.

Of Sequences and Strings

Since biological sequences are normally represented as strings, strings are probably a good starting point for our discussion of writing code to manage sequences in Python.

Here's a very simple DNA sequence:

```
mySequence = 'atcg'
```

Strings in Python have a lot of properties that make them a great vehicle for handling biological sequences. Listing 3-1 gives an example.

Listing 3-1. Strings in Python

```
mySequence = 'atcg'
print('Sequence length is ',len(mySequence))
```
Sequence length is 4

In Listing 3-1 we show how the Python len function returns the length of the string in characters, and as we shall see in other chapters, it can also be applied to other Python variable types such as lists.

If we want to do any computation with sequences, one thing we would definitely like to be able to do is to iterate through a sequence, one position at a time, so this would seem like an opportune moment to introduce Python loops. Here's an example in Listing 3-2, followed immediately by its output.

Listing 3-2. Loops in Python

```
mySequence = 'atcg'
for c in mySequence:
    print(c)
```

a

t

c

g

The code you just typed and executed translates into English as "for each item in 'mysequence', give the item the temporary name 'c' then print 'c' to the console." This kind of loop construction is known as an **iterator** in Python. Python knows that strings are made up of smaller items, in this case characters, so when you iterate over a string using the "for" command, the iterator returns each character in the string, in order of occurrence. I used the name c because the items in this case are characters, but I could just have easily used any other name like b or base since the sequence we are dealing with is a DNA sequence.

The indent in the print(c) line is significant. As we have seen in other chapters, indents are the way to create blocks of code in Python that are to be executed all together. Every line of code that is indented by one level underneath the for statement gets executed on each round trip through the loop. So, for example, see Listing 3-3.

Listing 3-3. Indents in loops

```
for c in mySequence:
    print('This line will be executed for each pass through the loop')
    print('So will this one')
print('This line will only be executed at the end')
```

```
This line will be executed for each pass through the loop
So will this one
This line will be executed for each pass through the loop
So will this one
This line will be executed for each pass through the loop
So will this one
This line will be executed for each pass through the loop
So will this one
This line will only be executed at the end
```

The two indented lines in the for code block are executed for every character in the sequence, while the unindented print statement is only executed after all of its iterations after completed. Listing 3-4 shows a slightly more real-world example of a code block in a for loop.

Listing 3-4. Code block in for loop

```
i = 0
for c in mySequence:
    i += 1
    print(i,c)
```

1 a

2 t

3 c

4 g

In the preceding example, we also initialized a variable i as zero and then incremented it by 1 for each pass through the loop, so that we could also print the index of each base in our DNA sequence. The expression with the Python increment operator i += 1 is a syntactic shorthand for writing i = i + 1 and there is a similar decrement operator -=.

Another feature of strings (and all list-based objects in Python) is that their characters (or items if it's a list) can also be accessed according to their numerical position in the object, starting from 0 (all lists, sequences, arrays, and so on in Python are numbered from 0) up to 1 minus the length of the object. You can also slice strings (and lists) up using a [from:to] syntax:

```
print(mySequence[0])
```

a

```
print(mySequence[3])
```

g

```
print(mySequence[-1])
```

g

```
print(mySequence[0:4])
```

atcg

```
print(mySequence[:4])
```

atcg

```
print(mySequence[2:3])
```

c

```
print(mySequence[2:4])
```
cg
```
print(mySequence[2:])
```
cg
```
print(mySequence[-3:])
```
tcg

Note the following features of Python indices: the last number in the [from:to] range is exclusive, for example, if you want to select a slice of your sequence up to and including position 41, the to specifier needs to be 42 (which position will *not* be included in the selected substring (or sub-list); if the from or to index is excluded, the beginning or end of the string (or list) is assumed; a negative index for a string (or list) denotes the position -n from the end of the string.

Now that we've introduced the Python string and list slicing notation, let's just take a moment to introduce Python lists, since they behave very much like strings in some ways, and we can apply the notation we have already learned for strings to lists as well.

Lists and More

A Python list is a sequence of items rather like a string is a sequence of characters, except that **Python list items can be any Python object** and not just characters. We also do not use quotes around Python lists, but rather square brackets like this:

```
mySequenceAsAList = ['a','t','c','g']
```

Notice here that we have stored the exact same sequence as in our previous string example, but this time in list format. Notice how the items are separated by a commas and enclosed in square brackets instead of quotes. Although this format looks quite different from the previous string version, we can see that the string slicing notation we used previously yields very similar results as before when applied to this list instead of to a string.

```
print(mySequenceAsAList[0])
```
a
```
print(mySequenceAsAList[3])
```
g
```
print(mySequenceAsAList[-1])
```
g

```
print(mySequenceAsAList[0:4])
```
['a', 't', 'c', 'g']
```
print(mySequenceAsAList[:4])
```
['a', 't', 'c', 'g']

```
print(mySequenceAsAList[2:3])
```
['c']
```
print(mySequenceAsAList[2:4])
```
['c', 'g']
```
print(mySequenceAsAList[2:])
```
['c', 'g']
```
print(mySequenceAsAList[-3:])
```
['t', 'c', 'g']

Our new list-based sequence contains characters, just as the previous string version did, so when we print an individual item in the list, for example, print(mySequenceAsAList[0]), we get the same result as before – a character. When we print slices of the list however, for example, print(mySequenceAsAList[2:4]), we get the result in list format instead of string format. Note that anytime we use the slice notation with a list, we always get a list-formatted result even if the result contains only a single item. For example, print(mySequenceAsAList[2:3]) returns ['c'] and not c. Strings are such a common and widely used idiom in programming languages that you can think of a Python string as a kind of specialized version of a Python list, designed specifically for representing sequences of characters, and with its own special syntax that is appropriate to strings.

But now let's look at some of the major differences between Python lists and Python strings. Firstly and perhaps most importantly, a Python list item can be any Python object, strings, numbers – even another list or a list of lists, or a list of lists of lists, or ... okay you get the idea. Here's a list with a completely disparate collection of object types including strings, lists, numbers, and even the Python True and None values. True is a built-in Python Boolean value that (not surprisingly) is the opposite of its sister Boolean value False. The None value is used to denote a Python object that has no assigned value – it is in effect a pointer to nothing. We'll come across these built-in values a lot in this book and get very familiar with them, but for now, let's just see how they can appear as elements in lists:

```
myList = ['atcg',['a','t','c','g'],42,True,None]
print('Length of myList is: ',len(myList))
```
Length of myList is: 5
```
print(myList[0])
```
atcg
```
print(myList[1])
```
['a', 't', 'c', 'g']
```
print(myList[2])
```
42

```
print(myList[3])
```
True
```
print(myList[4])
```
None

Just as a sort of curious little aside, notice that the second item in myList (myList[1]) is itself a list. How do you think you would reference the items in that inner list now that it is embedded in another list?

It's actually very logical and intuitive – so, for example:

```
print(myList[1][2])
```
c
```
print(myList[1][1:3])
```
['t', 'c']

Easy right?

How about something a little more difficult now?

A big difference between strings and lists in Python is that lists are mutable whereas strings are not.

Phew!

Just for the record, if you're not sure about what *"mutable"* means, it sounds like what it is – changeable, modifiable. It might seem counterintuitive to say that strings are immutable, since we're able to assign them a value in the first place, but once a string value has been assigned, it cannot be changed except by replacing it with another string.

When we say

```
correctSpelling = 'recognize'
```

and then

```
correctSpelling = 'recognise'
```

we're not actually modifying the string correctSpelling, we're essentially just creating a new one with the same name. If we declare correctSpelling as a list, we can do so exactly the kind of modification that is not possible with a string in Listing 3-5.

Listing 3-5. Modifying a list

```
correctSpelling = ['r','e','c','o','g','n','i','z','e']
correctSpelling[7] = 's'
print(correctSpelling)
['r', 'e', 'c', 'o', 'g', 'n', 'i', 's', 'e']
```

If we try to similarly edit the string version (**which is not allowed in Python**)

```
correctSpelling = 'recognize'
correctSpelling[7] = 's'
    correctSpelling[7] = 's'
TypeError: 'str' object does not support item assignment
```

we get an error message telling us that the string type (abbreviated 'str' in Python) does not allow the assignment of its individual items. There are actually some special functions for editing strings, but they all create a new string rather than editing the existing one, for example, in Listing 3-6.

Listing 3-6. Editing a string

```
correctSpelling = 'recognise'
correctSpelling = correctSpelling.replace('s','z')
print(correctSpelling)
recognize
```

Methods and Objects

The statement `correctSpelling.replace('s','z')` has a syntax that may look unfamiliar, but it introduces an aspect of Python that we haven't encountered before now. **Objects** in Python such as strings can have special functions unique to their particular **object type**, and these dedicated functions are referred to as **methods** (even more on objects awaits in Chapter 7 on object-oriented programming where we will see that you can define your own object types, and even redefine or extend existing Python object types).

A method for an object type can be applied to an *instance* of that type using the `object.method()` syntax shown previously. A method is just a *function* that is defined for a particular object type. It has a name and parentheses for passing arguments just like we saw when we described function declarations in Chapter 2. The big difference however is that a method always receives the object that is calling it as an argument. This might sound odd, but it makes perfect sense when you think about the fact that a method is a function dedicated to an object type. It is designed to do something for or with the object type it was defined for, and therefore, it is never used in any context that does not involve an object of the type for which it was defined.

In the example, `correctSpelling.replace('s','z')`, `correctSpelling` is the string object that is using the `replace()` method that was defined for string objects.

To round out our introduction to Python lists, let's look at some of the cool **list methods** (i.e., functions defined for list objects) that allow us to edit lists.

```
myList = ['apple','banana','pear','llama','orange']
print(myList)
['apple', 'banana', 'pear', 'llama', 'orange']

myList.append('peach')
print(myList)
['apple', 'banana', 'pear', 'llama', 'orange', 'peach']

myList.insert(2,'kiwi')
print(myList)
['apple', 'banana', 'kiwi', 'pear', 'llama', 'orange', 'peach']

myList.remove('llama')
print(myList)
['apple', 'banana', 'kiwi', 'pear', 'orange', 'peach']
```

There are also other modalities within Python for editing lists that don't use the `object.method()` syntax, for example:

```
myList[4] = 'lemon'
print(myList)
['apple', 'banana', 'kiwi', 'pear', 'lemon', 'peach']
print(sorted(myList))
['apple', 'banana', 'kiwi', 'lemon', 'peach', 'pear']
```

Lists are extremely versatile in Python, and there are many more ways to use them, as we will see in other chapters. For now however, if you want to sink your teeth a little deeper into what you can do with Python lists, have a look at this documentation on data structures[1] at the official Python web site.

The Python Dictionary is Your Friend

So now that we've started to see how we can store biological sequences as Python strings and access chunks of them using the **[from:to]** string slicing notation, let's see how one of the most useful Python features of all – dictionaries – can help us with the analysis of biological sequences.

Did we already mention that **the Python dictionary is your friend?**

A Python dictionary is a repository of labeled items. The order of the items is not paramount as it is in a string or a list, so instead of the items being labeled according to their numerical positions, they can be labeled pretty much any old way we choose – for example:

```
musician = {'name':'Nigel','instrument':'guitar','preferred volume':11,}
print(musician['name'])
Nigel
print(musician['instrument'])
guitar
print(musician['preferred volume'])
11
```

---

[1]`docs.python.org/2/tutorial/datastructures.html`

A Python dictionary is composed of **key-value** pairs where the **key** is the label by which the item is found and the **value** is obviously the value of the item. Dictionary values can be any *immutable* Python object - for example:

```
gene = {'name':'p53','taxonomy':9606,'metal binding':True, \
        'locations':['cytoplasm','nucleus']}
print(gene['name'])
```
p53
```
print(gene['taxonomy'])
```
9606
```
print(gene['metal binding'])
```
True
```
print(gene['locations'])
```
['cytoplasm', 'nucleus']
```
print(gene['locations'][0])
```
cytoplasm
```
print(gene['locations'][1])
```
Nucleus

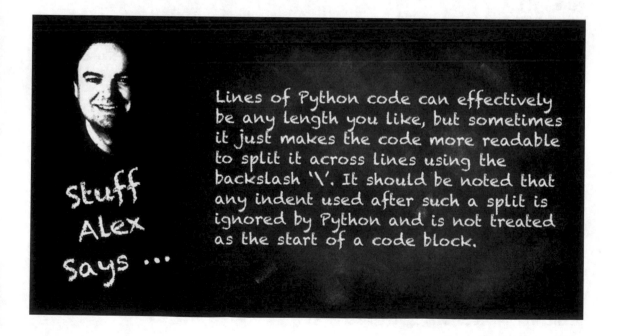

Lines of Python code can effectively be any length you like, but sometimes it just makes the code more readable to split it across lines using the backslash '\'. It should be noted that any indent used after such a split is ignored by Python and is not treated as the start of a code block.

In the example shown here, the **keys** are all strings, but the **values** include a string, an integer, a Boolean value, and a list. Notice how the logic for referring to items in lists embedded within dictionaries still holds – the only difference from our previous list-within-a-list example being that the dictionary item is referenced using a key instead of a numerical position.

Anyway, back to dictionaries...

Dictionary key names in Python **must be unique**, and can be of any **immutable** object type, so strings and numbers are allowed as dictionary keys, but lists (which are mutable as we have seen) are not. As a brief aside, there is actually a special immutable list type in Python called a **tuple**, which is written with regular parentheses around it to distinguish it from a mutable list. Tuples *can* be used dictionary keys, but we won't say any more about tuples for now.

New entries can be added directly to a dictionary by a simple declaration like

```
gene['name'] = 'homo sapiens'
gene['id'] = 96020344
```

and it's also possible to create an empty dictionary like this:

```
gene = {}
```

So in Listing 3-7, we create a dictionary of molecular weights of nucleotides (really useful if you're a biologist!), we then create a function that calculates the molecular weight of oligonucleotides, and then finally we test our new function using a short DNA sequence.

Listing 3-7. Calculating molecular weight

```
dnaMolecularWeight = {'a':313.2,'c':289.2,'t':304.2,'g':329.2}
def oligoMolecularWeight(sequence):
    dnaMolecularWeight = {'a':313.2,'c':289.2,'t':304.2,'g':329.2}
    molecularWeight = 0.0
    for base in sequence:
        molecularWeight += dnaMolecularWeight[base]
    return molecularWeight
dnaSequence = 'tagcgctttatcg'
print(oligoMolecularWeight(dnaSequence))
```
4002.59999999999

Sweet!

A DNA Restriction Digest Function Coded in Python

Now let's look at a somewhat more complex application in which we can use dictionaries and lists together – calculating the molecular weight of the DNA fragments that would result from a restriction digest.

The activity of a restriction enzyme can be defined by its recognition site on the DNA sequence and the position relative to the recognition site, at which it cuts the DNA. Let's create a dictionary that we can use to define these restriction enzyme parameters:

```
restrictionEnzymes = {}
```

and add a couple of restriction enzymes to it to get us going:

```
restrictionEnzymes['bamH1'] = ['ggatcc',0]
restrictionEnzymes['sma1'] = ['cccggg',2]
```

Notice that the **key** for each entry in this dictionary is the name of the enzyme and the value is a list whose first element is the enzyme's recognition site and second element is the position relative to the recognition site, at which the enzyme cuts the DNA.

You could imagine adding a whole bunch of restriction enzymes to this dictionary, and even using as a kind of simple restriction enzyme database with which you could do digital DNA restriction experiments. One thing you would almost certainly need however is a way to keep track of which enzymes are present in the dictionary and to be able to query whether or not the dictionary has the enzyme you are interested in using.

There are two very useful dictionary methods that you should know if you are going to use dictionaries in your code, and the best way to describe them is to see them in action:

```
print(restrictionEnzymes.keys())
['bamH1', 'sma1']
print('sma1' in restrictionEnzymes)
True
print('EcoR1' in restrictionEnzymes)
False
```

Here again, we are using the object.method() syntax to access the methods that are defined for dictionary objects. The method keys() returns a **list** of the dictionary's keys while checking to see if the specified key is in the dictionary returns True or False. Note that the list of dictionary keys returned by the keys() method is not necessarily in the order in which the keys were entered, or alphabetical or any other specific order for that matter. **Python dictionaries are not ordered in the same way as Python lists**, so you cannot refer to dictionary entries by position in the way that you can with lists.

Just as an aside, you could of course use the `sorted()` function that we used earlier to sort the keys alphabetically, like this:

```
print(sorted(restrictionEnzymes.keys()))
['bamH1', 'sma1']
```

Before we jump into the full code for our restriction digest function, we need to introduce another very useful string method called `find`. Here's how it works:

```
mySequence = 'gctgtatttcgatcgatttatgct'
print(mySequence.find('ttt'))
6
print(mySequence.find('gtgtgt'))
-1
```

Notice how the `mySequence.find` method returns the position in the string `mySequence` of the *first* occurrence of the substring `'ttt'` that we are searching for. If we search for a substring (`'gtgtgt'`) that is *not* in the sequence, `find` the method returns -1 to indicate that the substring was not found (note that `find` cannot use zero for "not found," since this is actually the index of the first position in a Python string and a zero would indicate that the substring was found at that position).

But also notice that there is a second occurrence of `'ttt'` in `mySequence`. What if we want to find all occurrences of `'ttt'` in `mySequence`? We will certainly need to be able to do something like this for the restriction digest function that we want to write.

We can still use the `find` method for our restriction digest function, but we need to know about some additional arguments that this method can take, and in the process, we will learn about **default arguments** in functions.

If we were to examine the code for the declaration of the `find` method, it would look something like this:

```
def find(self,substring,start=None,end=None):
```

Remember that methods are just functions that operate on specific objects for which they were defined (formally speaking, they operate on *instances of a particular class*, but more of this later when we get to **object-oriented programming** and **Python classes**).

So don't fret too much about the self argument at this point, this is just a special syntax that is unique to methods, by which the method receives the object as its first argument, so that it knows which object it is operating on.

What we are really interested in here are the two arguments start and end that are already predefined in the method declaration. Python allows us to declare default values for arguments to functions and methods, so that we don't need to enter them all of the time. This is very useful when a particular argument is almost always the same – for example:

```
def automobile(color,horsepower,wheels=4):
```

which allows us to use the function like this:

```
myCar = automobile('flaming grey',300)
```

in which the function defaults automatically to four wheels. But it also allows us to specify the number of wheels if we need to (e.g., to handle the relatively rare case of a three-wheeled automobile):

```
myCar = ('cobalt black',150,3)
```

In a similar way, we can override the default start and end arguments to the find method in order to force the search to be made over a different region of the string. That way, each time we find an occurrence of the 'ttt' substring, we can start the search again from the next position:

```
print(mySequence.find('ttt'))
6
print(mySequence.find('ttt',7))
16
```

In the simple example we are using here, we can see at a glance that there are only two occurrences of the 'ttt' substring, but what if we were working with a much longer sequence and/or a more complicated substring?

What we need is a way to successively iterate over an entire sequence to identify all of the substring positions from the beginning to the end. Let's see how we can do this by introducing the Python while operator:

```
found = 0
searchFrom = found
```

```
while found != -1:
    found = mySequence.find('ttt',searchFrom)
    if found != -1:
        print('Substring found at: ',found)
    searchFrom = found + 1
```
Substring found at: 6
Substring found at: 16

The Python while operator will continue to iterate through the indented block of code that follows it, so long as the condition that it contains is true. In this case, we are taking advantage of the fact that the find method returns -1 when there are no more substrings to be found. The working of the loop is very simple: we search for the substring, each time we find it we report it and update the position from which the next search is to be done and repeat until finally we get a -1 from the find method.

Now we are finally in a position to write the function that this chapter has been building to – a function that takes a DNA sequence and calculates the molecular weights of the DNA fragments that would result from a restriction digest.

We will use the oligoMolecularWeight function that we created earlier in the chapter to calculate the molecular weights of the fragments – we will also use the restriction enzymes dictionary that we created.

Within the function itself, we will store the fragments and their molecular weights as a **list of tuples** that the function will return. Remember from our earlier discussion that **a tuple is simply an immutable list** that is distinguished from a list in Python by having parentheses around it instead of square brackets. For example:

```
fruit = ['apple','orange']
print(fruit)
```
['apple', 'orange']
```
fruit[1] = 'pear'
print(fruit)
```
['apple', 'pear']
```
fruit = ('apple','orange')
print(fruit)
```
('apple', 'orange')
```
fruit[1] = 'pear'
TypeError: 'tuple' object does not support item assignment
This line will be executed for each pass through the loop
```

46

In all other respects however, tuples behave like lists, but once they have been created, they cannot be edited without creating a new tuple. As we mentioned previously, tuples can be used as dictionary keys because of this property, but they are also useful for creating lists that you know should not be edited once created, which seems appropriate for the results of our restriction digest function.

So without further ado, let's jump right into the DNA restriction digest function in Listing 3-8.

Listing 3-8. DNA restriction digest function

```
restrictionEnzymes = {}
restrictionEnzymes['bamH1'] = ['ggatcc',0]
restrictionEnzymes['sma1'] = ['cccggg',2]
def restrictionDigest(sequence,enzyme):
    motif = restrictionEnzymes[enzyme][0]
    cutPosition = restrictionEnzymes[enzyme][1]
    fragments = []
    found = 0
    lastCut = found
    searchFrom = lastCut
    while found != -1:
        found = sequence.find(motif,searchFrom)
        if found != -1:
            fragment = sequence[lastCut:found+cutPosition]
            mwt = oligoMolecularWeight(fragment)
            fragments.append((fragment,mwt))
        else:
            fragment = sequence[lastCut:]
            mwt = oligoMolecularWeight(fragment)
            fragments.append((fragment,mwt))
        lastCut = found + cutPosition
        searchFrom = lastCut + 1
    return fragments
```

Once more, let's break it down...

```
def restrictionDigest(sequence,enzyme)
    motif = restrictionEnzymes[enzyme][0]
    cutPosition = restrictionEnzymes[enzyme][1]
```

Our function takes two arguments: the DNA sequence and the name of enzyme from the `restrictionEnzymes` library. Just to make the code more readable, we then assign the restriction site sequence to `motif` and the cutting position to `cutPosition`.

```
    fragments = []
    found = 0
    lastCut = found
    searchFrom = lastCut
```

Next we create a list in which to store and eventually return the results of the digest, and we initialize some important variables that we will use to keep track of our progress through the sequence. The variable `found` is the position of the last found restriction site, initialized to the start of the sequence to begin with. The variable `lastCut` stores the position at which we last cut the DNA (which may not be the same as the starting position of the restriction site). This is needed to define the starting position of the current fragment (and the end of the last one). The variable `searchFrom` (again, included to make the code more readable) tells us from where we need to start the next search step, which is always the next position after the one in which we previously cut the DNA strand.

```
    while found != -1:
        found = sequence.find(motif,searchFrom)
        if found != -1:
            fragment = sequence[lastCut:found+cutPosition]
            mwt = oligoMolecularWeight(fragment)
            fragments.append((fragment,mwt))
        else:
            fragment = sequence[lastCut:]
            mwt = oligoMolecularWeight(fragment)
            fragments.append((fragment,mwt))
        lastCut = found + cutPosition
        searchFrom = lastCut + 1
```

The remaining part of the function loops through the DNA sequence using a `while` loop that continues as long as the `sequence.find` method manages to find another restriction site, in which case, the current fragment is computed and stored in the `fragments` list.

Notice that once the `sequence.find` method fails to find another restriction site, we need to finish out the current fragment which runs to the end of the sequence, and store it with the others.

At the end of each iteration through the loop, we update the position of the last DNA strand cut and the position from which we will start the search again on the next run through the loop (if there is one).

So let's try our restriction digest function with a made-up DNA sequence into which I have deliberately inserted two bamH1 restriction sites (you'll first need to execute the code in Listing 3-8, of course):

```
digestSequence =
'gcgatgctaggatccgcgatcgcgtacgatcgtacgcggtacggacggatccttctc'
print(restrictionDigest(digestSequence,'bamH1'))
[('gcgatgcta', 2800.7999999999997),
('ggatccgcgatcgcgtacgatcgtacgcggtacggac', 11478.400000000005),
('ggatccttctc', 3345.1999999999994)]
```

Nice!

Our function returns the restriction digest fragments as a list of tuples, each consisting of the fragment's sequence and its molecular weight. This is quite a useful function in and of itself, but we have still barely scratched the surface of what Python can do with biological sequences. Later on, we will see how **regular expressions**, one of Python's most powerful tools, can be used even for large-scale genomics and sequencing applications. But before we get there, we have a brief pitstop into Python mathematical expressions and string formatting by way of Bayes' theorem.

References and Further Exploration

- Mutable vs. immutable objects in Python[2]: a nice short blog post on the difference between mutable and immutable objects in Python

---

[2]codehabitude.com/2013/12/24/python-objects-mutable-vs-immutable/

CHAPTER 4

A Statistical Interlude

Of Bayes' Theorem and Biomarkers

"I'm Alice, what's your name?" said Alice to the queen.

"I am the queen!" replied the queen indignantly, "and it is customary to address me as 'Your Majesty'."

"Apologies, your majesty, but how could I have known that you're the queen?" asked Alice

"Hello!" said the queen snarkily, gesturing at herself. "Did you eat a big bowl of Duh! for breakfast? Crown – regal garb – stately bearing… are these things not evidence of queenliness?"

"Hmmm!" said Alice, pulling out a paper and pen and starting to scribble some equations while muttering softly to herself. "So if we consider the prevalence of queens in the entire population vs. the number of people in the population who wear crowns and stately garb, but who are NOT queens… divided by…."

"Nerd alert!" exclaimed the queen, exasperated. "Does anybody here have an aspirin?"

Functions, function arguments, string formatting, the % operator in string formatting

Drug and diagnostic development, null hypothesis, t-test, Bayes' theorem, cancer, ovarian cancer, biomarkers, CA-125, probability, conditional probabilities

A. Lancaster and G. Webster, *Python for the Life Sciences*, https://doi.org/10.1007/978-1-4842-4523-1_4

As life scientists, it is seldom that we ever get to deal with anything resembling certainty. The systems that we work with are typically nonlinear and chaotic, heterogeneous, non-binary – in a word, messy. In the world of commercial life science, it is common that the real value of an R&D investment of hundred of millions or even billions of dollars may ultimately ride on such a razor-thin edge between success and failure that it requires the calculation of something like a t-test to determine whether you really have a marketable product or just another placebo – or in the case of a diagnostic, a real indicator vs. background noise.

The development of a new drug or diagnostic is in essence a process of gathering evidence either for or against your working hypothesis that the use of your product will confer some net benefit over not using it. In such a case, the null hypothesis – that your product will confer no net benefit at all – is (and always should be) a core consideration in your approach. With each new piece of data that a drug company accumulates along the hopeful path to that blockbuster product, they are weighing the evidence for and against eventual success or failure.

The Reverend Bayes and his Famous Theorem

This process of weighing the evidence was mathematically formalized during the eighteenth century by Thomas Bayes, an English priest who was fascinated with statistics and probability. **Bayes' theorem**, the landmark formulation that bears his name, is such an important approach for weighing scientific evidence that we felt it worth dedicating its own small chapter to in the book, and we'll use Python for our numerical explorations of the Theorem. It has also been our experience that despite its centrality in any quantitative application of the scientific method, there are many biologists who have never encountered any formal introduction to Bayes' theorem in their training. An understanding of the implications of Bayes' theorem and its application to the myriad problems of truth, belief, and likelihood that our uncertain world challenges us with daily is something that every scientist (biologist or not) can put to good use in his or her own work, and so this chapter will be something of a Bayes' theorem tutorial in addition to the Python that you will learn when we implement it as code. Bayes' theorem is also a very convenient example for demonstrating simple Python mathematical functions.

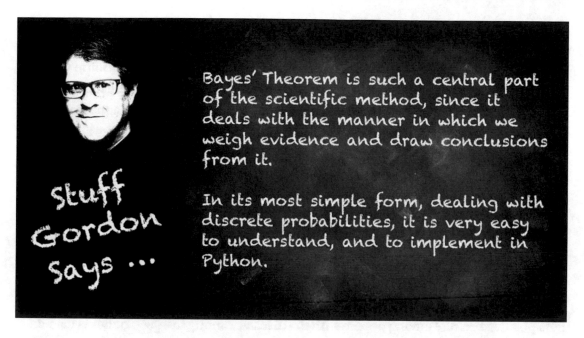

Bayes' Theorem is such a central part of the scientific method, since it deals with the manner in which we weigh evidence and draw conclusions from it.

In its most simple form, dealing with discrete probabilities, it is very easy to understand, and to implement in Python.

stuff Gordon Says ...

So why is Bayes' theorem so useful and what does it have to teach us as life scientists?

By way of a very simple and brief introduction to Bayes' theorem, let's take a look at the development of biomarkers – an area of life science research that is directly concerned with issues of prediction and likelihood.

Bayes' Theorem in Action: Biomarker Performance

Let's imagine that we are looking for a reliable early indicator for a disease which affects about 1.5% of the population and that our research has uncovered a biomarker whose presence is predictive of the disease in about 80% of sufferers. Sounds pretty good right? Most people would probably look at those numbers and conclude that a positive test for the biomarker was associated with something like an 80% chance of having the disease. Not too shabby.

Not so fast.

One very important question that remains unanswered is "How many people who do not have the disease would still get a positive test result with this biomarker?" A biomarker that produced a positive result (indicative of the presence of the disease) in 80% of all patients, with or without the disease, would obviously have no predictive power at all for signaling the presence of the disease. As with the inherent uncertainty that pervades most things in life, biomarkers are seldom if ever 100% reliable, but let's say for the purposes of our story that the biomarker in question produces false positives in about 4% of patients without the disease (i.e., the test result indicates disease where none is actually present). Things seem to be looking up. Armed with these numbers, we might feel that this biomarker has a bright future in the clinic based upon the following reasoning – it will only fail to detect the disease in about 2 out of 10 sufferers and it will only produce a misdiagnosis of the disease in about 4 out of 100 healthy patients.

So now we're in good shape right?

Once again – not so fast.

Let's think about this biomarker's performance from the perspective of a hypothetical population of 10,000 patients. Based upon the 1.5% incidence of this disease in the population, we would expect our population to have about 150 patients with the disease and, therefore, about 9850 without it. Of those 150 patients with the disease, we would expect about 120 to test positive for the biomarker based upon an 80% positive test rate among people with the disease. Among the 9850 patients who do not have the disease, we would expect about 394 to test positive based upon a 4% false-positive test rate for the biomarker.

Now put yourself in the position of one of those patients who just got a positive test result. The first question you're going to ask is "What is the probability that I have the disease given that I tested positive for it?"

This is really the key question. What does the test result actually mean?

To answer that question, let's look at the overall probability of getting a positive test result under any circumstances. We expect 120 patients with the disease to test positive and 394 without the disease to test positive. So out of a total of 514 positive tests, we expect 120 patients who test positive to actually have the disease, corresponding to a probability of about 23%. In other words, the answer to the question of the patient who had the positive test result is that they have only about one chance in four of actually having the disease based upon the positive test result. Put another (and perhaps more optimistic) way, despite the positive test result, there are still about three chances in four that they do not have the disease.

Or put in yet another way – despite the positive test result, the patient is still three times more likely not to have the disease than to have it.

In the light of this new analysis of the biomarker's performance, would you still conclude that this biomarker is a useful clinical diagnostic for this disease? If you were a physician, for example, would you schedule a potentially risky or expensive surgical procedure based upon the one in four chance of the disease indicated by the positive test result? Would you alternatively recommend doing nothing at all despite the positive test result?

You might be really surprised to learn that this "hypothetical" disease biomarker example is based upon the real numbers for the CA-125 biomarker that is actually used as a diagnostic indicator for ovarian cancer. A wealth of statistics have been published both for ovarian cancer incidence and for the use of CA-125 as a diagnostic marker. All that remained for us to do was to plug these numbers into a Bayesian model.

According to the American Cancer Society,[1] the lifetime risk of a woman developing ovarian cancer is about 1 in 72 (0.0134). In a recent study involving more than 78,000 women,[2] the use of CA-125 as a single indicator yielded 3285 false-positive results (~4%) in which healthy women were diagnosed as having ovarian cancer. It is worth noting by the way that the diagnostic probabilities obtained from this admittedly rather crude Bayesian model presented previously do nonetheless correlate rather well with the actual statistics obtained for true- and false-positive tests from studies of women who were tested with CA-125 for ovarian cancer.

Incidentally, if you think we were exaggerating about the naivety of people's interpretation of biomarker statistics, where, for example, a test that detected 80% of cases for diseased patients was equated in people's minds with an 80% probability of having the disease if the test is positive, well unfortunately we were not. In repeated studies, it has been consistently shown that even the majority of physicians, whose job it is to interpret these kinds of statistical results for their patients, struggle with their interpretation,[3] generally ascribing more confidence to their conclusions from them than is actually due.

---

[1]www.cancer.org/index
[2]www.livescience.com/14450-ovarian-cancer-screening-tests-reduce-deaths.html
[3]archinte.jamanetwork.com/article.aspx?articleid=1861033

Bayes' Theorem: The Mathy Bits

The intuitive "algorithm" that we used previously to determine the probability of an event (the patient has a disease), given some prior evidence (the patient tested positive for the disease), can be captured more formally in an equation. The formal description of Bayes' theorem is typically presented as an equation of the form

$$p(B|A) = \frac{p(A|B)p(B)}{p(A)}$$

In the preceding equation, the syntax p(B|A) denotes the conditional probability of outcome B given outcome A. If we plug in the same numbers that we used in our intuitive approach in order to re-calculate the probability of having the disease given a positive test result, they look like this:

*p(disease | positive) = p(positive | disease) * p(disease) / p(positive)*

Note that p(positive) is the total probability for all of the circumstances under which a positive test could occur – in our case, it is the sum of the probabilities for getting a positive test with and without the disease.

*p(positive) = p(positive | disease) * p(disease) + p(positive | no disease) * (no disease)*

*p (positive) = 0.8 * 0.015 + 0.04 * 0.985 = 0.0514*

Therefore, *p(disease | positive) = 0.8 * 0.015 / 0.0514 = 0.233* which corresponds to the 23% probability we arrived at using our intuitive approach.

A Bayesian Biomarker Function in Python

Let's implement this in Python. First, in Listing 4-1, we'll implement a function that is specific to the biomarker example we've seen in this chapter, and then we'll extend it to an implementation of the general form of Bayes' theorem as shown in the preceding equation.

Listing 4-1. Biomarker function

```
def biomarker(pDisease,pPosDisease,pPosNoDisease):
    pNoDisease = 1.0 - pDisease
    pPos = pPosDisease * pDisease + pPosNoDisease * pNoDisease
    return (pPosDisease * pDisease) / pPos
```

We've defined a function `biomarker` that takes three arguments, `pDisease`, the overall (population) probability of having the disease; `pPosDisease`, the probability of getting a positive test result when you have the disease; and, of course, the essential piece of information that we were missing in our initial consideration of a biomarker's performance, `pPosNoDisease`, the probability of getting a positive test result when you do not have the disease (i.e., the false-positive test rate).

Using elementary probability theory, we know that the probability of having no disease is 1.0 minus the probability of having the disease, so we can immediately calculate this quantity that we need for our equation, as seen in the first line of the function:

```
pNoDisease = 1.0 - pDisease
```

Now we are ready to calculate `pPos`, which is all of the ways that it's possible to get a positive test result. In our example, there are two ways – either with the disease or without it.

```
pPos = pPosDisease * pDisease + pPosNoDisease * pNoDisease
```

Finally, we can put it all together by calculating and returning from our function what is essentially the fraction of positive test results that correspond to somebody actually having the disease, out of all possible positive test results.

```
return (pPosDisease * pDisease) / pPos
```

In Listing 4-2, let's test our `biomarker` function with the input parameters corresponding to the real numbers from our ovarian cancer example

Listing 4-2. Biomarker function in action

```
def biomarker(pDisease,pPosDisease,pPosNoDisease):
    pNoDisease = 1.0 - pDisease
    pPos = pPosDisease * pDisease + pPosNoDisease * pNoDisease
    return (pPosDisease * pDisease) / pPos
```

```
pDisease = 0.015
pPosDisease = 0.8
pPosNoDisease = 0.04
print('Probability (disease | positive result) = ', \
biomarker(pDisease,pPosDisease,pPosNoDisease))
```
Probability (disease | positive result) = 0.23346303501945526

Looks good, so in the next section we'll finish up by rewriting our function to reflect the general form of Bayes' theorem as shown in the equation.

String Formatting Using a General Bayesian Function

Listing 4-3. A simple, general Bayesian function with Python string formatting

```
def bayes(outComeA,outComeB,pB,pAGivenB,pAGivenNotB):
    pNotB = 1.0 - pB
    pA = pAGivenB * pB + pAGivenNotB * pNotB
    pBGivenA = (pAGivenB * pB) / pA
    return 'p (%s | %s) = %.2f' % (outcomeB, outcomeA, pBGivenA)
```

In Listing 4-3 we show function that is functionally (no pun intended) the same as the more specific `biomarker` form we just implemented in Listing 4-2, except that we have now included two extra arguments `outComeA` and `outComeB`, so that we can provide to the function descriptions of the outcomes `pA` and `pB`, for which we're calculating the probabilities. These two descriptive arguments are used in the final `return` statement of the function to output the result in a more readable form than the general equation.

You will also see Python's nifty string formatting being used in the `return` statement here.

```
return 'p (%s | %s) = %.2f' % (outcomeB, outcomeA, pBGivenA)
```

This string formatting syntax allows you to put placeholders into a Python string for numbers or text or a variety of other Python data types, which can subsequently be programmatically inserted into the string as needed. In our function, we are outputting the two outcome descriptions as strings (`%s`) and the final calculated `pBGivenA` probability as a floating point number with two decimal places of accuracy (`%.2f`).

58

In Listing 4-4 we show some Python string formatting examples and their outputs to give you a sense of how the syntax works.

Listing 4-4. Python string formatting examples

```
geneName = 'TP53 tumor protein p53 [ Homo sapiens (human) ]'
geneID = 7157
matchProbability = 98.64756341
print('The gene to be analyzed is: %s' % geneName)
print('The gene ID number is: %d' % geneID)
print('The gene match probability is: %.3f' % matchProbability)
print('The results for geneId: %d: %s' % (geneID,geneName))
```
The gene to be analyzed is: TP53 tumor protein p53 [Homo sapiens (human)]
The gene ID number is: 7157
The gene match probability is: 98.648
The results for geneId: 7157: TP53 tumor protein p53 [Homo sapiens (human)]

Notice how the fields need to be contained in parentheses if you are inserting more than one of them into a formatted string (as you can also see in our bayes function output). Full details of the Python string formatting syntax are given in the documentation for Python strings[4] at the official Python web site.

To finish up, let's test our more general bayes function to make sure that it works in Listing 4-5.

Listing 4-5. Using string formatting within a function

```
def bayes(outComeA,outComeB,pB,pAGivenB,pAGivenNotB):
    pNotB = 1.0 - pB
    pA = pAGivenB * pB + pAGivenNotB * pNotB
    pBGivenA = (pAGivenB * pB) / pA
    return 'p (%s | %s) = %.2f' % (outcomeB, outcomeA, pBGivenA)
outcomeA = 'positive test result'
outcomeB = 'has disease'
pB = 0.015
pAGivenB = 0.8
```

```
pAGivenNotB = 0.04
print(bayes(outcomeA,outcomeB,pB,pAGivenB,pAGivenNotB))
```
p (has disease | positive test result) = 0.23

As life scientists, the weighing of evidence is always an important component of our work. I hope that the preceding example makes it clear that in the case of the biomedical sciences at least weighing the evidence naively can have the potential to be extremely costly and even life-threatening. In the life sciences, Bayes' theorem has been successfully applied to a vast array of biological areas as diverse as bioinformatics and computational biology, next-generation sequencing, biological network analysis, and disease evolution and epidemiology, to name but a very few examples.

The fundamentals of Bayes' theorem are extremely easy to grasp, especially when dealing with the point probabilities and binary outcomes that were discussed here, but the applications of Bayes' theorem are vast, not only in the life sciences but in any sphere of activity in which our beliefs and decisions are shaped by weighing the evidence.

Bayes' theorem can be used to analyze many different kinds of data, but hard-coding the data points into your Python program can get a little tedious. To help out, in the next chapter, we'll introduce Python's file handling features.

References and Further Exploration

- An intuitive, visual introduction to Bayes' theorem[5]: a YouTube video created by, yours truly, Amber Biology

- A more detailed explanation of Bayes' theorem, including its application to non-discrete probabilities

---

[5]www.youtube.com/watch?v=3kD6GyMuf4M

CHAPTER 5

Opening Doors to Your Data

Reading, Parsing, and Handling Biological Data Files

"Somebody, please help me!" cried Alice. *"Thanks to my research, I'm literally drowning in data."*

"No my child you are not," said a mysterious voice.

"What? Who are you?" said Alice in the general direction of the disembodied voice.

"I am the Grammar Fairy," said the voice, *"and I'm here to tell you that nobody can literally drown in data. You can literally drown in water, but you can only figuratively drown in data."*

"Oh puh-lease!" said Alice rolling her eyes.

"Sorry," said the Grammar Fairy, *"but people like you who misuse the word 'literally' drive me figuratively insane."*

 Files, **open()**, **close()**, *duck typing, casting,* **float()**, **int()**, *loops,* **for**, *exceptions,* **try**, **except**, *dictionaries,* **string strip()**

 Genes, gene sequences, DNA, FASTA files

© Alexander Lancaster and Gordon Webster 2019
A. Lancaster and G. Webster, *Python for the Life Sciences*, https://doi.org/10.1007/978-1-4842-4523-1_5

So you've been enjoying writing your loops, creating variables and all kinds of other programming delights. But now let's imagine that you now want to start really crunching a lot of data. This chapter is all about pulling that kind of data from ***external files***, where most of that data will most likely "live." To see what your life would be like without reading data from a file, let's imagine we had a list of genes with expression values and you wanted to calculate the mean. Well, you could create a bunch of variables like this:

```
expr1 = 2.1
expr2 = 0.9
expr3 = 0.1
```

And then calculate the mean

```
mean = (expr1 + expr2 + expr3) / 3
```

but that would get old very quickly, especially if we had any more than a few genes to average. And copying and pasting all this data manually into variables would start to get a little tedious. In addition, it would mean that we would be "hard-coding" the gene expression values into the Python code itself. Now ***hard-coding*** doesn't mean that it's difficult to code, it means that the values are *baked into* the code, much the way desiccated coconut is baked into a lamington.[1]

But as delicious as lamingtons are, your code will be much more flexible if we can read that same data from a file. There are by the way cases where it *is* desirable to hard-code things, but let's leave that for another time. Python has got you covered in this department.

Let's put the gene expression data in a simple text file using your favorite text editor and call it gene_expression.txt. Put in the following contents (each level on a new line):

```
2.1
0.9
0.1
```

Opening Files with Python

The first concept to get your head around is that of a file *handle*. Think of it like the handle for the pot that is cooking the sauce for those delicious lamingtons. The handle is just a way to get those yummy ingredients together, they aren't the ingredients

---

[1]A delicious Australian cake

themselves. So let's first create a file handle called f for the file gene_expression.txt using the open() command:

```
f = open("gene_expression.txt", 'r')
```

Let's unpack this a bit. The first of the two arguments to the open() command is pretty clear: it's just the file name, the second argument refers to whether or not we want to modify the *contents* of the file. 'r' means we want the file be *read-only*. We won't be changing the contents of the file, we just want the data: no messing with our ingredients here!

We now can access the ingredients of the file using the f handle. Text files, like our gene_expression.txt friend here, can basically be treated like a "list" of lines. But first of all we have to get the list of ingredients, as it were, from the file handle, and the trusty command to do so is called, wait for it... readlines():

```
lines = f.readlines()
```

The variable lines now contains a list of lines with each element of the list containing the contents of each line as a string. We are now ready to put this together with our knowledge of loops to retrieve all those yummy file contents in Listing 5-1.

Listing 5-1. Opening a file in Python

```
f = open("gene_expression.txt", 'r')
lines = f.readlines()
for line in lines:
  print(line)
```

The code in Listing 5-1 opens the file, gets the lines, and then loops through each line and simply prints the contents of that line back to the screen. If you run the preceding code you should... ah, wait. We forgot to clean up! It's important to remember that like any good chef, we should put away our pots and pans. This means remembering to close() our file handles! This tells the computer that we don't need the contents of that file any more.

OK, now we have the following code in Listing 5-2 that fixes that.

Listing 5-2. Opening a file in Python – with a correct close() function

```python
f = open("gene_expression.txt", 'r')
lines = f.readlines()
for line in lines:
  print(line)
f.close()
```

Running the code should produce the following output:

2.1

0.9

0.1

This is all well and good, but how can we actually *use* the data that we just read in? The first thing to realize is that the numbers output to the screen are not actually numbers! "What's that you say? That's crazy talk! I can see that they are numbers just as plain as day."

Actually they are really strings[2] in disguise, and one way we can see that this is so is that when we print each of the lines to the screen, it includes what is called the *end-of-line* character. No that's *not* the end of the subway line (like Alewife or Braintree on the Red Line of the 'T' in our beautiful hometown Boston[3]). It's the *invisible character* that tells the computer that we are now done with the characters on the line and are ready to start on the next one. This is why there is a space between each of the lines of output, but not in the original file.

So the actual *contents* of the first line in the loop is "**2.1\n**" where **\n** represents the aforementioned end-of-line character. You don't need to know the details of end-of-line character just for the moment, but we will be returning to it later when we get into the really fun stuff like output, so keep it in your back pocket.

So file handles, end-of-line characters, invisible characters, enough with all these abstractions already, how do I get to the actual *values*?

---

[2]https://docs.python.org/2/library/functions.html
[3]www.mbta.com/schedules_and_maps/subway/

Changing Variable Types for Fun and Profit: Casting

Now we need to digress a little to talk about *casting*, no this is not the kind of casting you do for your upcoming big budget Hollywood flick, this kind of casting is about converting variables from one **type** (say a string) to another type (say an integer). You'll recall from Chapter 2 that Python uses **duck typing**, that is, variables get set to a particular type without explicitly having to tell the computer beforehand to expect variables of that type.

So how does casting help us out in our present case?

In our particular case, this is actually really easy. What we really want out of the string **"2.1\n"** is the floating point number **2.1** embedded within. So we simply use the function float() to convert the string to floating point number. You can try this for yourself:

```
line = float("2.1\n")
print(line)
2.1
```

Note that float() has magically extracted the floating point number and removed that unsightly end-of-line character. You have now successfully casted the original string into a floating point number, now contained with the variable line. If, instead of floats, you happened to have had a bunch of data that were all integers, you could have used a similar function called int(), or you can convert integers, or numbers back into strings using the str() function; see the documentation for Python built-in functions[4] for more details.

So, brief digression ended, let's incorporate casting back into our original loop, and note that we are now *storing* the newly re-casted value into a new variable level that we can use later. In Listing 5-3 is the new and improved loop.

Listing 5-3. Opening file and converting to floating point numbers

```
f = open("gene_expression.txt", 'r')
lines = f.readlines()
for line in lines:
  level = float(line)
  print(level)
f.close()
```

---

[4]https://docs.python.org/2/library/functions.html

We also output that data back to the screen using the print() function. If you run the program, you'll now see a much abbreviated output:

2.1

0.9

0.1

Ta da! You've now got actual values from a file into your program! Congratulations. Time to grab some coffee. Don't worry, I'll wait.

Back? OK, so we have a small admission to make, we can't *quite* move on to the fun stuff of doing stuff *with* the data just yet. Yes, we have to deal with the small matter that sometimes there may be *errors* in your input file.

Crikey mate!

Yes, dear reader, you understand that we're not talking about errors in *your* code, but errors that might be introduced into your input data file by *other* people, those who are obviously much less careful and possibly not quite as truly upstanding citizens as yourself.

Perhaps that other person gave you a file that looked like this:

2.1
0.9
3.1xx
0.1

And you were now to run the same code, it would screech to a halt with the following:

2.1
0.9
```
Traceback (most recent call last):
  File "./File_IO.py", line 8, in <module>
    level = float(line)
ValueError: invalid literal for float(): 3.1xx
```

Ouch!

You must guard against these miscreants as much as possible through the magic of error checking. But to avoid hurting the feelings of those other people (who might happen to be otherwise very nice people, collaborators, or maybe your lab PI), we'll adopt the kinder, gentler Python description: exception handling.[5]

When Things Go Wrong: Python Exception Handling

If you were writing programs where everything was hard-coded and there was no external input, you might never need to worry about exceptions. But those would be very boring programs: every time the program ran, it would do exactly the same thing. And you certainly wouldn't be able to do anything very interesting in life science or computational biology if you weren't able to handle data! Even if you are using Python for some theoretical models, you would want to be able modify parameters or read in model specifications.

It's a truism in life sciences as much as in life itself that things might not always go according to plan, so it's worth building in some robustness to your programs as early as possible. Yes, dealing with these exceptions isn't the most fun, it's a little bit like taking some medicine, but trust us, you'll thank us later.

The basic format of handling errors is that we first try to *do our original thing*, which is done in every case except if we get an error, in which case we *do something else*. Makes sense, right? The structure looks like this:

```
try:
    do our original thing
except SomeKindOfError:
    do something else
```

Let's return to our original example. The offending line was in the casting of the float to a floating number. The float() function didn't know what to do with the string, because it wasn't obviously a number. Our original error message in grey, shown earlier, told us that the kind of error we got was a ValueError, so we need to add an exception to deal with this case. We could choose what we want to do if the except happens, the simplest

---

[5]https://docs.python.org/2/tutorial/errors.html

thing would be to just ignore it. To do this you would call the pass function, which amounts to telling the computer "move along, nothing to see here":

```
try:
  level = float(line)
except ValueError:
  pass
```

But it's good debugging practice to identify the offending line, this way you can report back to those who sent you the file, the error of their ways.

```
try:
  level = float(line)
except ValueError:
  print("line is not a number:", line)
```

Note that it's possible that you could have multiple different types of errors, and you could deal with each of them differently by having multiple except clauses, but we're keeping it simple for the time being.

Now the full program is beginning to come into focus (remember to keep your indenting straight) in Listing 5-4.

Listing 5-4. Opening file with exception handling

```
f = open("gene_expression.txt", 'r')
lines = f.readlines()
for line in lines:
  try:
    level = float(line)
  except ValueError:
    print("line is not a number:", line)
    print(level)
f.close()
```

Now let's do some real computation! To return to our original example of calculating an average, we can now do this by keep tracking of the total expression level (sum) and the number of expressions (count) in Listing 5-5.

Listing 5-5. Computing averages from a file on the fly

```
f = open("gene_expression.txt", 'r')
lines = f.readlines()
sum = 0
count = 0
for line in lines:
  try:
    level = float(line)
  except ValueError:
    print("line is not a number:", line)
  print(level)
  sum += level
  count += 1
print("average:", sum/float(count))
f.close()
```

This outputs the following:

2.1

0.9

0.1

average: 1.03333333333

So we've reached our original goal, reading a file in and calculating the average of a bunch of expression levels. But, now you ask, couldn't I have just done the same thing in a spreadsheet? Why do I need all this Python stuff? Yes, that's true, but calculating averages is just the beginning. You get all kinds of data from all kinds of files, and they may be in many different kinds of formats. Python will give you the flexibility to handle just about anything. Next we will build upon our skills and show to parse one of the most common sequence data files: the FASTA file.

We recommend writing your own routines from scratch because it's important to get a granular feel for file handling. At some point, you'll probably find yourself needing to parse files for which there is no existing parser, and if the file format is useful, you may want to incorporate your parser into an open-source package like Biophython since you now have the coding chops to be able to contribute to the ever-expanding universe of open-source bioinformatics!

Reinventing the Wheel: Parsing a FASTA File

FASTA files are one of the most common sequence formats used throughout bioinformatics, genomics, and evolutionary biology. We should say at the outset that if you end up in the world of sequence analysis for a living, you will probably find yourself drawing on existing parsers such as those provided in Biopython[6] that both *read* and *write* a multitude of sequence formats. We highly recommend you investigate these packages when you have the basics we present here firmly under your belt. For example, parsing a FASTA file[7] would as simple as running the code in Listing 5-6 (the import statement will be described more fully in Chapter 6). Note also that this code will not run without having first installed the Biopython package (see how to install Biopython using pip in Chapter 1); however, we are *not* expecting you to execute this code yourself right now, we are showing this simply as an example of the brevity of the code.

---

[6]http://biopython.org/
[7]http://biopython.org/wiki/SeqIO

Listing 5-6. Parsing a file using Biopython

```
from Bio import SeqIO
handle = open("example.fasta", "rU")
for record in SeqIO.parse(handle, "fasta"):
    print(record.id)
handle.close()
```

So, imagine that you want to read some sequences from an organism into your program so that you can ultimately search it for various motifs or genes (this is a topic we'll dive into more deeply in Chapter 7 on Python regular expressions). The *first* step will be reading the sequences from a file. We've created a test data file `Sequences.fasta`, located in the genomes subdirectory to play with. Note that the extension of FASTA files varies considerably; sometimes it might be `.fasta`, as in this case, or sometimes `.fas`, or `.fna`: (a **FASTA** file designator for **n**ucleic **a**cids). So let's jump in and look at the first few lines:

```
>Gene1
AGCTTTTCATTCTGACTGCAACGGGCAATATGTCTCTGTGTGGATTAAAAAAAGAGTGTCTGATAGCAGC
TTCTGAACTGGTTACCTGCCGTGAGTAAATTAAAATTTTATTGACTTAGGTCACTAAATACTTTAACCAA
TATAGGCATAGCGCACAGACAGATAAAAATTACAGAGTACACAACATCCATGAAACGCATTAGCACCACC
ATTACCACCACCATCACCATTACCACAGGTAACGGTGCGGGCTGACGCGTACAGGAAACACAGAAAAAAG
CCCGCACCTGACAGTGCGGGCTTTTTTTTCGACCAAAGGTAACGAGGTAACAACCATGCGAGTGTT
```

As you can see, the basic format of each sequence in a FASTA file is pretty simple:

1. *An identifier*: Starting with a ">" followed by a unique string (the identifier itself).

2. *The sequence*: Which starts on line following the identifier. This sequence consists of multiple symbols (nucleic acids or amino acids) that may appear on a single line, or wrapped across the multiple lines.

The devil, however, is in the details, and because the FASTA format is pretty loose (e.g., it allows blank lines between sequences), our parser should be reasonably robust to these kinds of minor variations in formatting. Obviously there are many more wrinkles that a full FASTA parser might need to handle, for example, catching letters that aren't part of the standard nucleotide "alphabet." But before getting into all the exceptions, we will present our parser in Listing 5-7. Its goal is to read in a FASTA formatted file, save each sequence to a **dictionary,** and print that dictionary.

Listing 5-7. Parsing a FASTA file using standard Python library

```python
f = open("Sequences.fasta", 'r')
lines = f.readlines()
seq_dict = {}
seq_name = None  # initially we have not found a gene
for line in lines:
  if line[0] == '>':
    # get name of the gene to use in the dictionary
    seq_name = line[1:].strip()
    seq_dict[seq_name] = "
  else:
    if seq_name:  # we have a sequence!
      # append the sequence to the dictionary
      seq_dict[seq_name] = seq_dict[seq_name] + line.strip()
print(seq_dict)
f.close()
```

As you can see, the file opening part and the for loop through each of the lines in the file is the same as for our previous example. The key challenge we need to solve is deciding, based on the current line, which of the following three different states we are currently in: (**i**) *no* sequences have been started, (**ii**) we're *starting* a new sequence, or (**iii**) we're adding to an *existing* sequence. We can use the name of the current sequence seq_name to keep track of the state.

At the beginning of the file, no sequences have yet been found, so before we start the for loop, we set seq_name to the None Python constant.[8] As we have already mentioned in previous chapters, None is most often used to indicate when values are *missing* and it is useful in this case because we can refer to the seq_name variable *before* we actually assign a value to it. We also initialize an empty dictionary seq_dict.

---

[8]https://docs.python.org/2/library/constants.html

Now we're ready for the loop. The *first* thing we do *within* the loop is check to see whether the current line contains the sequence start character ">"; if it does, then we're in business! We can now assign seq_name to everything in the line *after* first character using this Python slice: line[1:]. Note that, similar to the previous section on reading gene expression data we need to get rid of the pesky end-of-line character. Here we can use the built-in strip() function which operates on strings to remove all *leading and trailing spaces* and special characters[9] (like end-of-line character). We also initialize the dictionary using that new seq_name to the empty string **"**. This is the empty vessel that we will begin to fill with sequence data.

If the line did *not* start with the sequence start character, then we need to first check to see if a seq_name is currently set. This handles the case wherein we have not yet found a sequence identifier – for example, if the first line of the file was a blank line, then seq_name will be set to None, and this is an example of the need to make sure your code is robust. If it *is* set, then bingo! – we're ready to start adding those sequences to the current dictionary entry in seq_name. This is achieved by extracting the current sequence and using the "+" operator to extend the string by adding a strip()ed version of the current line – also note that this magically handles the case in which the line is blank or composed only of whitespace. Lastly we print out the dictionary.

To put the program through its paces, let's create the test file Sequences.fasta that isn't just a standard FASTA file, but one that deliberately contains a few wrinkles:

```
>Gene1
AGCTTTTCATTCTGACTGCAACGGGCAATATGTCTCTGTGTGGATTAAAAAAAGAGTGTCTGATAGCAGC
TTCTGAACTGGTTACCTGCCGTGAGTAAATTAAAATTTTATTGACTTAGGTCACTAAATACTTTAACCAA
TATAGGCATAGCGCACAGACAGATAAAAATTACAGAGTACACAACATCCATGAAACGCATTAGCACCACC
ATTACCACCACCATCACCATTACCACAGGTAACGGTGCGGGCTGACGCGTACAGGAAACACAGAAAAAAG
CCCGCACCTGACAGTGCGGGCTTTTTTTTCGACCAAAGGTAACGAGGTAACAACCATGCGAGTGTT

>Gene2
GGCGCGCGTCTTTGCAGCGATGTCACGCGCCCGTATTTCCGTGGTGCTGATTACGCAATCATCTTCCGAA
TACAGTATCAGTTTCTGCGTTCCGCAAAGCGACTGTGTGCGAGCTGAACGGGCAATGCAGGAAGAGTTCT
AGGTGATGGTATGCGCACCTTACGTGGGATCTCGGCGAAATTCTTTGCCGCGCTGGCCCGCGCCAATATC
AACATTGTCGCCATTGCTCAGGGATCTTCTGAACGCTCAATCTCTGTCGTGGTCAATAACGATGATGCGA
CCACTGGCGTGCGCGTTACTCATCAGATGCTGTTCAATACCGATCAGGTTATCGAAGTGTTTGTGAT
```

---

[9]https://docs.python.org/2/library/stdtypes.html#str.strip

AAAACTGGCGTGCGCGTTACTCATCAGATGCTGTTCAATACCGATCAGGTTATCGAAGTGTTTGTGAT

> Gene 3 (other comment)
TACAGTATCAGTTTCTGCGTTCCGCAAAGCGACTGTGTGCGAGCTGAACGGGCAATGCAGGAAGAGTTCTATTTC
CCAATTTTTAGGAACCC

Note that we have introduced an additional two sequences with differing formatting: Gene2 has a line space between the identifier and the sequence, and Gene 3 contains identifiers with additional spaces, as well as having the sequence on a single line (as opposed to being separated into multiple lines). If we run the program PFTLS_ Chapter_05_02.py, we should see the sequences being printed as a dictionary:

{'Gene1':'AGCTTTTCATTCTGACTGCAACGGGCAATATGTCTCTGTGTGGATTAAAAAAAGAGTGTCTGATA
GCAGCTTCTGAACTGGTTACCTGCCGTGAGTAAATTAAAATTTTATTGACTTAGGTCACTAAATACTTTAACCAA
TATAGGCATAGCGCACAGACAGATAAAAATTACAGAGTACACAACATCCATGAAACGCATTAGCACCACCATTAC
CACCACCATCACCATTACCACAGGTAACGGTGCGGGCTGACGCGTACAGGAAACACAGAAAAAAGCCCGCACCTG
ACAGTGCGGGCTTTTTTTTCGACCAAAGGTAACGAGGTAACAACCATGCGAGTGTT','Gene2': 'GGCGCGC
GTCTTTGCAGCGATGTCACGCGCCCGTATTTCCGTGGTGCTGATTACGCAATCATCTTCCGAATACAGTATCAGT
TTCTGCGTTCCGCAAAGCGACTGTGTGCGAGCTGAACGGGCAATGCAGGAAGAGTTCTAGGTGATGGTATGCGCA
CCTTACGTGGGATCTCGGCGAAATTCTTTGCCGCGCTGGCCCGCGCCAATATCAACATTGTCGCCATTGCTCAGG
GATCTTCTGAACGCTCAATCTCTGTCGTGGTCAATAACGATGATGCGACCACTGGCGTGCGCGTTACTCATCAGA
TGCTGTTCAATACCGATCAGGTTATCGAAGTGTTTGTGATAAAACTGGCGTGCGCGTTACTCATCAGATGCTGTT
CAATACCGATCAGGTTATCGAAGTGTTTGTGAT',Gene 3 (other comment)': 'TACAGTATCAGTTT
CTGCGTTCCGCAAAGCGACTGTGTGCGAGCTGAACGGGCAATGCAGGAAGAGTTCTATTTCCCAATTTTTAGGAA
CCC'}

Note that the program has handled each of the test cases like a champ, with all identifiers correctly being used as dictionary keys and all sequences consisting of contiguous nucleotide identifiers.

So good work, people! In the next chapter, we'll introduce Python **regular expressions**, which will supercharge our searches for sequence needles (like in this chapter) in the genomic haystacks.

References and Further Exploration

- Biopython[10]: the granddaddy of bioinformatics toolkits in Python, it contains parsers for multiple bioinformatics file formats, among many other features.

- PyCogent[11]: a newer toolkit for analyzing sequences, interaction with third-party applications with a special focus on molecular evolution and genomics

---

[10]http://biopython.org/
[11]http://pycogent.org/

CHAPTER 6

Finding Needles in Haystacks

Regular Expressions for Genomics and Sequencing

"Oh dear!" said the White Rabbit. "I'm running late for the lab meeting and I still have a mountain of gene sequencing data to process."

Having abandoned his calculator and spreadsheets and forked over a king's ransom for some fancy desktop application for handling gene data, the White Rabbit was still frustrated. The application that had seemed like it wanted to be all things to all people was, when push came to shove, simply unable to do the particular kind of analysis that he needed to process his experimental data.

Suddenly and without warning, a large, wise old toad sitting on a lily pad in the middle of the pond croaked a single word: "Python!"

"What, no, no, no!" exclaimed the very harried White Rabbit. "Everybody knows that Python is slow because it's an interpreted language, and time is something that I do not have any surplus of."

"Hey, you're the rodent with the fancy waistcoat and pocket watch, and I'm just some old guy who eats flies. What do I know?" said the elderly toad hopping into the water in search of his next meal.

Regular expressions, the **re** *module, Python modules and submodules,* **import***, the Python* **MatchObject***, iterators, Python bytecode, Python interpreter, the* **random** *module, the year 2038 problem, the* **time** *module, Cython, SWIG, Python standard library*

Next-generation sequencing, gene promoters, restriction enzymes, restriction sites, genomes, DNA, nucleotides, chromosomes, consensus sequences, mismatches

A. Lancaster and G. Webster, *Python for the Life Sciences*, https://doi.org/10.1007/978-1-4842-4523-1_6

Those of you who are involved in genomics or next-generation sequencing are particularly going to enjoy this chapter in which we introduce regular expressions, one of the most powerful text-handling features of Python.

The best way to think of a regular expression is as a **searchable pattern** in a character sequence. The simplest kind of pattern is a straight sequence of characters like the kind we saw for defining DNA restriction sites in Chapter 3 on sequences. Remember that we defined a restriction site as a recognition motif and a position relative to it, at which the enzyme cuts the DNA, like this:

```
restrictionEnzymes['bamH1'] = ['ggatcc',0]
```

And although we didn't actually use regular expressions in that chapter, the small sequence **'ggatcc'** that we searched for would be a valid regular expression – a regular expression in which every position in the searchable pattern is uniquely and unambiguously defined by a character.

But let's think about a slightly more complex example – one in which we might want to have more than one possible character at a given position. The restriction enzyme *NciI* recognizes the DNA sequence **CC(C or G)GG** (and cuts the DNA after the second C). How could we represent this restriction enzyme in our Python library?

One way to do it would be to search for both of the possible sequence variants **CCCGG** and **CCGGG**. This would work, but it would be very inefficient as it would require running the entire search for each sequence variant. Now imagine doing that for a restriction enzyme like *ScrFI* which has the recognition site CC(A,T,C or G)GG! This would require separate searches for the sequence variants **CCAGG, CCTGG, CCCGG,** and **CCGGG,** and this enzyme only has ambiguity at a single position! Some restriction enzymes recognize multiple bases at multiple positions in their recognition sites, creating tens or even hundreds of possible sequence variants that would need to be searched.

Fortunately, there is a much (much) better, faster, and more efficient way to do it, and regular expressions are it.

The Python Regular Expressions Library and `import`

In order to use regular expressions in Python, we need to ***import*** the Python regular expressions library[1] re and cannot rely on simple string searching methods like `find`. What does it mean to `import` a library? Well, by using the re library, we are stepping outside of the *core* language features (things that are built in) and are using features that are part of the **Python standard library**. Think of this as if the core language is the inner solar system (Mercury, Venus, Earth, Mars), the standard library could be thought of as the outer planets (Jupiter, Saturn, Neptune, Uranus). They are still part of the Python Solar System, but they just happen to be orbiting a bit further out. Importing modules is simple, simply type at the beginning of your program

```
import re
```

And you're done! (Of course if you are using a different module, you will replace re with that module name.) If you simply need to use a global function in that module, as we do in this chapter, this is all you need. (In practice, many modules consist of various *submodules,* we will talk about submodules and the associated concept of *namespaces* in Chapter 7, but until then this simple form of import should be sufficient.)

So in Listing 6-1, let's jump in and use the Python regular expression library's equivalent of the string find method. We'll also use the library of restriction enzymes that we created in the chapter about working with sequences, except that we can now expand its functionality to work with DNA restriction sites that allow more than one base at any given position.

Listing 6-1. Creating regular expressions (with output shown inline)

```
import re
restrictionEnzymes = {}
restrictionEnzymes['bamH1'] = ['ggatcc',0]
restrictionEnzymes['sma1'] = ['cccggg',2]
restrictionEnzymes['nci1'] = ['cc[cg]gg',2]
restrictionEnzymes['scrF1'] = ['cc[atcg]gg',2]
```

---

[1]docs.python.org/2/library/re.html

79

```
sequence1 = 'atatatccgggatatatcccggatatat'
print(re.findall(restrictionEnzymes['bamH1'][0],sequence1))
[]
print(re.findall(restrictionEnzymes['nci1'][0],sequence1))
['ccggg', 'cccgg']
print(re.findall(restrictionEnzymes['scrF1'][0],sequence1))
['ccggg', 'cccgg']
```

First we import the Python regular expression library with the import re statement, and then we create our restriction enzyme library (we've just recreated the code from Chapter 3 here for completeness). You will see that we've now also added the two new restriction enzymes that we discussed previously, which allow more than one base at one position in their recognition sites.

Next we defined a sequence into which we deliberately added the two variants of the *NciI* recognition site which we also separated with stretches of **at** pairs just to make them easy to see.

Finally, we use the re module's findall method to search the sequence for the regular expressions that corresponds to the recognition sites for ***BamH1***, ***NciI***, and ***ScrF1***. Let's take a look at each of them.

The regular expression for BamH1 is just a simple string: 'ggatcc'.

The regular expressions for ***NciI*** and ***ScrF1*** contain a position defined by square brackets with a set of characters inside them. This is the regular expression syntax for specifying what characters are permissible at that position in the pattern. You can think of the square brackets as a kind of OR statement – for example:

'cc[cg]gg' means "**cc** followed by **c** or **g** and then **gg**"
'cc[atcg]gg' means "**cc** followed by **a** or **t** or **c** or **g** and then **gg**"

In our example code in Listing 6-1, we can now see why the ***BamH1*** search failed to produce any hits and why both ***NciI*** and ***ScrF1*** matched the two recognition sites we inserted into the sequence, since they satisfy the search criteria for both enzymes – the two possible sites that match ***NciI*** are actually a subset of the sites that match ***ScrF1***, with ***ScrF1*** also allowing **a** and **t** at the central position in the recognition site.

Turns out, there's actually an even simpler regular expression syntax to allow any of the four bases at the central position in the ***ScrF1*** recognition site.

```
restrictionEnzymes['scrF1'] = ['cc.gg',2]
```

A period in a regular expression means that any character is able to match the search pattern at that position. In our DNA sequence world, this would mean any of **a, t, c,** or **g,** but be careful here – it would also accept any other character, including characters that would *not* be elements of a valid DNA sequence.

Identifying Gene Promoters with Regular Expressions

Let's look at a slightly more complex example of how the power of regular expressions can be harnessed for working with DNA sequences – searching for biologically interesting sequences in a genome such as **gene promoters** (we'll explore the varied and interesting ways promoters can be used to control gene expression levels in Chapter 12 on biochemical kinetics). Gene promoters often consist of relatively conserved recognition sequences separated by a spacer sequence, often of variable length. Many bacterial gene promoters, for example, consist of two distinct recognition sequences upstream of the gene to be transcribed like in Figure 6-1.

```
5' ----PPPPPP------------------PPPPPP----GGGGGGGGGGG … 3'
        |                        |        |
       -35                      -10     start of gene
```

Figure 6-1. *Typical bacterial gene promoter*

The consensus sequence for the recognition site at the -10 position is **tataat**, while the -35 site has a consensus sequence of **ttgaca**. We can quite easily craft a Python regular expression that would search a genome for such consensus promoter regions like this:

```
promoter = 'ttgaca.................tataat'
```

This would match any sequences that consisted of exactly the two consensus recognition sites separated by a fixed number of bases (with any of the four bases being allowed at those positions). Since these sequences are the consensus sequences for motifs that are themselves actually subject to some variability, we could extend the search to account for this variability by allowing mismatches at sites in the consensus sequences that we know to be more variable, like this:

```
promoter = 'ttga.a.................ta...t'
```

But what if the spacer between the consensus sequences is of variable length?

It turns out that regular expressions give us a simple and efficient way to deal with this situation as well. We can create search patterns that allow a variable number of bases between the recognition sites like this:

```
promoter = 'ttgaca.{15,25}tataat'
```

The curly brackets after the period are used to indicate a repeat of between 15 and 25 occurrences of the character preceding the brackets – in this case the period that matches any base. This search pattern would match any stretch of the genome consisting of the two consensus recognition sites, separated by between 15 and 25 bases of any kind.

```
sequence2 = 'cccccttgacaccccccccccccccccccctataatccccc'
sequence3 = 'cccccttgacaccccccccccccccccccccccctataatccccc'
print(re.findall(promoter,sequence2))
['ttgacaccccccccccccccccccctataat']
print(re.findall(promoter,sequence3))
['ttgacaccccccccccccccccccccccctataat']
```

As we can see from the preceding code, the regular expression `'ttgaca.{15,25}tataat'` matches both `sequence2` and `sequence3` which differ only in the length of the spacer between the two consensus sequences.

The MatchObject: Our First Real Encounter with Python Objects

Now you're probably looking at the results from the `re.findall` method and thinking that there's something missing. Sometimes it's enough to know whether or not a matching pattern is present in a sequence and to see what it is, but what if I also want to know *where* it is in the sequence? Fear not, for the `re.finditer` method is your friend for this problem. The `finditer` method does not return a simple list of matches in the way the `findall` method does, since the `finditer` method is capable of running a more sophisticated kind of search that yields a set of richer and more structured results. Here's what it looks like if we try to just directly print the result from a `finditer` search:

```
print(re.finditer(promoter,sequence2))
<callable-iterator object at 0x100409290>
```

Uh, okay – what's a "callable-iterator object" and what do I do with it?

In order to handle this additional complexity, the `finditer` method returns an iterable collection of Python **MatchObject** objects instead that allows the search results to be stepped through one at a time and each one analyzed more extensively. Technically, the `finditer` method returns an object that is a kind of ordered list of other objects. The top-level result of the method is an **iterator** that can be stepped through by calling each of its contained objects in turn using the `for element in object` syntax that we've already seen for strings and lists. Each of the elements referenced in the **iterator** object is actually a Python `MatchObject` which is kind of like a mini database for each search hit that can be queried to extract and analyze the information about the match that it contains.

In addition to the more traditional *procedural* programming style that is essentially blocks of instructions for the computer to follow, Python also supports *object-oriented* programming (often abbreviated as OOP). We've already had a little taste of this with the object methods we have used (like string.find), and in Chapter 7, we'll really get into the nuts and bolts of OOP. For now though, it is sufficient to think of Python **iterator** and `MatchObject` as other kinds of Python objects like a `String` or an `int`, each with its own attributes and methods.

In Listing 6-2 we show some code that shows how to iterate through the list of search hits returned by the `finditer` method (this assumes that the variables have already been defined as above) and interrogate each corresponding `MatchObject`.

Listing 6-2. Iterating through regular expression matches

```
matches = re.finditer(promoter,sequence2)
for m in matches:
    print(m.group())
    print(m.start(),m.end())
ttgacaccccccccccccccccctataat
5 34
```

There is actually only one search hit to iterate through in our simple example, and we print the matching sequence and its start and end positions using the `MatchObject` methods, `group()`, `start()`, and `end()`. This gives you a flavor of how regular expression search results can be handled, but there's a lot more that you can do with them than we've discussed here. If you'd like to know more, check out the official Python documentation on MatchObjects.[2]

Regular expressions have a long history in computer science and are pretty much ubiquitous in computer programming languages. The regular expression patterns that we have seen so far in this chapter barely scratch the surface of what they can do – indeed, it would be possible to fill an entire book[3] with a discussion of regular expressions. For the purposes of this brief introduction to regular expressions however, if you're looking for a good path for getting deeper into regular expressions, it's probably best to start with the official Python documentation. This Python regular expression "how-to"[4] is a really great place to start.

But Python is Too Slow for Real Genomics Work Right?

Now, some of you may be saying that is all well and good for searching really small sequences of the kind we have seen in the examples shown here, but can it work for the kind of sequences that researchers in the fields of genomics and next-generation sequencing are interested in? Sequences that can often run to many millions of base pairs in length?

The answer is yes.

I raise this point because you might one day hear (or have already heard) someone say something like this: "Python is an interpreted language and therefore too slow for intensive computational work." While this blanket statement is largely a big, steaming pile of you know what, it does contain a germ of truth insofar as there are under certain circumstances, some downsides to interpreted programming languages that have to do with performance.

Compiled programming languages like C and Fortran are converted into a set of machine-executable instructions prior to running the code, so that when you hit "run," the hardware can immediately go to work executing the code. These compiled languages generally have a performance advantage as a result of this. With an interpreted language like Python by contrast, the code must be both parsed and converted into executable

---

[2]https://docs.python.org/2.0/lib/match-objects.html
[3]regex.info/book.html
[4]docs.python.org/2/howto/regex.html

code on the fly before the code can actually be run by the hardware. This explanation of compiled vs. interpreted languages is however very simplistic. There are languages including Python that also use an intermediate layer of code called bytecode in which the original programming language has already been converted into a set of instructions that are very close to the machine's own executable instruction set. Bytecodes can be run extremely efficiently as a result, since there is very little overhead in converting them on the fly into machine-executable instructions. This means that you can have some parts of your Python code being parsed and interpreted at runtime, and some parts of it that are already compiled to bytecode for more rapid and efficient execution.

But wait (as the infomercials love to say), there's more!

The situation with Python is further complicated by the fact that Python modules can also be written in other languages like C and then compiled into machine-executable instructions and linked to the Python interpreter. This means that your Python code can be run as interpreted code, from bytecodes, or directly as machine-executable instructions – all from within the same application!

The official Python interpreter is actually written in C, as are many of the modules that come with it as part of the Python standard library.[5] This means that when you call these standard library modules from your code that is running in the Python interpreter, the functions and methods that these modules contain can be run directly (and very efficiently) as compiled machine-executable instructions (so long as they are able to run without encountering a reference to anything back into the interpreted code).

Perhaps you can guess where we're going with this brief detour into computer science.

The regular expression library in Python that we brought into our code by importing the module re in which it resides is written in C and compiled. It is also highly optimized code and extremely efficient, as we hope to demonstrate in the next block of code that we show you.

Let's look at an example from human genomics.

The largest contiguous sequence in the human genome is chromosome 1 with its 250 million base pairs. In Listing 6-3, let's create a random, synthetic chromosome 1 and use Python regular expressions to probe its sequence.

---

[5]https://docs.python.org/2/library/index.html

Listing 6-3. Creating random synthetic chromosome

```python
import random
bases = ['a','t','c','g']
sequenceList = []
for n in range(0,250000000):
    sequenceList.append(random.choice(bases))
chromosome = ''.join(sequenceList)
```

First we import the Python random module which contains code for generating random numbers and sequences. In this code we are going to build a random, 250 million base sequence. Since Python strings, as we know from Chapter 3, are immutable, it is more efficient to build a very large string as a list and then to convert the list to a string.

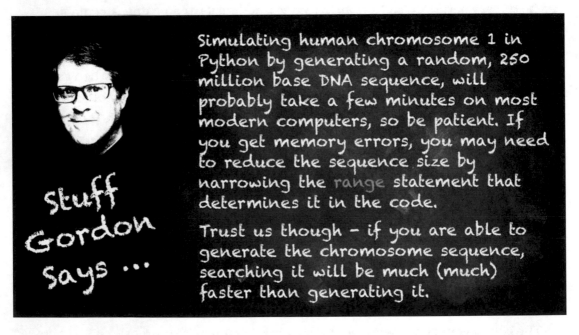

Simulating human chromosome 1 in Python by generating a random, 250 million base DNA sequence, will probably take a few minutes on most modern computers, so be patient. If you get memory errors, you may need to reduce the sequence size by narrowing the range statement that determines it in the code.

Trust us though – if you are able to generate the chromosome sequence, searching it will be much (much) faster than generating it.

Our random sequence will be composed of the 4 DNA bases a, t, c, and g, and we will use the random.choice method to randomly add them to our list one at a time, until we have our required length of 250 million bases. We can then use the join method to take our list and convert it to the string that we will use as our synthetic chromosome. Note that the join method on the empty string " takes each element of the list specified in its argument and adds it to the resulting string using the empty string as the separator.

We use the empty string in our case, because we don't want any separators between the bases in the sequence.

When you run this block of code, don't be surprised if it takes a few minutes to complete. This is a big string to assemble. The code to create our synthetic gene sequence will be by far the slowest part of the code in this chapter.

Once we have our synthetic chromosome assembled as a string, let's append some code to Listing 6-3 to see how long it takes to search it using Python regular expressions. To start our testing, let's search our 250 million base synthetic chromosome for the downstream consensus sequence **'tataat'** from our gene promoter example that we saw earlier. The full code is shown in Listing 6-4.

Listing 6-4. Creating synthetic chromosome and searching for regular expression

```
import time
import random
bases = ['a','t','c','g']
sequenceList = []
for n in range(0,250000000):
    sequenceList.append(random.choice(bases))
chromosome = ''.join(sequenceList)
searchPattern = 'tataat'
t1 = time.time()
result = re.finditer(searchPattern,chromosome)
t2 = time.time()
print('Start time =',t1,'seconds. End time =',t2,' seconds.')
```

So here we introduce another Python, the `time` module, which, as the name implies, handles time. The `time.time()`method returns the number of seconds since an arbitrary fixed date and time referred to in the Python documentation as the start of the epoch. This all sounds very prehistoric and/or apocalyptic, but you might be surprised to learn that this grand dawn of history is actually January 1, 1970.

Stuff Gordon Says ...

The standard approach to counting time on computers was defined by the engineers of Unix - one of the first real computer operating systems, and it has been inherited by virtually all other computer platforms as a kind of de facto standard for time. Since the first Unix systems appeared in the early 1970s, Unix engineers decided that the oldest possible date for a Unix file system was midnight on January 1st 1970, which became the official "dawn of time" for pretty much all computer systems everywhere.

If you're interested in learning more about this, you might want to read about the upcoming Year 2038 Problem which is the end of the epoch for Unix time, unless operating systems make some changes to the way that time values are stored and handled.

Anyway, after that little aside about Unix time, back to genomics...

We're going to use the time() method to see how long our regular expression search code takes to search the 250 million bases of our synthetic chromosome for the '**tataat**' consensus sequence. We will record the time in seconds just before the start and again as soon as the code has run, and we can then compare the result (your numbers will look a bit different to these numbers, because you'll be running the code in the future relative to when this book was published):

```
Start time = 1446646598.11 seconds. End time = 1446646598.11 seconds.
```

Okay – that's fast. If you look at the start and end times, they're the same – at least to two decimal places of precision. Let's do a more appropriate benchmark by running our search many times over and averaging the results to get a better idea of how long the search is really taking. We'll also subtract the start time from the end time and average over the number of search repeats, so that we get a direct measure of how long the search took.

The fact that we are going to repeat our timed search **one million times** in Listing 6-5 should give you a sense of how fast this regular expression search really is.

Listing 6-5. Timing a repeated search one million times (output is interspersed)

```
import time
import random
bases = ['a','t','c','g']
sequenceList = []
for n in range(0,250000000):
    sequenceList.append(random.choice(bases))
chromosome = "".join(sequenceList)
searchPattern = 'tataat'
nsearch = 1000000
t1 = time.time()
for n in range(0,nsearch):
    result = re.finditer(searchPattern,chromosome)
t2 = time.time()
print('Average search time was ',(t2-t1)/float(nsearch),' seconds')
```
Average search time was   1.06230282784e-06   seconds
```
nmatches = 0
for match in result:
    nmatches += 1
print('Number of search hits = ',nmatches)
```
Number of search hits = 60951

You can see that was fast! – about 1 microsecond for each complete search. Wait a minute though. Was this search fast just because it didn't find any matches?

Let's see. In the end part of Listing 6-5, we iterate through the search hits (remember, **finditer** returns an iterable object) and we count them. Based upon our timing numbers, **the finditer search is identifying more than 60,000 matches in our 250 million base sequence in about a microsecond**. Python regular expression searches are just really fast!

Let's do one more timing test in Listing 6-6, this time with a slightly more complicated regular expression which will allow any base in the fourth position.

Listing 6-6. Second timing test

```
import time
import random
bases = ['a','t','c','g']
sequenceList = []
for n in range(0,250000000):
    sequenceList.append(random.choice(bases))
chromosome = ''.join(sequenceList)
searchPattern = 'tat.at'
nsearch = 1000000
t1 = time.time()
for n in range(0,nsearch):
    result = re.finditer(searchPattern,chromosome)
t2 = time.time()
print('Average search time was ',(t2-t1)/float(nsearch),' seconds')
```
Average search time was   1.0852959156e-06   seconds
```
nmatches = 0
for match in result:
    nmatches += 1
print('Number of search hits = ',nmatches)
```
Number of search hits =   239051

As we can see, the number of hits we get has now ballooned to almost 240,000 which is not surprising since we are using a more permissive search pattern. The average time for each search is however still close to a microsecond.

So next time somebody tells you that Python is too slow for any kind of intensive computation, you can politely show them the impressive performance of its regular expression searches – searches furthermore that you were able to run by simply typing a few lines of code and hitting "run" instead of having to go through the separate steps of compiling and linking your code as you would for a compiled language. Did I also mention that your Python code will run "as is" on any computer with a standard Python distribution on it?

Like much of the Python standard library, the re module that handles regular expressions is actually written in C, so while the initial function call to the search may be handled by the Python interpreter, the subsequent search is actually being run in compiled native code, which explains its efficiency. Indeed, one of the great strengths of the Python language is that it interfaces very easily with natively compiled languages like C, allowing computationally intensive parts of your code to be run down "on the bare metal" with regard to CPU and memory, largely free of the overhead of the Python interpreter.

There are even modules like Cython that allow you to write Python code, convert it to C, and compile it as a machine-executable module that you can just `import` into your application in the way that you would do for any other Python module. There is also a framework called SWIG that allows you to write modules in C and compile and link them to the Python interpreter (see references at the end of the chapter for more information on both of these modules). A certain degree of additional technical knowledge is useful to have if you're interested in using one of these approaches to create some high-performance code for your Python project, so we'll mention them in passing here, with the caveat that these are somewhat more advanced Python coding topics that are really beyond the scope of this introductory book.

The next chapter will continue our introduction core features of the Python language by entering the mysterious world of object-oriented programming (OOP). We will stay in the land of biological sequences for the time being – they will be our guidepost as we learn just how useful object-oriented programming is to quantitative explorations of biology.

References and Further Exploration

- Cython[6]: a module for converting Python code to C
- SWIG[7]: the Simplified Wrapper and Interface Generator

---

[6]cython.org/

[7]www.swig.org/Doc1.3/Python.html

CHAPTER 7

Object Lessons

Biological Sequences as Python Objects

"I don't need to organize my stuff," declared the Mad Hatter. "I have a system all of my very own that looks totally chaotic if you're not me, but trust me – I know exactly where everything is."

"What happens when you come back from your holidays?" asked one of the dinner guests. "Can you still recall where everything is?"

"What if somebody else moves something?" asked another of the dinner guests.

"Or you move something yourself and neglect to put it back in exactly the same place?" asked yet another.

"Or!" snapped the Mad Hatter, red-faced. "Everything gets moved around by a bunch of your ungrateful dinner guests poking their big noses into it all when they should know better!"

In the uncomfortable silence that followed, all of the dinner guests just stared into their teacups.

Object-oriented programming, functional programming, procedural programming, objects, classes, instances, methods, inheritance, decorators, the Python **Object**, **__init__()**, **self**, *constructors, class and instance variables, overriding,* **__str__()**, **print**

DNA, RNA, protein, sequences, sequence searching, transcription, translation, genetic code, codons, molecular weight, nucleotides

A. Lancaster and G. Webster, *Python for the Life Sciences*, https://doi.org/10.1007/978-1-4842-4523-1_7

In this chapter, we're going to give you a very concise introduction to object-oriented programming (OOP), a programming idiom that you're probably going to want to learn if you ever need to write more than relatively simple scripts with Python. There's a great deal of talk about OOP with plenty of accompanying hype on both sides of the argument for and against it. In much the same way as we saw in the case of regular expressions, entire books have even been devoted to the subject. The simple truth is that OOP is a way to organize your code that done right will generally make it cleaner, easier to understand, easier to maintain, and more reusable. If you're thinking that we fall into the positive camp with regard to OOP, based upon that description of it, you would be right. It's important to stress however that it's *one* way of writing code but not the *only* way. OOP is not perfect for all situations. For small scripts, for example, OOP can feel like using a sledgehammer to crack a nut.

Why Object-Oriented Programming?

There's also a hotly debated issue that lies at the core of all computer programming languages, about how to manage the states of all of the entities (variables, functions, etc.) that are created in code, in such a way that the robustness and consistency of the code scales with its complexity. In a nutshell, there's a good argument to be made that the OOP paradigm is not the best approach to managing code as it gets really complex and you start to have a lot of moving parts. The alternative to OOP that is often put forward is functional programming. This debate is way beyond the scope of this book, but we wanted you to be aware of it, lest you should think that we are presenting OOP as a panacea for all ills. OOP may not be perfect, but it is the paradigm within which the vast majority of programmers around the world are currently writing code at the time of writing of this book.

In our experience, having used OOP and non-OOP programming idioms, we would say that OOP succeeds pretty well in its stated goals of helping the programmer to better manage the complexity of larger coding projects with lots of moving parts. If you're asking yourself at this point, "Should I learn OOP?" we would say a definitive "Yes" if you ever want to pursue any kind of larger project in Python, or indeed any other OOP programming language (like Java).

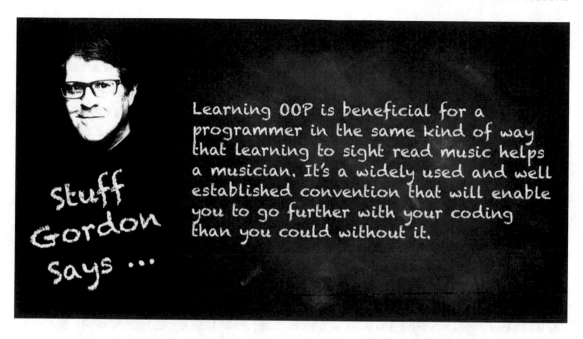

Learning OOP is beneficial for a programmer in the same kind of way that learning to sight read music helps a musician. It's a widely used and well established convention that will enable you to go further with your coding than you could without it.

Stuff Gordon Says ...

Becoming conversant in the OOP paradigm will also serve you well if you ever need to learn other programming languages since most modern and popular languages (Java, C++, Ruby, C#, etc.) are OOP-centric.

What we aim to provide in this chapter is an introductory guided tour of the OOP landscape and how OOP is implemented in Python. Our intention in this is to give you enough information to get you started in OOP programming with Python, without burdening you with an exhaustive (and exhausting) survey of the field, that in any case could fill this entire book and leave no room for anything else!

So to start our discussion of what OOP is, let's start with what it is *not* – in other words, how is OOP different from most what we have seen so far in this book?

OOP is all about Organizing Our Programs

Much of the code we have seen so far is written in a procedural programming style which, as the name suggests, essentially consists of blocks of code organized into procedures for the computer to follow. These procedures are mainly functions and methods in Python, but in other programming languages, they might be called subroutines or blocks. The common feature they all share is that they organize the code into smaller units or tasks – for example, reading in a data table for a 96-well plate from a file or calculating the molecular weight of an oligonucleotide from its sequence.

To be clear, the hardware that runs the code doesn't really give a fig about organizing code. When everything is working as it should, the hardware will simply execute the instructions it is given in their specified order, with no concerns about how sensible, tidy, or organized the code is. The way that the code is organized by the programmer might in certain circumstances impact its efficiency of execution (if there's unnecessary redundancy, for example), but assuming that the code is correct insofar as it actually does what the programmer intends it to do, and is free of bugs, it will be run by the hardware whether or not it is efficient or well organized.

So, as a general principle, we could say that **organizing code is mainly for the programmer's benefit** (and also for the benefit of anybody else who might need to read, understand, use, collaborate on, or modify her code).

OOP is a *conceptual model* for whatever it is the programmer is trying to implement in his or her code that, as its name suggests, uses *objects* as its core building blocks.

We've actually already encountered Python objects in earlier chapters when we used the **object.method** syntax – the `list.append()` method, for example, for appending items to the end of a list. The `list` object is already defined for you in the Python standard library, but to really get behind the scenes and understand Python objects, let's design one or two of our own, for an application area that we're very familiar with – biology.

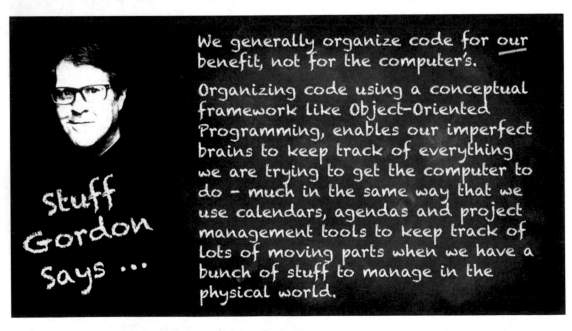

We generally organize code for our benefit, not for the computer's.

Organizing code using a conceptual framework like Object-Oriented Programming, enables our imperfect brains to keep track of everything we are trying to get the computer to do – much in the same way that we use calendars, agendas and project management tools to keep track of lots of moving parts when we have a bunch of stuff to manage in the physical world.

Stuff Gordon Says ...

An OOP Implementation for Handling Biological Sequences

Let's imagine that we're creating an application that manages biological sequences and that the application must handle DNA, RNA, and protein sequences. These all seem like good candidates for Python objects in our code, so let's use them as an example.

So if you're sitting comfortably and paying attention, here's the first really big thing you need to know as a newcomer to OOP.

When we describe an object in OOP code, **we're actually describing a template for that object which is called a** class. This makes perfect sense if you think about it. Our application may handle hundreds or even thousands of sequence objects, so it makes sense to write one master description for all of them.

A class is a template for an object that defines all instances of that object. We refer to each actual object an *instance* of the class to which it belongs. In this sense then, when we talk about objects in Python, what we are referring to are **instances of a particular class**.

Before we can create instances (objects), we first need to describe the class in terms of (**i**) what properties it stores – these are often referred to as fields, instance fields, or instance variables – and (**ii**) what it can do, that is, its methods. The best way to explain each of these is to consider what they would look like in our sequence class (we're going to start using the term **class** from here on when we're describing the template for the object and **instance** when we're describing an actual object which is an instance of a class).

Each sequence object is going to have to be able to store the actual sequence of nucleotide bases if it's a DNA and RNA sequence, or peptides if it's a protein, but what else might a sequence object need to have? Maybe a name as well, or an accession number for the database from which it was extracted. The fields in a class can also be used to set the *states* of the objects that it defines – for example, if the object is an amino acid in a protein, you could imagine having a Boolean (True/False) field that defines whether or not it is phosphorylated. You can probably think of many more fields that we could include in our sequence example, but for now we'll assume that our Sequence class includes a name field and a sequence field.

Namespaces and Modules

We need to pause here for a brief detour to talk about **namespaces** and **modules**. What are those I hear you asking? Well, namespaces we briefly mentioned in Chapter 6 when we introduced the `import` statement. If you've ever "surfed" the Internet (hey, remember the 1990s?), and come across a little web site called Google, you'll have encountered these namespaces all the time, you just won't have called them that. google.com itself is a namespace, and these familiar sites

news.google.com
images.google.com

are really just elements within the overall **google.com** namespace. Within a namespace, everything must be unique. For example, there can't be two **images** in the **google.com** namespace but obviously **images.yahoo.com** is OK since it's in completely different namespace. Namespaces are used in several different ways in Python, they allow you to refer to elements using a shorthand, as well as grouping classes and functions into **modules**.

For example, all the classes we are creating in this chapter are contained within the file `PFTLS_Chapter_07.py`, this file itself constitutes both a **module** *and* a **namespace** (for even more details and examples on modules and namespaces, consult the trusty Python language manual's section on modules[1]). We will return to modules and namespaces when we discuss ways of importing individual classes and functions from modules in Chapter 11, but for the time being, it suffices to say that each Python class must have a unique name within this module (see also the Python tutorial[2]). All that said, let's return to our discussion of the classes.

Structure of the Class Definition

Notice how we are now writing the name of our class in Python coding style, and by convention, Python programmers tend to start class names with an uppercase character (this is not mandatory, but rather a practice that is widely agreed upon by Python programmers to make everybody's code more widely readable and easy to understand).

---

[1]`https://docs.python.org/2/tutorial/modules.html`
[2]`https://docs.python.org/2.7/tutorial/classes.html`

If the class name consists of more than one word, for example, ProteinSequence, the general Python convention is to use so-called CamelCase, where the first letter of each word is uppercase.

The convention for fields by contrast is that they generally start with lowercase letters and only use uppercase letters to mark the start of a new word, for the sake of readability. So, for example, our Sequence class might contain the fields sequence and sequenceName. You can already see how this helps make the code more readable since you can now distinguish between the Sequence class and the sequence field that it contains.

Don't worry too much about these conventions right now, but it's a good practice to start using them early on in your code. Forgetting or confusing them might make your code harder to read, but it will not break it.

Figure 7-1 shows what our Sequence class looks like so far, sketched out as a little diagram.

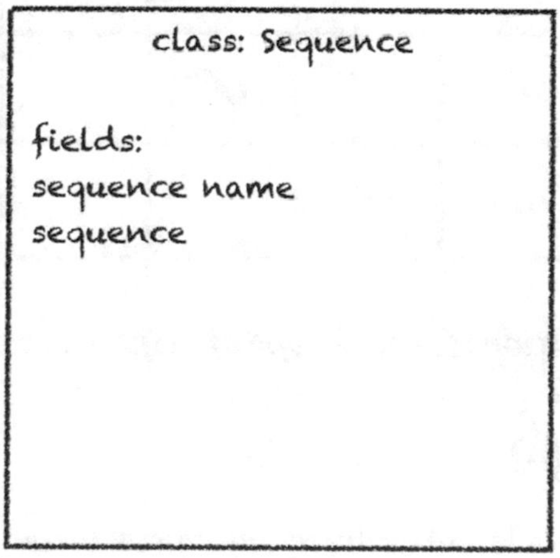

Figure 7-1. *Sequence class overall structure*

We have two fields, but no methods yet. Methods, as we saw in the string.find() example in Chapter 3, are functions that are specific to a particular class. Methods define what the class can do, and they generally act upon or with an object of that class. For example, we used the string.find() method like this: mySequence.find('ttt') to locate the pattern 'ttt' in the string mySequence.

So what do we need our Sequence class to be able to do?

We'll probably need to implement a search method for locating patterns of interest in the sequence, but now we come to a little conundrum...

Are we going to use our Sequence class for all three types of sequence?

The reason we're asking is that there might be some methods that aren't applicable to all three types – for example, a function to translate a DNA sequence into a protein sequence would make no sense being applied to a sequence that was already a protein sequence to begin with. Maybe we will need to code three separate classes in our application, one for each type of sequence. Wait a minute though – would that mean having to code the search method that we want for all sequence types separately for each type?

Okay, hold that thought for a minute and we'll draw up a table in Figure 7-2 that shows what methods we would like to have for each sequence type.

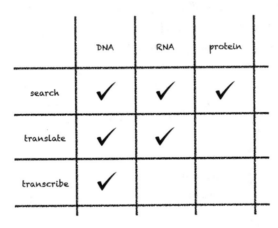

Figure 7-2. *Desired functions for each type of Sequence subclass*

Class Inheritance

One way for sure that we could satisfy the requirements of this table would be to code each sequence type as a separate class, but with the caveat that we would have to create some redundant code. There is however a feature of OOP that was designed to help the programmer out with this kind of problem and it's called inheritance.

Just as parents have children who inherit their attributes, OOP classes can have *child classes* that inherit the fields and methods from their *parent classes*. As OOP programmers, we can even choose which attributes get inherited by the child classes and which don't. Similarly, we are free to endow our child classes with new attributes that their parent classes do not have. What this means for us in practice is that every attribute we want to have as common to all of our child classes, we can put into the parent class from where it will be inherited. In our example, this means that the search method which we want to have in the DNA, RNA, and protein classes need only be written once in the parent class for it to be inherited as a method in each sequence type.

We'll see how this works in more detail in a minute, but let's jump in and see how we create classes in Python by coding the parent class for DNA, RNA, and protein sequences. We'll call this parent class **Sequence** since it's a kind of generic class that isn't a specific sequence type. This need not even be a class that we actually intend to use, but rather it can be just a kind of generic placeholder class from which the specific classes that we actually want to use can inherit some of their fields and methods. In some programming languages, these generic classes can even be specified as *abstract classes* which means that they cannot be *instantiated* directly (i.e., used to create instances (objects) of the class), but can only be invoked via their child or *subclasses*. Python does actually have a way of specifying abstract classes using a feature of the Python language called decorators[3] which we will not discuss here because they are a more advanced Python topic that is beyond the scope of this beginner's introduction.

So in Figure 7-3 is the design for our top-level or parent class for biological sequences. Remember that its two fields and one method will be inherited by all of the subclasses that we create from it.

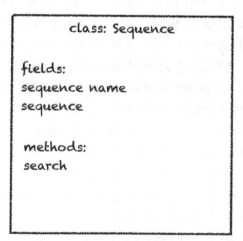

class: Sequence

fields:
sequence name
sequence

methods:
search

Figure 7-3. *Design of parent Sequence class*

[3]https://wiki.python.org/moin/PythonDecorators

And in Listing 7-1 is the code to create our parent class for biological sequences.

Listing 7-1. Parent class for biological sequences

```
# A Python class for handling biological sequences
class Sequence:
    def __init__(self,name,sequence):
        self.name = name
        self.sequence = sequence
    def search(self,pattern):
        return self.sequence.find(pattern)
```

It is important to remember that this code just defines the Sequence class, it does not create any instances (objects) until we instantiate it. A Python class definition starts with the **class** keyword, followed by the name and a colon. As we will see in a minute, if the class we are creating is a subclass that inherits from a parent class, we would also include the name of the parent class in parentheses after the current class name. Since Sequence however is a top-level class, we don't need this additional syntax.

What we just told you is not strictly speaking true. The very top-level class in Python is pyObject from which all other classes inherit. When you create your top-level class in Python, it *automatically and invisibly* inherits from pyObject, a bunch of useful properties that are inherent to all Python objects, for example, the __init__ method that is used to create an instance of the class (a class definition that contained no methods for instantiating the class would not be very useful right?).

So the __init__ method is pretty much always the first method to be defined in your new class, since it contains the instructions that tell the class how to create instances of itself. You will also notice that the rather strangely named self is always the first argument that is passed to __init__. This is just the reference to the object that we are creating. You can think of it like a kind of address at which the object is to be stored. You don't need to know what the actual address is – Python handles all of that for you behind the scenes.

The __init__ class method in Python, is the starting point for all instances of any Python class.

In OOP terminology, __init__ is known as a constructor, and it is always the first class method to be executed upon instantiation of a Python class.

stuff Alex Says ...

You can see how all of this works in the next two lines of __init__. You will notice that for our Sequence class, the __init__ method requires the two arguments name and sequence which are passed to it from outside. The first thing that the Sequence class does when it creates a new instance is to use these two external variables to define its own name and sequence fields. These are its own versions of name and sequence that are unique to the object itself and no longer need correspond with the values of those external variables or, indeed, with the name and sequence variables of any other instances of the Sequence class. This is really what self means. Whenever you refer to it within the contact of an object, it always means that object's version of that field. This allows you to distinguish between the object's version of a field (e.g., self.name) and, for example, an external variable (e.g., name) with the same name or, indeed, the same field from another object.

As a little aside to explain self more fully, imagine that you had a class with a method that allows the object to compare itself with another object of the same class (a very common scenario in programming, for example, to determine if two strings or numbers are equal). The external object is passed to the current object's method as an argument – the (non-mandatory) convention among Python programmers in such a situation is to call the external object other to make the distinction with self really clear. Now the current object's method can do the comparison between its own version of the field and the other object's version of it, something like the code in Listing 7-2.

Listing 7-2. Function to compare names between two objects

```python
def compareNames(self,other):
    if self.name == other.name:
        return True
    else:
        return False
```

So when you initialize your new object with the __init__ method, you always use the argument self to essentially establish the reference to that object that will enable you to refer unambiguously to its fields and methods in your code. In some OOP languages, self is passed to the constructor as a hidden variable, but in Python we have to explicitly pass it.

You can see that in our very simple example, all that the __init__ method does for the Sequence class is to define the name and sequence fields. Following the __init__ method, we have also included the search method which we want to be inherited by all of the subclasses of Sequence. Notice that like all instance methods, it takes self as the first argument. The search method also takes a second argument pattern which is as its name suggests is the pattern that will be searched in the object's self.sequence.

Since Sequence is a real class, even though we intend to use it more like an abstract class, let's go ahead and create an instance of it to test our parent class code and make sure it works (make sure you've first executed the code to define the class in Listing 7-1):

```python
mySequence = Sequence('Some made up sequence','cgtatgcgct')
print(mySequence.name)
```
Some made up sequence
```python
print(mySequence.sequence)
```
cgtatgcgct
```python
print(mySequence.search('gcg'))
```
5

So far so good. Our parent class Sequence works as expected. We were able to create an instance mySequence of the class, and we could then use the **object.property** syntax to access its fields and methods.

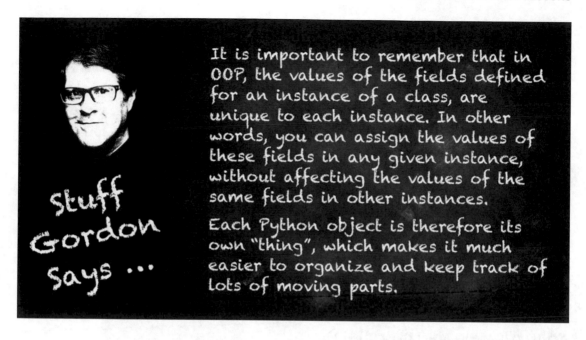

It is important to remember that in OOP, the values of the fields defined for an instance of a class, are unique to each instance. In other words, you can assign the values of these fields in any given instance, without affecting the values of the same fields in other instances.

Each Python object is therefore its own "thing", which makes it much easier to organize and keep track of lots of moving parts.

Stuff Gordon Says ...

Now let's go ahead in Listing 7-3 and create our first subclass of Sequence which will be specifically designed to handle DNA sequences (note that the code in Listing 7-1 needs to be executed first).

Listing 7-3. Defining a subclass of Sequence: DNASequence

```
class DNASequence(Sequence):

    def __init__(self,name,sequence):
        Sequence.__init__(self,name,sequence)

    def transcribe(self):
        return self.sequence.replace('t','u')
```

Notice firstly how we now have the parent class in parentheses after the current class name to indicate that this new class DNASequence is a subclass of Sequence. You'll also notice that the code from our __init__ method has been replaced with a single line that simply passes the name and sequence arguments back up to the __init__ method that we already wrote for the Sequence parent class. It's important to note that we could also include more code in the __init__ method for our DNASequence subclass to add additional steps to the initialization of the object that are not present in the parent class – but for now, we'll content ourselves to just use the steps already present in the __init__ method from the parent class to initialize instances of our subclass as well.

You will also notice that the search method is not present in the subclass definition since we want to inherit it from the Sequence parent class and we also have a new method transcribe that is not in the parent class. This makes sense since the transcribe method is specific to DNA sequences, and we would not want it to be inherited by the other sequence types (which it would be if we put it in the parent class).

As before (after executing the code in both Listing 7-1 and Listing 7-3), let's create an instance of our new DNASequence subclass and test it:

```
myDNASequence = DNASequence('My first DNA sequence','gctgatatc')
print(myDNASequence.name)
```
My first DNA sequence
```
print(myDNASequence.sequence)
```
gctgatatc
```
print(myDNASequence.search('gat'))
```
3
```
print(myDNASequence.transcribe())
```
gcugauauc

Nice!

Even though we didn't explicitly include the search method in our DNASequence subclass, we can see that it was successfully inherited from the Sequence parent class, as we expected it would be. We also have a new method transcribe that is specific to the DNASequence subclass. Subclasses inherit from parent classes, not the other way around, so the transcribe method will not be inherited back to the parent Sequence class nor to any of its subclasses. If you're the empirical type who values only knowledge based upon experience, you can verify this last statement by attempting to use transcribe from the parent class.

```
print(mySequence.transcribe())
AttributeError: Sequence instance has no attribute 'transcribe'
```

Let's continue and create an RNASequence class, which will include a translate method for translating its nucleotide sequence into a peptide sequence. For the sake of efficiency when working with long sequences, the translate method will initially create a list of peptides and use the join method on the empty string to turn it into a single string. In order to translate the RNA codons, we will also create a Python library containing the standard genetic code that will serve as a lookup table for translation.

In Listing 7-4 is the code for the RNASequence class (requires also executing the code in Listing 7-1 for this to work).

Listing 7-4. Defining a subclass that includes a class variable

```
import string
rnaToProtein = {'uuu':'F','uuc':'F','uua':'L','uug':'L',
                'ucu':'S','ucc':'S','uca':'S','ucg':'S',
                'uau':'Y','uac':'Y','uaa':'STOP','uag':'STOP',
                'ugu':'C','ugc':'C','uga':'STOP','ugg':'W',
                'cuu':'L','cuc':'L','cua':'L','cug':'L',
                'ccu':'P','ccc':'P','cca':'P','ccg':'P',
                'cau':'H','cac':'H','caa':'Q','cag':'Q',
                'cgu':'R','cgc':'R','cga':'R','cgg':'R',
                'auu':'I','auc':'I','aua':'I','aug':'M',
                'acu':'T','acc':'T','aca':'T','acg':'T',
                'aau':'N','aac':'N','aaa':'K','aag':'K',
                'agu':'S','agc':'S','aga':'R','agg':'R',
                'guu':'V','guc':'V','gua':'V','gug':'V',
                'gcu':'A','gcc':'A','gca':'A','gcg':'A',
                'gau':'D','gac':'D','gaa':'E','gag':'E',
                'ggu':'G','ggc':'G','gga':'G','ggg':'G'}
class RNASequence(Sequence):
    def __init__(self,name,sequence):
        Sequence.__init__(self,name,sequence)

    def translate(self):
        peptide = []
        for n in range(0,len(self.sequence),3):
            codon = self.sequence[n:n+3]
            peptide.append(rnaToProtein[codon])
        peptideSequence = ''.join(peptide)
        return peptideSequence
```

The code for the translate method is slightly more complicated, but if you look carefully, you will see that it is simply iterating through the RNA sequence three bases at a time and using the rnaToProtein dictionary to translate each three-base codon into a peptide.

Let's test the new subclass (be sure to execute code in Listing 7-1 and Listing 7-4 first) to see how it works:

```
myRNASequence = RNASequence('My first RNA sequence','gcugauauc')
print(myRNASequence.name)
```
My first RNA sequence
```
print(myRNASequence.sequence)
```
gcugauauc
```
print(myRNASequence.search('gau'))
```
3
```
print(myRNASequence.translate())
```
ADI

Finally and for completeness, we'll round out our set of biological sequence subclasses with a ProteinSequence class in Listing 7-5 (requires executing code in Listing 7-1 first).

Listing 7-5. ProteinSequence subclass

```
class ProteinSequence(Sequence):
    def __init__(self,name,sequence):
        Sequence.__init__(self,name,sequence)

myProteinSequence = ProteinSequence('My first protein
sequence','MDVTLFSLQY')
print(myProteinSequence.name)
```
My first protein sequence
```
print(myProteinSequence.sequence)
```
MDVTLFSLQY
```
print(myProteinSequence.search('LFS'))
```
4

Rather than just having the class methods transcribe and translate produce a string with the transcribed or translated sequence, we could of course directly output the appropriate class. In Listing 7-6 we show an updated DNASequence class which provides an alternative to the transcribe method that outputs a new RNASequence instead of just the RNA sequence as a string (note that the Sequence and RNASequence classes need to be first defined by executing the code in Listing 7-1 and Listing 7-4).

Listing 7-6. Updated DNASequence that returns an RNASequence object

```
class DNASequence(Sequence):
    def __init__(self,name,sequence):
        Sequence.__init__(self,name,sequence)
        self.residues = {'a':313.2,'c':289.2,'t':304.2,'g':329.2}
    def transcribe(self):
        return self.sequence.replace('t','u')
    def transcribeToRNA(self):
        rnaSequence = self.sequence.replace('t','u')
        rnaName = 'Transcribed from ' + self.name
        return RNASequence(rnaName,rnaSequence)

newRNASequence = myDNASequence.transcribeToRNA()
print(newRNASequence.name)
```
Transcribed from My first DNA sequence
```
print(newRNASequence.sequence)
```
gcugauauc

In the new `transcribeToRNA` method, we can see that it's actually an instance of the RNASequence class that gets returned instead of just a string encoding an RNA sequence. This is just to illustrate that from a Python perspective, there's really nothing special about instances of user-defined classes. Instances of a class can be returned from functions and methods, they can be passed to them as arguments, and **classes can even appear as fields inside other classes**.

To show you how much easier classes and objects can make your life, in Listing 7-7 let's expand our parent class a little with a couple of extra methods and new field.

Listing 7-7. Expanding the parent class

```
class Sequence:
    def __init__(self,name,sequence):
        self.name = name
        self.sequence = sequence
        self.residues = {}

    def search(self,pattern):
        return self.sequence.find(pattern)
```

```
def molecularWeight(self):
    mwt = 0.0
    for residue in self.sequence:
        mwt += self.residues[residue]
    return mwt

def validSequence(self):
    for residue in self.sequence:
        if not residue in self.residues:
            return False
    return True
```

Most of this code is the same as before, but you can see that we've added an additional line to the __init__ method to define a field called residues. We are going to use this field to define the one-letter codes and molecular weights of the residues in the sequences of the subclasses, but in the parent class which you'll remember is essentially a generic sequence class that we don't plan to use directly, residues is just an empty dictionary. Strictly speaking, we did not need to add residues to the parent class at all, but we like to put these kind of placeholder fields into parent classes, even if we don't intend to ever actually instantiate the parent class. It serves as a kind of reminder to us that we need to include this field in the subclasses.

The other big changes are two methods molecularWeight and validSequence which use the residues dictionary to calculate the molecular weights and to validate the sequence, respectively. Validating the sequence in this case means verifying that all of the residues in the sequence are valid for that particular sequence type. We can see what this means if we modify residues field to the __init__ method of the DNASequence class as in Listing 7-8 (you'll need to first load the Sequence and RNASequence classes by running the code in Listing 7-7 followed by the code in Listing 7-4).

Listing 7-8. Add residues to DNASequence subclass

```
class DNASequence(Sequence):
    def __init__(self,name,sequence):
        Sequence.__init__(self,name,sequence)
        self.residues = {'a':313.2,'c':289.2,'t':304.2,'g':329.2}
    def transcribe(self):
        return self.sequence.replace('t','u')
```

```
def transcribeToRNA(self):
    rnaSequence = self.sequence.replace('t','u')
    rnaName = 'Transcribed from ' + self.name
    return RNASequence(rnaName,rnaSequence)
```

The dictionary keys of `residues` are just the four DNA nucleotides, and their corresponding values are their molecular weights (we haven't included any molecular weights for terminal or modified residues in this simple example). Now we can have a DNASequence object calculate its own molecular weight and also validate its sequence, like this:

```
print(myDNASequence.molecularWeight())
```
2775.8
```
print(myDNASequence.validSequence())
```
True

Class Variables, Instance Variables, and other Classes as Variables

Okay – we have to come clean here and admit that we probably just did something somewhat silly, at least from an OOP perspective. The way we included the `residues` dictionary in the `__init__` method means that each instance of the class DNASequence will have its own copy of the residue properties. This is dangerous from the perspective that we could, in principle, accidentally reassign the values of these properties in any particular instance of the DNASequence class and thus create a DNASequence object that no longer shares common properties with other DNASequence instances (by the way, there could be circumstances under which we might actually *want* this, in which case we are not so stupid). The approach we used is also inefficient, since we now have to store duplicate copies of the same dictionary in every DNASequence instance. This is not a big deal for tens or even hundreds of sequences, but it might be for millions of sequences.

Wouldn't it be nice if there was a way to do the one-time creation of a field for an entire class, to which all instances of that class would have access, without having to carry their own, individual copies of that field? It turns out that there is a way to do exactly this in Python, using a construct known as a **class variable**, of which we'll learn more in just a moment – so stay tuned.

Notice that once we had added the two extra methods to the parent Sequence class, all we had to do was add a single line in the DNASequence subclass to define the residues for that sequence type, and then we had the extra functionality on tap. In order to extend this functionality to the RNASequence and ProteinSequence subclasses as well, all we need to do is to similarly add the residues dictionary to the __init__ methods of each of them as well, obviously including the residue definitions that are appropriate to each sequence type.

These last changes show how well objects can help not only to organize your code but also to make it more consistent and easier to use. All of our sequence classes have the same syntax and functionality for searching, calculating molecular weights, and validating the sequence. Each of the subclasses also has additional functionality that is consistent with its specific sequence type – there's no way, for example, to inadvertently have your application try to transcribe a protein sequence, which would make no sense and, if allowed to proceed unchecked, could cause errors and inconsistent behavior in subsequent parts of the application that might be much harder to trace and debug. Remember how we previously remarked upon the common and consistent functionality and syntax for Python string and list objects with the **[from:to]** syntax? You've just seen exactly how you can bring that kind of clean organization and consistency to your own code by using classes.

It's important to realize that there's nothing fundamentally different in Python about a class you create yourself vs. one of the core classes that are provided in the Python library, like strings, ints, and floats. A class you create can even be used as a field inside another class. For example, let's take the residues field in the DNASequence class and make it a class of its own, with its own functionality.

In Listing 7-9 is the definition of our new class: DNANucleotide.

Listing 7-9. Class to handle nucleotides

```python
class DNANucleotide:
    nucleotides = {'a': 313.2, 'c': 289.2, 't': 304.2, 'g': 329.2}
    def __init__(self,nuc):
        self.name = nuc
        self.weight = DNANucleotide.nucleotides[nuc]
```

By way of illustrating the manner in which classes can be used in a nested manner (where classes appear as fields within other classes), we will keep this example really simple, but we will also use this example to craftily introduce Python class variables.[4] You can see a class variable definition in the line

```
nucleotides = {'a': 313.2, 'c': 289.2, 't': 304.2, 'g': 329.2}
```

that appears within the class definition. Notice however that **it does not appear in the code for actually instantiating the class**. This makes it a variable that is shared by all instances of the class DNANucleotide, rather than being a field in one of those instances.

Why would we want this? A little more explanation is due...

It would be very convenient if the DNANucleotide class were somehow able to contain its *own* definition of DNA nucleotides that is separate from any definitions contained anywhere else in the code. This means that the class DNANucleotide would always be using the same set of consistent data, and it also breaks the potentially dangerous dependency of a programmer using the DNANucleotide class in their code, but failing to provide anywhere in their code the definition of the nucleotides that it needs.

One way to achieve this would be to give each instantiation of the DNANucleotide class its own copy of the nucleotide definition – within the __init__ routine, for example. This would work fine, but it could also be a little wasteful. If we're building, for example, the DNA sequence of human chromosome 1, we might end up with about 250 million nucleotides, each of which would need storage for its own copy of the nucleotides data definition. Furthermore, our goal in embedding this data in the DNANucleotide class is to make coding with this class safer, more robust, and more consistent. We don't therefore really want every single instance of DNANucleotide having its *own* definition of this data – rather, we would like them all to share one copy of the *same* data.

Hence the **class variable** – a single definition that is in effect shared by all instances of the class, rather than each instance having to carry its own copy.

---

[4]https://docs.python.org/3/tutorial/classes.html#class-and-instance-variables

When writing code to tackle small to medium-sized projects, it's tempting not to worry too much about how efficient or robust your code would be for larger-scale projects.

Sometimes this is okay, but there can often be a big payback down the line, in taking a little extra time to adopt good coding practices that make your code scalable to larger tasks.

We will see how to reference a class variable in a moment, but just think about it for a moment. Since the definition is not made within the class instance, we cannot use the self.field syntax that we're used to for working with fields in class instances.

If we look at the **__init__** routine, we can see that it takes a single nucleotide and then uses the dictionary contained in the nucleotides class variable to also add the molecular weight property.

Like so:

```
def __init__(self,nuc):
    self.name = nuc
    self.weight = DNANucleotide.nucleotides[nuc]
```

So now you can see how to reference the nucleotides class variable.

```
self.weight = DNANucleotide.nucleotides[nuc]
```

Like all class variables, it's just the class name followed by the variable name.
Let's do a quick test to make sure our new class works.

```
nucleotide = DNANucleotide('g')
print(nucleotide.name, nucleotide.weight)
g 329.2
```

Great!

In the interests of keeping things simple, we're only adding a couple of fields to DNANucleotide, making it a minimally functional class. In practice, when you're going to all the trouble of creating a new class in Python, you would probably have in mind a great degree of data encapsulation and functionality than we have shown in this simple example.

Now we'll use our new DNANucleotide class inside a class for DNA sequences, and just to continue to keep things simple, we'll temporarily create a new DNA sequence class of its own as well in Listing 7-10 – one that does *not* inherit all of the stuff from the former Sequence class.

Listing 7-10. New parent class

```
class NewDNASequence():
    def __init__(self,name,sequence):
        self.name = name
        self.sequence = []
        for s in sequence:
            d = DNANucleotide(s)
            self.sequence.append(d)

    def molecularWeight(self):
        mwt = 0.0
        for s in self.sequence:
            mwt += s.weight
        return mwt

    def __str__(self):
        nucs = []
        for s in self.sequence:
            nucs.append(s.name)
        return ".join(nucs)
```

If you look at the __init__ routine, you will see that we're reading in a sequence string as previously, but now we're actually looping through the sequence one letter at a time and using each letter to create a new instance of the DNANucleotide class. We're then appending that new class instance to a list that we established when we instantiated the class. The sequence field in this new class is therefore no longer just a character string, but a list of class instances.

Before we move on to discuss the other details of this new class, take a moment to consider that there's actually a great deal of embedding of classes going on here. Not only are we embedding the DNANucleotide class as a field in the NewDNASequence class, but we're using the Python list class to store the sequence of DNANucleotide classes!

Let's create an instance of our NewDNASequence class and examine it in detail (after first executing the code in Listing 7-10).

```
myDNASequence = NewDNASequence('My new DNA sequence','gctgatatc')
print(myDNASequence.sequence[0])
```
<__main__.DNANucleotide instance at 0x10cd7cf38>

Interesting!

When we try printing the first element in the class sequence field, instead of getting a letter, we actually get the kind of printed representation that Python uses to show you that you referenced a class – in this case a DNANucleotide instance with the ID 0x10cd7cf38. Don't worry too much about the ID – it's essentially just a pointer that Python uses under the hood for whenever your code needs to reference that particular class instance. In other words, it tells the code where to look when it encounters a reference such as s.name where s would be, for example, an instance of DNANucleotide with the ID 0x10cd7cf38.

We can confirm that the sequence field of myDNASequence is a list of DNANucleotide instances by simply printing out the instance fields for one of the elements in the list, like this:

```
print(myDNASequence.sequence[0].name)
```
g
```
print(myDNASequence.sequence[0].weight)
```
329.2

You will see that we also added a molecularWeight method to our new class to show that the functionality to calculate molecular weights is now kind of embedded or *enshrined* if you prefer within the DNANucleotide class, and we don't need to provide any additional nucleotide molecular weight tables in the code to access this functionality. Note that we couldn't really write the molecularWeight method within the DNANucleotide class, because it only makes sense in the context of a sequence of DNANucleotide instances. However, the essential core of what the enclosing NewDNASequence class needed to create this method was provided by the DNANucleotide class.

```
print(myDNASequence.molecularWeight())
```
2775.8

This is an important aspect of good coding practice because it is what programmers would call a *portable implementation*. For example, another programmer could take your DNANucleotide class and drop it in their code and use it without having to worry about dependencies like the need for a table of nucleotide molecular weights that has a nomenclature and format that make it compatible with the code for your class.

A Little More about Inheritance and Overriding Inherited Methods

Before we finish this chapter on OOP, we would like you to cast your minds back to earlier in this chapter when we told you that under the hood, all Python objects automatically and invisibly inherit from a master Python class called pyObject.

This turns out to be incredibly useful in many ways, one of which is that the creators of Python could use pyObject to define placeholder fields that are universal to all Python objects. Here's a concrete example.

When you use the Python print command, it seems to automagically know how to render to the console output stream a printed representation any kind of object from a simple integer or a string to a list or even a class.

Try running this code and you'll see what we mean:

```
a = 10
b = 10.0
c = 'DNA'
d = [1,2,3,4,5]
print(a, b, c, d)
```
10 10.0 DNA [1, 2, 3, 4, 5]

The trick that Python is using here is that there is a special method in every object called __str__() that, when run, returns the string representation for that class. When you write your own classes, this method is present, but it will default to the __str__()

method that it inherits from either pyObject or from a superclass (i.e., a class of which is a direct or indirect subclass). If you create your own Python class, for example, Python has no idea how best to render an instance of it in a meaningful form as text using the print function so it defaults to the safe option of just saying in effect: "**This is an instance of class x and its ID is y**".

The trick here is that the print function runs the object's __str__() method in order to get the appropriate string representation that it needs to write to the output stream of the Python console.

The even more interesting trick is that you, as the programmer, can override the __str__() method for a class if you want a different string representation of it when you print it. All you have to do to override this (or any) inherited method is to simply supply your own version of it in your class definition. If you look back at the class definition that we wrote for NewDNASequence, you will see that we did exactly that.

When we wrote our class definition for the DNANucleotide class, we did not bother to override __str__(); hence, when we tried to print it out, we got that kind of default "this is an instance of class x" message along with the ID of the class instance, like this:

<__main__.DNANucleotide instance at 0x10cd7cf38>

Since we did take the time to supply our own version of __str__() in our NewDNASequence class, effectively overriding the generic class version of it that it inherits from pyObject, we will see that if we try to print an instance of the NewDNASequence class, we get exactly the string representation that we specified in our overridden __str__() method – in this case, a string of characters representing the sequence, like this:

```
print(myDNASequence)
```
gctgatatc

So that concludes our introduction to object-oriented programming with Python. In subsequent chapters in this book, we will build further on the ideas presented here. As always though, it is well worth while looking at the official Python documentation[5] for classes. And even beyond the Python programming language, if you really want to deepen your understanding of object-oriented programming, it is well worth reading one of the many excellent books that discuss the OOP paradigm in more depth (see the following section).

---

[5]https://docs.python.org/2.7/tutorial/classes.html

In the next chapter, we'll explore genomic data in even more depth: examining how we can use Python to analyze large-scale data consisting of billions of "short sequences," sometimes called next-generation sequence (NGS) data.

References and Further Exploration

- Gamma, Helm, Johnson, and Vlissides, *Design Patterns: Elements of Reusable Object-Oriented Software*[6] (Addison-Wesley. 1994). This is a classic text on different forms of object-oriented patterns (often referred to as "The Gang of Four" after its four authors).

- Harold Abelson, Gerald Jay Sussman, and Julie Sussman, *Structure and Interpretation of Computer Programs*[7] (MIT Press, 1996). This book is something of a computer science bible. The authors discuss computer programming tools like abstraction and modularity that are used in the family of conceptual models for computer programs, of which OOP is a member.

---

[6]www.amazon.com/Design-Patterns-Elements-Reusable-Object-Oriented-ebook/dp/B000SEIBB8/ref=mt_kindle

[7]www.amazon.com/Structure-Interpretation-Computer-Programs-Second/dp/0070004846

CHAPTER 8

Slicing and Dicing Genomes

Next-Generation Sequencing Pipelines

"A caterpillar sitting on a mushroom, smoking a hookah," said Alice. "Now that's not something you see every day!"

"You want to know why I sit on this mushroom?" said the caterpillar. "It's because I'm a fun guy!"

Alice groaned. "Really?"

"Not really," said the caterpillar. "It's just because the authors of this book really liked this picture of us and wanted to use it – but being too lazy and unimaginative to find a witty connection between a smoking caterpillar and next-generation sequencing, which by the way is the subject of this chapter, they resorted instead to making some lame mushroom jokes."

"Wow! That's really meta-insightful," said Alice impressed. "What's next-generation sequencing?"

"Oh no you don't!" exclaimed the caterpillar. "Now you're just enabling them. Fictional characters we may be, but pandering to those pedestrian hacks is still way beneath our dignity."

---

 with *statement,* **subprocess**, **argparse**, **pysam** *libraries*

 Short-read sequencing, mapping, alignment, BWA, VCF, BAM and SAM formats

---

A. Lancaster and G. Webster, *Python for the Life Sciences*, https://doi.org/10.1007/978-1-4842-4523-1_8

In this chapter we'll take you into the world of **deep sequencing**, sometimes called next-generation sequencing **(NGS)** or **short-read sequencing**. Look it even sounds futuristic, it has a subtitle from the *Star Trek*[1] franchise in the phrase! Most working biologists have probably heard about this technology, and you may be keen to get your hands on this kind of data to ask your own questions. But you may also be daunted by the intimidating terminology and word salad of tools and acronyms involved – BWA, NGS, VCF – and the equally intimidating list of technologies – Illumina, pyrosequencing, SOLiD, and so on. Never fear, we're here to help.

The basic process of deep sequencing at its heart is quite conceptually simple:

1. Take some biological sequences: The DNA of chromosome, messenger RNA, and so on.

2. Find a way to turn the sequence into DNA (e.g., mRNA can be changed into cDNA).

3. Break or **fragment** the DNA into random pieces (depending on the size of the original sample).

4. Massively **amplify** those copies of DNA, producing many millions or billions of fragments.

5. **Sequence** parts of those fragments, generating billions of short *reads*, which typically vary from 40 to 200 base pairs.

The key notion is that the reads are produced in **massively parallel** fashion. What do we mean by this? It means that the same region of the original sequence is typically sequenced (or *covered*) by many different reads, as opposed to just one. These reads also do not simply start or stop at the same point, but they *overlap*.

---

[1]`www.startrek.com/`

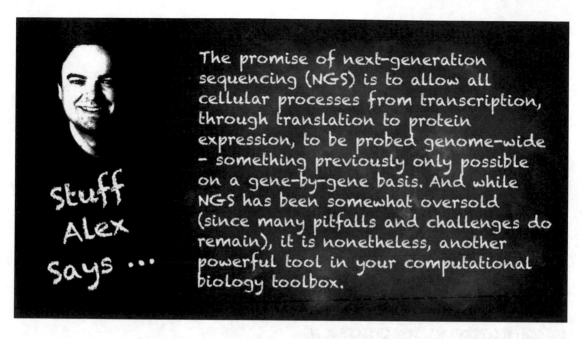

The promise of next-generation sequencing (NGS) is to allow all cellular processes from transcription, through translation to protein expression, to be probed genome-wide – something previously only possible on a gene-by-gene basis. And while NGS has been somewhat oversold (since many pitfalls and challenges do remain), it is nonetheless, another powerful tool in your computational biology toolbox.

This is important because any individual read can contain a sequencing error, even if it is in just one base. Having many dozens of overlapping reads allows us to reduce the chance of identifying the wrong base (false positives). This also reinforces another theme that we will return to throughout the book and that is that biology is a very noisy affair! Whether it is in a cell, ecosystem, or population you are studying, or in the experimental process that you use to study them, noise is ever present, and getting comfortable with noise is a big part of working in computational biology.

This is all very interesting, but how can Python help me? This is a good question. A lot of the tools used for NGS analysis are command-line based; however, Python can be used to drive many of these processes, and indeed there are plenty of excellent packages and frameworks designed to do this on a large scale (see a list at the end of chapter). In line with our overall philosophy, we aren't planning to introduce you to all the cutting-edge libraries (which can go quickly out of date anyway), but instead our goal is twofold: (1) giving you simple example to whet your appetite to explore further and (2) introducing new Python features to help you with that goal. The chapter will be in four parts:

- Introducing the basic formats used for raw sequence: The FASTQ and BAM and SAM

- How to use Python **subprocess** to drive an external command-line program to *align* reads to a genome

- Slicing and dicing the genome: Using a Python library to **extract** reads from an alignment

- Showing you how to wrap up all the preceding functionality into an executable program that uses Python's `argparse`[2] to parse command-line arguments

Going Next-Generation: From FASTA to FASTQ

Let's dive in with the workhorse of sequence data files, the **FASTQ** file, which contains all the raw sequences, normally referred to as **reads**. This is basically an enhanced version of the FASTA file that we first met in Chapter 5 of this book. In most NGS technologies, each read is of the same length:

```
@r0
GAACGATACCCACCCAACTATCGCCATTCCAGCAT
+
EDCCCBAAAA@@@@?>===<;;9:99987776554
```

Each read is represented by a four-line stanza:

1. The first line starts with the symbol **@** and uniquely identifies the read. It usually contains information about the machine it was generated on and other information like the position on the "flow cell" (which is the slide that the original sequence identification was made). For many purposes we don't need to know this information, except in the cases where reads come in "pairs." This effectively serves the same kind of purpose that the information in the ">" line of the FASTA format files.

2. The second line contains the actual sequences of **GAACGATA** identified by the machine.

3. The third line starts with the symbol **+** and separates the sequence information from the following line that contains quality scores.

---

[2]https://docs.python.org/2.7/library/argparse.html

4. The last line are the quality scores: These are the scores that the original machine uses to assess the quality of the base calls in the second line. These are important because they are used by downstream algorithms when putting all the sequences together.

In theory we could write a Python program that directly reads the FASTQ files, but in practice, FASTQ files are rarely analyzed directly. Instead, they are used as input to other tools. One of the most common tasks in analyzing NGS data is **alignment**. Alignment consists of taking all the individual reads in a FASTQ file and finding their *location* in a given genome. This genome is called the **reference genome**. There are many tools that perform this task, so many that somebody once quipped on Twitter that eventually every lab will have its own alignment algorithm. Two of the most common are **bowtie** and **bwa** (for Burrows-Wheeler transform). For our purposes, we merely want to demonstrate the process, so we will arbitrarily select the bwa aligner.

The aligner generates an **alignment file**, for bwa it generates a **SAM** file (which stands for **Sequence Alignment/Map**). This is an *uncompressed text file* with a line for each read containing the aligners "best guess" for the original location on the genome that the sequence came from. SAM files also include reads that were not aligned at all (**unaligned reads**). Figure 8-1 reviews the steps graphically.

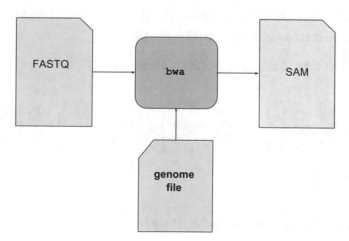

Figure 8-1. *Inputs and outputs of the bwa step in the NGS pipeline*

BAM files: **viewing**, **sorting**, and **indexing**

SAM files are of limited use in practice, since NGS is massively parallel, each alignment may contain many *billions of reads*; therefore, SAM files are often incredibly massive. This brings us to another workhorse of the NGS menagerie: the **BAM** file (for **Binary Alignment/Map**), which is basically just a *compressed version* of the SAM file. But even after conversion to BAM, for efficient later processing BAM files also need another *two* additional steps: sorting and indexing. All three of these steps are achieved via suite of tools called, not surprisingly, samtools.[3] Let's break 'em down:

1. View: Conversion from **SAM** to **BAM** is done using the samtools view command.

2. Sort: Sorting puts all reads that are closer to ends of chromosomes toward the beginning of the file; this makes it faster to find all the reads in a particular region because they are all adjacent to each other in the file. This is achieved by use of the samtools sort command.

3. Index: Indexing, which must always come *after* sorting, creates an additional **BAI** file – this is basically a lookup table so that reads can be retrieved easily by chromosome name, again without having to search the entire file from beginning to end. Here the command samtools index is your friend.

Let's expand our graphical representation (Figure 8-2).

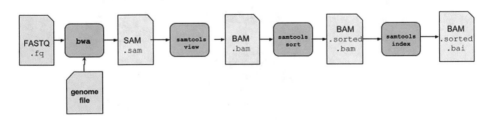

Figure 8-2. *Full NGS pipeline for generating a sorted BAM file*

OK, this is great conceptually, how do you actually run these tools? Here we need a detour into the command-line tools.

---

[3]http://samtools.sourceforge.net/

A full step-by-step installation guide for `samtools` and `bwa` is beyond the scope of this chapter, but each of the tools has fairly complete installation instructions for each supported platform on their web sites (for samtools, visit samtools.sourceforge.net; for bwa, visit bio-bwa.sourceforge.net). For example, if you are running on a Linux platform, it may be as simple as running `sudo dnf install samtools bwa` (on Fedora) or `sudo apt install samtools bwa` (on a Debian/Ubuntu-based system).

The example we'll present uses two input files that are included in the associated codebase (see Chapter 1 for details):

1. An input FASTQ file containing 10,000 reads originally taken from a genome sequence of *E. coli.*

2. A *reference genome:* We use the complete genome for *E. coli* encoded in the file **NC_008253.fna** (this was originally downloaded from the NCBI[4]: the associated indexes have been pre-built for you).

All of these files are located in the **genomes** subdirectory of our codebase. The following are the series of commands that you would run from the terminal:

```
bwa mem NC_008253.fna e_coli_10000snp.fq > e_coli_10000snp.sam
samtools view -b -S e_coli_10000snp.sam > e_coli_10000snp.bam
samtools sort e_coli_10000snp.bam e_coli_10000snp.sorted
samtools index e_coli_10000snp.sorted.bam
```

You should be able to go ahead and run these commands and generate two final output files: the output BAM file `e_coli_10000snp.sorted.bam` and index file `e_coli_10000snp.sorted.bam.bai`.

Phew! Let's stop and take stock. You may have noticed that there appear to be a lot of different tools and steps you need to run to basically accomplish the one actually *interesting* biological analysis step, that of alignment. You might think that it would be better for all of this to be built into bwa, saving you all these additional "bookkeeping" steps, and maybe you'd be right, but NGS tools have evolved, like many pieces of scientific software in a piecemeal way. In some ways it is still a cottage industry.

---

[4]www.ncbi.nlm.nih.gov/nuccore/NC_008253

This is where Python comes in (astute readers will have noticed somewhat of an absence of Python thus far!). We can use Python's ability to call out to command-line tools to "wrap" or to use another term of art, *encapsulate,* a lot of that complexity to make more *reusable* pipelines.

Calling with a Subprocess

The module subprocess[5] is Python's workhorse for command-line interactions. We won't recapitulate the interface here, but we'll dive in with an implementation of the first step, the alignment itself in Listing 8-1.

Listing 8-1. Using the with statement to send a file to a subprocess

```
import subprocess
with open('e_coli_10000snp.sam', "w") as output_sam:
  # do the alignment
  subprocess.check_call(['bwa', 'mem', 'NC_008253.fna',
  'e_coli_10000snp.fq'], stdout=output_sam)
```

The first thing you'll notice is the opening of the output file is different to the way we showed you how to create files in Chapter 5. We make a quick detour here to explain with. Basically a with statement declares a variable that is only valid within the block of code below it (for more details, see the Python docs on with[6]). This is a handy way to make the code for reading a file nice and compact, since we only need the file handle for the time that the subprocess call runs. This avoids having to have separate open() and close() statements. The traditional way would need three lines as in Listing 8-2.

Listing 8-2. Sending an input file to subprocess not using a with statement

```
output_sam = open('e_coli_10000snp.sam', "w")
subprocess.check_call(['bwa', 'mem', 'NC_008253.fna', 'e_coli_10000snp.
fq'], stdout=output_sam)
output_sam.close()
```

---

[5]https://docs.python.org/2/library/subprocess.html
[6]https://docs.python.org/2/reference/compound_stmts.html#the-with-statement

Neither one is intrinsically better, but using with has the advantage that you won't forget to close the file, because with does it for you! with also has a number of other uses beyond using files, such as allowing code blocks to be reused, but we won't get into that here, you can see the previously mentioned Python docs on with for more details.

Now back to the subprocess call itself... within the with clause, we pass in each of the command-line parameters described in the preceding section as a list and then assign the standard output stdout (i.e., what would be otherwise be output to the console) to that file handle. If you run this code in the genomes directory that contains the test FASTQ and genome files, you should see the output of the **bwa** tool, which should resemble the following:

```
[M::main_mem] read 10000 sequences (350000 bp)...
[M::mem_process_seqs] Processed 10000 reads in 0.244 CPU sec, 0.245 real sec
[main] Version: 0.7.9a-r786
[main] CMD: bwa mem NC_008253.fna e_coli_10000snp.fq
[main] Real time: 0.638 sec; CPU: 0.276 sec
0
```

OK, we've successfully run an external tool via Python to perform alignment. Congratulations to us! We can now *extend* this pipeline by wrapping the samtools command to convert the SAM file into the BAM file, using the code in Listing 8-3 (note that this assumes you have already run the code in Listing 8-1).

Listing 8-3. Calling samtools using subprocess

```
# convert back to the binary (compressed) BAM format using samtools
with open("e_coli_10000snp.bam", "w") as output_bam:
    subprocess.check_call(['samtools', 'view', '-b' '-S',
    "e_coli_10000snp.sam"], stdout=output_bam)
```

Again, notice the use of the creation of the BAM file using the with command that would normally be created through the direction of the standard output (stdout). Let's pause and regroup briefly. We have successfully used Python to process a raw FASTQ file e_coli_10000snp.fq, and generated two alignments to the genome:

e_coli_10000snp.sam, e_coli_10000snp.bam,

uncompressed and compressed, respectively. However, as we mentioned previously, we are not really able to *use* these files for further genomics analysis until we have sorted and indexed them. In principle we could "wrap" the samtools calls using the same scheme as the preceding one, but there is an external library we can use for this purpose. It's called pySam.

pySam: Reading Alignment Files the Pythonic Way

By using pySam we are briefly departing from our usual practice of coding as many of our examples using only the Python standard library, but we feel it is useful for you to have a familiarity with the use of external libraries, since you will encounter many of the more advanced tools if you end up specializing in genomics analyses. Also note that we have already shown you how to use and create the wrappers manually in Python, so you should be able to easily code replacements should these libraries ever become obsolete. In addition, using pySam has the virtue of making our examples a little more compact. To install pySam from the command line, you should first make sure you have Python pip installed (see Chapter 1), then run:

```
$ pip3 install --user pysam==0.15.2
```

(note that we specifically require version 0.15.2 of pysam, which works at the time of testing!) depending on how your system is set up:

```
$ python3-pip install --user pysam==0.15.2
```

With that prelude out of the way, let's add a function sort_and_index whose sole purpose is to... wait for it!... sort and index a BAM file. Making this a function as shown in Listing 8-4 is useful because it is a task that we will need over and over, it also hides some of the complexities and idiosyncrasies of samtools making it easier for you to focus on the flow of the actual analysis steps.

Listing 8-4. Function to sort and index a BAM file

```
import os.path
import pysam
def sort_and_index(bam_filename):
  prefix, suffix = os.path.splitext(bam_filename)

  # generated sorted bam filename
  sorted_bamfilename = prefix + ".sorted.bam"
```

```
# sort output using pysam's output
print("generated resorted BAM:", sorted_bamfilename)
pysam.sort("-o", sorted_bamfilename, bam_filename)

# index output using pysam's index
print("index BAM:",sorted_bamfilename)
pysam.index(sorted_bamfilename)

return sorted_bamfilename
```

As input we give the function the name of the BAM file that was generated in the previous step. Let's go through the function:

1. We first use the `splitext` command from the `os.path` standard library to extract the *prefix* of the file name (the e_coli_10000snp part), as well as the *suffix* (the bam part).

2. We then use it to generate the sorted output name by concatenating the prefix with the suffix `.sorted.bam`.

3. We are now ready to use the `pysam.sort()` function, which is very easy: simply give it the output filename prefixed by the `"-o"` followed by the input `bam_filename`.

4. We then use `pysam.index()` to index the file generated in the previous step, which outputs a `.bam.bai` file.

5. Lastly we `return` the name of the newly created BAM file to the calling function: this will come in use later on and also allows to centralize the code to generate this name just *once*.

Note that we have now successfully encapsulated some of the routine functions that may be used over and over again.

If you are building your own pipelines, you will probably find yourself noticing certain pieces of code that you are using over and over again, maybe you're even cutting and pasting them verbatim. If you find yourself doing this a lot, *stop*. These are ripe candidates for plucking from the bare vines of code to be planted into nice fertile functions that will reap reusable benefits down the track. So think of the preceding example as a way to get you familiar with this process. This is actually so common in programming that it has its own name: refactoring.

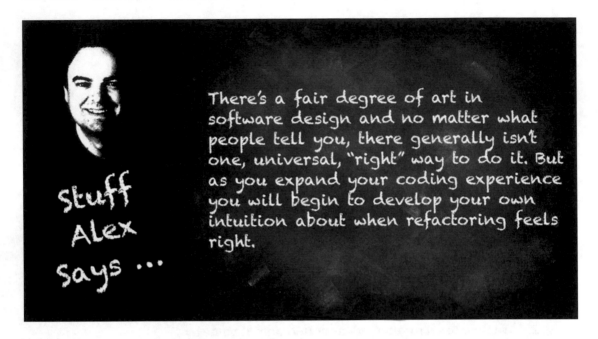

There's a fair degree of art in software design and no matter what people tell you, there generally isn't one, universal, "right" way to do it. But as you expand your coding experience you will begin to develop your own intuition about when refactoring feels right.

Of course, it's possible to go mad with this process and start prematurely refactoring code that doesn't need it, or find yourself writing a lot of functions that aren't really useful.

Let's see the functions we've created so far, all put into practice in Listing 8-5.

Listing 8-5. Python version of NGS pipeline: aligning and sorting and indexing

```python
import os.path
import pysam
import subprocess

def sort_and_index(bam_filename):
  prefix, suffix = os.path.splitext(bam_filename)

  # generated sorted bam filename
  sorted_bamfilename = prefix + ".sorted.bam"

  # sort output using pysam's output
  print("generated resorted BAM:", sorted_bamfilename)
  pysam.sort("-o", sorted_bamfilename, bam_filename)

  # index output using pysam's index
  print "index BAM:",sorted_bamfilename
```

```
pysam.index(sorted_bamfilename)
return sorted_bamfilename

# alignment
with open('e_coli_10000snp.sam', "w") as output_sam:
  subprocess.check_call(['bwa', 'mem', 'NC_008253.fna',
  'e_coli_10000snp.fq'], stdout=output_sam)

# convert to BAM
with open("e_coli_10000snp.bam", "w") as output_bam:
    subprocess.check_call(['samtools', 'view', '-b' '-S',
    "e_coli_10000snp.sam"], stdout=output_bam)

# sort and index
output_sorted_bamfilename = sort_and_index("e_coli_10000snp.bam")
```

If you run this code, you will generate the same outputs that we achieved using the command-line tools. Now, this might seem like overkill, since we did the same with only four lines in the shell, but we now have the building blocks for doing more interesting analyses.

Read on...

Visualizing Sequencing Reads

If you want to actually visualize the reads contained in the BAM file, a useful tool is the Integrative Genomics Viewer[7] (IGV). A step-by-step guide for installing and using this tool is beyond the scope of this chapter, but we provide the following pointers to the relevant parts of IGV's own instructions.[8] You need to first create your own .genome file following IGV's loading a genome instructions[9] by uploading the genome that we provide in the FASTA file NC_008253.fna. Then follow the instructions for viewing alignments[10] using the e_coli_10000snp.sorted.bam as input (you'll note that our pipeline has already done the sorting and index creating that the instructions require).

---

[7]www.broadinstitute.org/igv/

[8]www.broadinstitute.org/software/igv/UserGuide

[9]www.broadinstitute.org/software/igv/LoadGenome

[10]http://software.broadinstitute.org/software/igv/AlignmentData

Counting the Number of Sequencing Reads

Let's back up to the original biology that motivates these genomics analyses. We've now successfully aligned our reads with the original genome. In this particular case, the reads were derived from *E. coli's* genomic DNA, and therefore if all regions of the originally sequenced DNA were amplified *uniformly*, we would see more or less an even distribution of the reads at each site. We can even test this idea by extracting reads between some random coordinates and *counting* how many reads are present at each location and then *extracting* these reads into a *new* BAM file for future visualization.

The pysam library we just introduced has a very nice way to achieve this via the fetch() function as we show in Listing 8-6:

Listing 8-6. Counting the number of reads using pysam

```
import pysam
chrom = "gi|110640213|ref|NC_008253.1|"; start = 20; end = 200
output_final_bamfilename = "e_coli_subset.bam"
read_count = 0
all_reads = pysam.AlignmentFile("e_coli_10000snp.sorted.bam", 'rb')

# create final output file
output_final_bam = pysam.AlignmentFile(output_final_bamfilename, 'wb',
template=all_reads)

# use pysam to extract the reads from the given coordinates
output_reads=all_reads.fetch(chrom, start, end)

for read in output_reads:
  read_count += 1
  output_final_bam.write(read)
all_reads.close()
output_bam.close()
print("saving new BAM:",output_final_bamfilename, " with", read_count,
"reads aligning in %s:%d-%d" % (chrom, start, end))
sort_and_index("e_coli_subset.bam")
```

If we run this, we should see that in the region of the chromosome between 20 and 200 we have 216 reads:

saving new BAM: e_coli_subset.bam with 216 reads aligning in gi|110640213| ref|NC_008253.1|:20-200

Let's break this down:

1. We first set the coordinates and initialize the read count.

2. We next read in the alignment using pySam's `AlignmentFile()` function using `'rb'` to indicate that this is an *input* **r**ead-only **b**inary file. This returns a Python object `all_reads` that allows the reads to be accessed as a Python list (for more details, see the Pysam documentation[11]).

3. We again use pysSam's `AlignmentFile()` function to generate an *output* BAM file using the `'wb'` to indicate that this is a **w**riteable **b**inary file. Note that we also provide the newly initialized `all_reads` from the preceding step to the template keyword in the `AlignmentFile` call. This ensures that the original header metadata information about the chromosomes and so on in the original BAM file are transferred over to the new output BAM.

4. Got all that? Now we can get down the business of actually getting the reads in the given region using the `fetch()` function, by passing in the chromosome name and coordinates start and end.

5. We loop through each of the reads, incrementing the `read_count` and writing the read to the new BAM file.

6. We then close both the original input BAM and the new output BAM.

7. Lastly we call `sort_and_index()`. Look our original refactoring is paying off!

We now have the reads counts and the original BAM in a format that can again be visualized using IGV (see the preceding box).

---

[11]`pysam.readthedocs.org/en/latest/usage.html`

Building a Command-Line Tool

Now imagine that you find yourself needing to do this kind of genome "slicing and dicing" on a regular basis. Say for some reason, you'd like to visualize just the reads in a certain segment of a genome. Wouldn't it be nice to have a handy **command-line tool** that you could just point at a BAM file and say: "genie please give me just the reads in this region"? Well, Python is (still) your friend. (This is not just a made-up toy example, we have had cases where it is useful to extract a genomic subset of reads as input to other tools. This is especially true if the total BAM file is massive, or if other analysis or visualization tools cannot handle the large file size.) In the rest of example, we'll show you how to take the functionality we've developed thus far and build a command-line tool that can be run via a shell or terminal.

The first new piece of Python we need to introduce is the argparse library which is part of the Python standard library (more details than you can poke a burnt stick are at the official argparse tutorial[12]). The basic idea is to create an ArgumentParser object, which is initialized with a description of the command-line program that will be presented to the user at runtime. Here it is:

```
parser = argparse.ArgumentParser(description="""
Given an input FASTQ file, align to genome,
extract reads for specified region: CHROM:START-END
and write to sorted indexed bam to OUTPUT""")
```

Since the line is long, we can use Python's built-in triple quoting that is used for long strings (you can get more details of this from this online tutorial[13]). Once we have created this object, we can begin to add the individual command options. These come in two flavors: **_positional arguments_**, that is, arguments that are the primary input to the script, typically the input file, and **_option-style arguments_**, which are arguments that are provided in the form of command-line "switches" in the form of "--chromosome". Our first argument is positional:

```
parser.add_argument('input_fastq', help='input FASTQ file name')
```

---

[12]https://docs.python.org/2/howto/argparse.html
[13]https://docs.python.org/2/tutorial/introduction.html#strings

This is the required input FASTQ file name, this is the "main" argument. We also provide a little help function that will be displayed nicely for the user. We next add the options:

```
parser.add_argument('-o', '--output', dest="output_final_bam_filename",
 help='output BAM file name', default="final.bam")
parser.add_argument('-c', '--chrom', help='chromosome name', required=True)
parser.add_argument('-s', '--start', type=int, help='start position on
  chromosome', required=True)
parser.add_argument('-e', '--end', type=int, help='end position on
 chromosome', required=True)
```

The first thing to note is that all command-line options except the first "option" are actually *required* by setting `required=True`. This means that the script will fail to run unless the user provides those options and input arguments. Let's go through them one by one:

1. The first option `--output` is the name of the final output BAM file, the reason this is not required is because we provide a `default=final.bam`. This and each subsequent option has a short form and a long form, in this case `-o` and `--output`, respectively.

2. The second option `--chrom` is the name of the chromosome and is *required*. The use of the `--chrom` *automatically* creates an associated variable in the argument parser object which we will return to later. The short form is `-c`.

3. The third option `--start` is the starting position on the chromosome and is also *required*. Because this is an integer, we assign `type=int`, which will automatically convert the type. (This was not necessary for the previous options because they were strings, which is the default type.)

4. The last option `--end` is the end position on the chromosome and follows the same logic as the `--start` option.

Now, we've set up the arguments, all that remains is to actually do the parsing and assign them to the variables used in the rest of the program:

```
# next get and parse args and assign to our local files
args = parser.parse_args()
input_fastq = args.input_fastq
output_final_bam_filename = args.output_final_bam_filename
chrom = args.chrom
start = args.start
end = args.end
```

This should be mostly self-explanatory. We first get the arguments by calling parse_args on the parser object. Once we have this object, we can assign each of the input arguments to their corresponding names in the rest of the program. (Note that there is no requirement for the variables to have the same names as the arguments, but we keep them the same for clarity.)

Now here is the argument parser in full in Listing 8-7.

Listing 8-7. Creating a command-line tool using argparse

```
import argparse
parser = argparse.ArgumentParser(description="""Given an input FASTQ file,
align to genome, extract reads for specified region: CHROM:START-END
and write to sorted indexed bam to OUTPUT""")

parser.add_argument('input_fastq', help='input FASTQ file name')
parser.add_argument('-o', '--output', dest="output_final_bam_filename",
help='output BAM file name', default="final.bam")
parser.add_argument('-c', '--chrom', help='chromosome name', required=True)
parser.add_argument('-s', '--start', type=int, help='start position on
chromosome', required=True)
parser.add_argument('-e', '--end', type=int, help='end position on
chromosome', required=True)

# next get and parse args and assign to our local files
args = parser.parse_args()
input_fastq = args.input_fastq
output_final_bam_filename = args.output_final_bam_filename
```

```
chrom = args.chrom
start = args.start
end = args.end
```

If you take the program in Listing 8-7 and put it into an executable file with the name of the current chapter, and run it with the built-in "help" function activated using -h or --help, you should see the following:

```
$ ./PFTLS_Chapter_08.py -h
usage: PFTLS_Chapter_08.py [-h] [-o OUTPUT_FINAL_BAM_FILENAME] -c CHROM -s
                           START -e END
                           input_fastq

Given an input FASTQ file, align to genome, extract reads for specified
region: CHROM:START-END and write to sorted indexed bam to OUTPUT

positional arguments:
  input_fastq             input FASTQ file name

optional arguments:
  -h, --help              show this help message and exit
  -o OUTPUT_FINAL_BAM_FILENAME, --output OUTPUT_FINAL_BAM_FILENAME
                          output BAM file name
  -c CHROM, --chrom CHROM
                          chromosome name
  -s START, --start START
                          start position on chromosome
  -e END, --end END       end position on chromosome
```

Woo-hoo, we now have a functioning script! It will catch you also if you fail to provide any input:

```
$ ./PFTLS_Chapter_08.py
usage: PFTLS_Chapter_08.py [-h] [-o OUTPUT_FINAL_BAM_FILENAME] -c CHROM -s
                           START -e END
                           input_fastq
PFTLS_Chapter_08.py: error: the following arguments are required: input_
fastq, -c/--chrom, -s/--start, -e/--end
```

Or if you miss an argument

```
$ PFTLS_Chapter_08.py -o final.bam -c 'gi|110640213|ref|NC_008253.1|' -s 20
e_coli_10000snp.fq
usage: NGS_Genome_Slicing.py [-h] [-o OUTPUT_FINAL_BAM_FILENAME] -c CHROM -s
                             START -e END
                             input_fastq
test.py: error: argument -e/--end is required
```

The Final Pipeline: Putting it all Together

Let's pause again and regroup, as we've gone a long way now. We now have all the pieces for our complete pipeline: the *command-line parser*, the *alignment calls* using bwa, the function for *sorting and indexing*, and the *extraction* of the reads using pySam. We are now ready for the full program in Listing 8-8.

Listing 8-8. Full NGS Python pipeline

```python
#!/usr/bin/env python3
import sys
import os.path
import pysam
import argparse
import subprocess

def sort_and_index(bam_filename):
    prefix, suffix = os.path.splitext(bam_filename)
    sorted_bamfilename = prefix + ".sorted.bam"
    print("generate sorted BAM:", sorted_bamfilename)
    pysam.sort("-o", sorted_bamfilename, bam_filename)
    print("index BAM:", sorted_bamfilename)
    pysam.index(sorted_bamfilename)
    return sorted_bamfilename

parser = argparse.ArgumentParser(description="""Given an input FASTQ file,
align to genome, extract reads for specified region: CHROM:START-END
and write to sorted indexed bam to OUTPUT""")
```

```
parser.add_argument('input_fastq', help='input FASTQ file name')
parser.add_argument('-o', '--output', dest="output_final_bam_filename",
help='output BAM file name', default="final.bam")
parser.add_argument('-c', '--chrom', help='chromosome name', required=True)
parser.add_argument('-s', '--start', type=int, help='start position on
chromosome', required=True)
parser.add_argument('-e', '--end', type=int, help='end position on
chromosome', required=True)

# next get and parse args and assign to our local files
args = parser.parse_args()
input_fastq = args.input_fastq
output_final_bam_filename = args.output_final_bam_filename
chrom = args.chrom
start = args.start
end = args.end

# get prefix and extension from FASTQ file
prefix, suffix = os.path.splitext(input_fastq)
output_sam_filename = prefix + '.sam'
output_bam_filename = prefix + '.bam'

# using subprocess need to generate the standard output *first*
with open(output_sam_filename, "w") as output_sam:
  # do the alignment, hardcode the genome to the bacterial genome
  print("generated SAM output from:", input_fastq)
  subprocess.check_call(['bwa', 'mem', 'NC_008253.fna', input_fastq],
  stdout=output_sam)

# convert back to the binary (compressed) BAM format using samtools
with open(output_bam_filename, "wb") as output_bam:
  subprocess.check_call(['samtools', 'view', '-b', '-S', output_sam_
  filename], stdout=output_bam)
output_sorted_bamfilename = sort_and_index(output_bam_filename)
```

```python
# get ready to extract reads
read_count = 0
print("now extract reads from:", output_sorted_bamfilename)
all_reads = pysam.AlignmentFile(output_sorted_bamfilename, 'rb')

# create final output file
output_final_bam = pysam.AlignmentFile(output_final_bam_filename, 'wb',
template=all_reads)

# use pysam to extract the reads from the given coordinates
print("extract reads from chromosome:" + chrom + "at coordinates:", start, end)
output_reads= all_reads.fetch(chrom, start, end)

for read in output_reads:
  read_count += 1
  output_final_bam.write(read)
all_reads.close()

print("saving new BAM:", output_final_bam_filename, " with", read_count,
"reads aligning in %s:%d-%d" % (chrom, start, end))
output_bam.close()  # finally close the output bam file
sort_and_index(output_final_bam_filename) # sort and index
```

All the pieces are now present, the final program takes the file names that were previously hard-coded in the earlier snippets and uses the input files from the command line. We are ready. Here's what an example run of our final command-line using the same genomic coordinates as previously looks like:

```
$ cd genomes
$ ../PFTLS_Chapter_08.py -o final.bam -c 'gi|110640213|ref|NC_008253.1|' -s
20 -e 200 e_coli_10000snp.fq
generated SAM output from: e_coli_10000snp.fq
[M::main_mem] read 10000 sequences (350000 bp)...
[M::mem_process_seqs] Processed 10000 reads in 0.247 CPU sec, 0.247 real sec
[main] Version: 0.7.9a-r786
[main] CMD: bwa mem NC_008253.fna e_coli_10000snp.fq
[main] Real time: 0.347 sec; CPU: 0.270 sec
[samopen] SAM header is present: 1 sequences.
```

```
generate sorted BAM: e_coli_10000snp.sorted.bam
index BAM: e_coli_10000snp.sorted.bam
now extract reads from: e_coli_10000snp.sorted.bam
extract reads from chromosome:gi|110640213|ref|NC_008253.1|at coordinates:
20 200
saving new BAM: final.bam  with 216 reads aligning in gi|110640213|ref|
NC_008253.1|:20-200
generate sorted BAM: final.sorted.bam
index BAM: final.sorted.bam
```

At the end of this process, you should have a sorted BAM containing just the reads of interest from those coordinates contained in the file **final.sorted.bam**. It should now be possible to load those reads back into IGV for visualization.

Where to Next?

In this chapter we have just scratched the surface of what can be achieved using these kinds of data. Alignment is just one of the many kinds of investigations that massively parallel sequencing technologies enable. Two other areas worthy of note are as follows:

- Variant calling[14]: This builds on the kinds of alignments we have already done, the "pileups" of reads can be used to infer the presence of SNPs and indels. The basic intuition being that if you see a SNP relative to the reference in many of the reads, it's a likely candidate for a true SNP. The Genome Analysis Toolkit[15] (GATK) is a common tool in this area.

- Assembly: Assembly process where the raw reads are used to construct a ***reference genome*** (in the case of DNA) or ***transcriptome*** (the set of all mRNA transcripts expressed in the cell at a given time). In both cases this is like trying to reassemble the puzzle without the original picture on the box: you have to rely on the shape of the pieces themselves. Sometimes this can be partially guided by

---

[14]www.bioconductor.org/help/course-materials/2014/CSAMA2014/3_Wednesday/lectures/
VariantCallingLecture.pdf
[15]www.broadinstitute.org/gatk/

existing alignments if there is a reference genome for a closely related organism, the hardest is de novo assembly, where there is no picture at all. Tools that you can investigate include Trinity assembler,[16] Velvet/Oases,[17] ALL-Paths LG,[18] and many others. Each has their pros and cons. The forums SEQanswers[19] and BioStar[20] are good starting places to look for resources and discussions.

It's important to realize the "next-generation" sequencing space is a very fast moving area of technology with new companies being formed and new tools being released almost every other month. Reads lengths are getting longer with new forms of sequencing from companies such as PacBio,[21] Dovetail Genomics,[22] and 10x Technologies[23] and will probably eventually become more accurate. It's entirely possible that at some point the tools developed for this kind of short-read sequencing will become obsolete, because we'll be able to read an entire chromosome or mRNA molecule in one hit.

But we're betting that it won't be for a while and that the basic NGS concepts and formats will probably be here for the duration. How many times have people predicted the death of vinyl? Who knows, maybe your bearded barista will be rediscovering the joys of hand-tooled artisanal NGS pipelines around 2030. So the kinds of nitty-gritty, roll-up-your-sleeves approach with these data formats and Python that you've developed in this chapter should stand you in good stead in the future, because it gives you a granular view on the lowest level of the process even as the technology and tools change.

Speaking of nitty-gritty and rolling up your sleeves, in the next couple of chapters, we will show you how Python can be used to visualize and manipulate data from a real biological lab workhorse: the 96-well plate.

---

[16]https://trinityrnaseq.github.io/

[17]www.ebi.ac.uk/~zerbino/oases/

[18]www.broadinstitute.org/software/allpaths-lg/blog/

[19]http://seqanswers.com/

[20]www.biostars.org/

[21]www.pacb.com/

[22]http://dovetailgenomics.com/

[23]www.10xtechnology.com/

References and Further Exploration

Tutorials and discussion

- Titus Brown's NGS tutorial[24]

- Brad Chapman's Blue Collar Bioinformatics Blog[25] (**bcbio**)

- BioStar: general bioinformatics forum

- SEQanswers: forum focusing mainly on NGS technologies

Tools

- Bowtie[26]: including links to tophat, cufflinks, and others

Pipelines/frameworks

- Python-based pipeline **bcbio-nextgen**, associated with Brad Chapman's previously mentioned Blue Collar Bioinformatics blog: code repository[27] documentation[28]

- Python-based workflow system (COSMOS[29]) and associated genome-variant calling pipeline (GenomeKey[30])

---

[24]http://ged.msu.edu/angus/tutorials-2013/
[25]https://bcbio.wordpress.com/
[26]http://bowtie-bio.sourceforge.net/index.shtml
[27]https://github.com/chapmanb/bcbio-nextgen
[28]https://bcbio-nextgen.readthedocs.org/
[29]http://cosmos.hms.harvard.edu/
[30]https://github.com/LPM-HMS/GenomeKey

CHAPTER 9

The Wells! The Wells!

Microtiter Plate Assays I: Data Structures

The tiny bell above the door rang as Alice entered the little shop, which also happened to be the local post office. *"Could you check to see if any mail came for me?"* asked Alice of the elderly shopkeeper.

"And what is your surname dear?" inquired the shopkeeper.

"Why? Everybody just calls me Alice," said Alice bemused.

"My mailboxes are arranged in a grid that is sorted by surname," said the shopkeeper with obvious pride. *"From A at top left to Z at bottom right."*

"I guess you should just look under A for Alice then," said Alice.

The shopkeeper took down the bundle of mail in the top left box and started to riffle through it. *"Well look at that!"* she said. *"This one's for you and it says right here on the envelope that you might already be a winner in their grand prize draw!"*

"With 'might' being the operative word," said Alice sarcastically. *"Like 'I might' get struck by a meteorite as I exit your shop."*

The **csv** module, comma-separated values, OOP, classes, constructors, **import**, **matplotlib**, class and instance variables, Python types, **type()**, tuples, **range()**, advanced string formatting, exceptions, ordered collections, conditionals, the **math** module, **None**, iterators

Plate assays, 96-well plates, robots, lab automation, Arduinos, grid coordinate systems

A. Lancaster and G. Webster, *Python for the Life Sciences*, https://doi.org/10.1007/978-1-4842-4523-1_9

What book aimed at the modern life scientist could avoid mention of that trusty workhorse of biology labs everywhere – the 96-well plate? There's scarcely a lab you could walk into these days without seeing these little guys (also referred to as microtiter plates) everywhere. The burgeoning numbers of high tech instruments that use 96-well (and other configuration) plates has only added to their proliferation in the lab in recent years. Furthermore, these instruments are often capable of scanning these plates and reading large volumes of data from them in relatively short order. We therefore felt it would be worth giving the humble 96-well plate two chapters of its own, just to demonstrate some of the ways that we can use Python to work with and visualize plate data and also to show how it can be used to create software that can interface with laboratory automation systems.

Just to be clear, the 96-well format is probably the most commonly used plate right now, but there are plenty of plates with other grid layouts as well, and if we're going to write good, reusable code, we should probably ensure that it is able to handle plates with fewer or more wells, or plates with different ratios of rows to columns. Don't worry. We will.

This last paragraph is a nice segue into the first fundamental property of these assay plates that we would like to capture in our code – the organization of the data points on a two-dimensional grid. Every well on the plate may actually comprise a number of data points all grouped and related by their common coordinate on this two-dimensional grid. You could, for example, imagine the well's volume, optical density, or the concentrations of any of its contents as separate data points. This two-dimensional grid coordinate could be expressed as a simple one-dimensional parameter – well **15,** for example – based upon reading the plate from left to right and top to bottom in the same way that we read text in most Indo-European languages. Alternatively it could be read in the common **letter:number** format that is used for rows and columns – for example, **A6, B12,** and so on. If we want to write flexible and versatile code for handling plates, we are probably going to want to be able to switch between these different two-dimensional coordinate systems for the purposes of navigating the plate data. But there's another good reason to want to do this...

Did we Mention Robots?

Biology labs are full of instruments and plate readers that have robotic components capable of moving, scanning, sampling, or even loading plates on a well-by-well basis. This introduces a whole new challenge for software that handles plate data. Yes, the data will be organized on this two-dimensional grid, but the software may also need to physically handle the plate itself or the scanner or pipette head that reads/samples or loads the wells. In the second chapter on plate assays (that follows this one), we're not going to show you how to write the very low-level code for driving Arduinos or the other kinds of physical devices that are used for robotic applications, but we will write our code such that it can produce the kind of high-level instructions needed to drive a robot, with the expectation that it may well at some point need to be hooked up to some machine control software capable of driving a robot, or at least receiving and interpreting positional data from one.

Introducing the 96-well Plate

So let's take a quick look at a 96-well plate just to remind ourselves what we're dealing with.

In Figure 9-1, you can see from the embossed letters from A to H down the left hand side of the plate and the embossed numbers from 1 to 12 across the top, that this plate follows the convention we have already described, of using alphabetic labels for rows and numerical labels for columns. This plate also shows the 8 row by 12 column rectangular format of a typical plate. It is worth noting that this rectangular format is almost universal, but there are plates that exist in other formats – square, for example, with identical numbers of rows and columns.

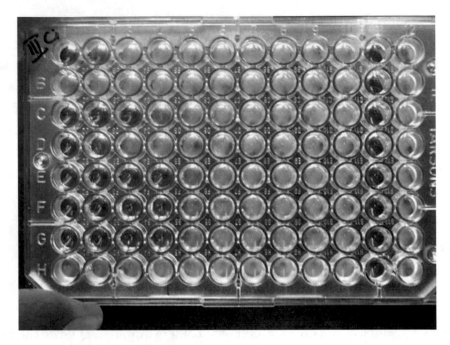

Figure 9-1. *Standard 96-well plate*

We will write our code under the assumption that a plate can have any aspect ratio corresponding to more or less any number of rows and columns, but we will assume that a plate always has a fixed *x,y* axis orientation in which the *x* **axis corresponding to the plate's columns is labeled numerically** and the *y* **axis corresponding to the plate's rows is labeled alphabetically**. So, for example, a particular well might have the coordinates **D10** corresponding to row **D** on the y axis and column **10** on the x axis.

If you've been paying attention here, you will see that we will always be referring to a location on the plate in a **row:column** format – in other words, a **y:x** format. This is in keeping with the way that we tend to organize tabular data, which in turn probably stems from some choices that we in the Western hemisphere collectively made a few thousand years ago about the layout of our written text.

Since a plate is also a good example of an object that aggregates a bunch of properties and parameters, the concept of a plate lends itself well (no pun intended) to representation as a Python object. Similarly, each well on the plate can itself be considered an aggregation of properties, not the least of which are its coordinates on the plate. Based upon these considerations, we will use an object-oriented programming (OOP) approach for our plate management code.

A Python Class for Multi-well Plates

This discussion of coordinate systems is a nice segue into one of the foundational properties that we would like our multi-well plate class to have. Since the wells of the plate are laid out on a grid as it were, we need to be able to say where we are on the plate, in other words, which well we're talking about. We also need to know the order of the wells and how we progress from one well to the next. For example, if we're reading plate assay data from a comma-separated values (CSV) file to assign each data point to the correct well, we need to be able to move virtually through the plate, mapping the data in the file correctly to the Python plate object. Furthermore, if we want our code to be capable of driving a robot for the purposes of reading data from the plate (e.g., with a spectrophotometric sensor), or pipetting liquids into the wells, we need to know how to move around the plate horizontally and vertically. On a 96-well plate with 12 columns, for example, when the robot has horizontally traversed a row of 12 wells, it needs to know that the next well is positioned 1 row down and 12 columns back from its current position in order to be able to move there.

There are at least three useful coordinate systems that we could use for a multi-well plate: a two-dimensional coordinate system might seem like the most intuitive for the two-dimensional layout of a plate. We could do this using a **row:column** notation either numerically, using a simple number for the row and column, or alphanumerically, using the alphabetical labels for the rows and numbers for the columns. The coordinates of the first system would look like this:

> **(1,1), (2,3), (6,10)**

The coordinates of the second system would look like this:

> **A01, B03, F10**

Largely self-explanatory, but why the zeros in front of column integers?

This is just a small trick to make all the well labels the same length, the reasons for which might not seem obvious now but bear with us and all will be explained!

It might not be so obvious why we would want to use a one-dimensional coordinate system for a two-dimensional object like a plate, but this simpler coordinate system also has its uses as we will see very soon. The one-dimensional coordinate system simply reflects the order of the wells on the plate in a linear fashion, from the first to the last. In keeping with our left-to-right, up-to-down system that seems natural based upon the way we write and read, for a 96-well plate, this system would label the top, left well as

151

number 1 and the bottom, right well as number 96 – reading across each entire row from left to right and then moving down and left to the leftmost well of the next row below.

The one-dimensional coordinate system is very useful from a **processing** viewpoint, since it is often the case when we're handling multi-well plates physically (e.g., with robots), or virtually (e.g., reading plate assay data from an input stream) that we need to know **what is the next well in the sequence**, so that we can transition through all of the wells on the plate.

Finally, we will need to be able to map these coordinate systems onto one another, so that we can consistently switch between them for different applications. What all of this boils down to is that in our code for implementing a Python class to handle multi-well plates, a lot of our class constructor method will be dedicated to setting up the layout of the plate and the coordinate systems that we use to move around in it.

So let's jump in and write our __init__ constructor method for a Python class that handles multi-well plates in Listing 9-1.

Listing 9-1. Constructor for Plate class

```python
import math, os, string, csv
import matplotlib.pyplot as plt

class Plate:
    rowLabels = "ABCDEFGHIJKLMNOPQRSTUVWXYZ"
    mapPositions = {'position1D':0,'position2D':1,'wellID':2}
    def __init__(self,id,rows,columns):
        self.id = id
        self.rows = rows
        self.columns = columns
        self.size = self.rows * self.columns
        self.validate = {}
        self.data = {}
        for key in Plate.mapPositions:
            self.validate[key] = []
        for n in range(1,self.size+1):
            self.data[n] = {}
            m = self.map(n,check=False)
            for key in Plate.mapPositions:
                self.validate[key].append(m[Plate.mapPositions[key]])
```

The first thing you will notice is that we are importing some other Python modules (such as matplotlib) that we will need later on, but we'll get those as we need them.

In the code for the Plate class, you will see that we are using **class variables**, a concept that we introduced in Chapter 7 on OOP. You will recall that these are not unique to each instance of the class, but are shared between all instances of the class. For the Plate class, we have two class variables rowLabels and mapPositions. The rowLabels variable defines the row labels that we can use for a plate, so already you can see that although a plate as represented in our class could in theory have any number of rows and columns – by introducing this list of permitted row labels, we are making the tacit assumption that a plate would never have more than 26 rows. We could expand this if we wished, but this might unnecessarily complicate matters – for example, we might need to expand our code to handle row labels of two and more letters. For the purposes of this chapter however, we will stick with uppercase A–Z as row labels and assume that all plates have at most 26 rows.

The mapPositions class variable requires a little explanation. If you think about the fact that we wish to support three-plate coordinate systems in our class, and that we wish to be able to map any one of them to any of the others – one straightforward and obvious approach to achieve these goals would be to write a family of six mapping functions as shown in Figure 9-2.

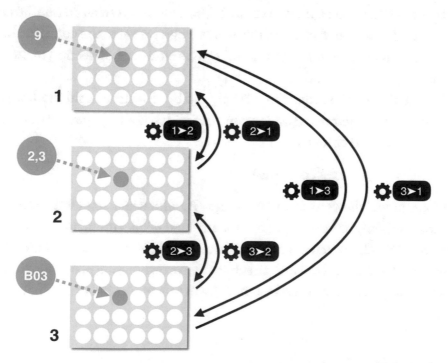

Figure 9-2. *Mapping functions for a 96-well plate*

Firstly, this would be a lot of code to write and maintain, and in the situation where we might need more than one mapping for a well, it would also force us to store, keep track of, and use the output coordinates of each of these functions separately. Furthermore, we would also need to keep track of the input coordinates and use them correctly, since each function would expect only one coordinate type as an input.

One clean and elegant solution to this multiplicity of functions, inputs and outputs, is to write a master mapping function that will accept any one of the three coordinate types as input and would also output all three mappings in a single, structured variable, such as a tuple. Some of our more farsighted readers may already have realized that this entails a small degree of redundancy, since one of this function's computed outputs will be the same as its input, but this is a small price to pay for the convenience of a function that takes any coordinate type as input and gives all the possible mappings in one go.

Finally then, the *raison d'être* for the mapPositions class variable is to define globally the order of the mapped coordinate types in the output from the coordinate mapping function. If you are a little unsure exactly how this will work, don't worry since it will all become clear when we get to the actual code for the mapping function.

In the interests of transparency, we should also admit that part of our reason for choosing this approach is to have the opportunity to introduce Python types[1] and to demonstrate how they can be used to create Python functions that can handle different kinds of inputs. You will soon see how this works when we get to the code that does the actual coordinate mapping, but for now, let's continue our dissection of the class constructor.

If we look at the function signature of the __init__ constructor method, we can see that it takes three arguments (aside from self which is always passed to instance methods): id, rows, and columns.

```
def __init__(self,id,rows,columns):
```

The id argument allows us to enter a unique ID with which to identify the plate. This would almost certainly be very important for any kind of lab automation process (e.g., using robots) in which the actual physical plates would likely have some kind of tracking ID that we would need to record and attach to the corresponding plate data. Note that this ID has nothing to do with class instance IDs or any other kind of internal Python references.

---

[1]https://docs.python.org/2/library/stdtypes.html

The rows and columns arguments are pretty self-explanatory and will be used to define the layout of the plate and also for the coordinate mappings.

The validate field declared as an empty dictionary will be used to check whether a coordinate input in the format of any of our three supported coordinate systems is valid for the current plate (we'll see in a minute how this works). The data field (also a Python dictionary) will be used to hold the actual data for each well. These might be, for example, laboratory measurements of optical density or pH, or parameters that describe the conditions that were set up in the well such as chemical concentrations or whether the well is a control sample or not.

Next, we set up the validate dictionary. This will consist of three lists of valid input coordinates, one for each of the three plate coordinate systems that we wish to support. The keys for this dictionary of **key-value** pairs will be the keys from the class variable mapPositions. For each key, we define the initial value to be an empty list, like this:

```
for key in Plate.mapPositions:
    self.validate[key] = []
```

The rest of the code in our __init__ constructor method simply iterates through each position on our plate from **1** to **n** (where **n** is the number of wells) and uses the mapping function to generate the set of three equivalent coordinates that represent each position.

Navigating the Plate

We'll see how the mapping method works in just a moment, but let's look at its code in Listing 9-2 and what it returns before we jump into the mechanics of the method.

Listing 9-2. map method in Plate class

```
def map(self,loc,check=True):
    if type(loc) == type(15):
        if check:
            if not loc in self.validate['position1D']:
                raise Exception('Invalid 1D Plate Position: %s' %
                str(loc))
        row = int(math.ceil(float(loc)/float(self.columns))) - 1
        col = loc - (row * self.columns) - 1
```

```
    elif type(loc) == type((3,2)):
        if check:
            if not loc in self.validate['position2D']:
                raise Exception('Invalid 2D Plate Position: %s' %
                str(loc))
        row = loc[0] - 1
        col = loc[1] - 1
    elif type(loc) == type('A07'):
        if check:
            if not loc in self.validate['wellID']:
                raise Exception('Invalid Well ID: %s' % str(loc))
        row = Plate.rowLabels.index(loc[0])
        col = int(loc[1:]) - 1
    else:
        raise Exception('Unrecognized Plate Location Type: %s' %
        str(loc))
    pos = self.columns * row + col + 1
    id = "%s%02d" % (Plate.rowLabels[row],col+1)
    return (pos,(row+1,col+1),id)
```

There's a lot of great Python learning stuff in the code for the map function, so we'll go through it in some detail in a moment. The first thing to look at however is the function's closing return statement.

```
return (pos,(row+1,col+1),id)
```

We can see that map returns a tuple containing three values – one for each coordinate system. This is how we avoid having to write six separate functions with six separate inputs and outputs, as described in the previous figure. Our map function takes any one of the three coordinate types as input and outputs a tuple with all three mappings. We can also keep track of which position in the tuple corresponds to which coordinate system, using our mapPositions class variable.

Here's a little question for you, dear reader...

You will notice that we have hard-coded the output from the mapPositions method – in other words, we just directly inserted each coordinate type in the output tuple without using the mapPositions class variable directly. This solution is quick to code, but it lacks a certain robustness. For example, what if we decided to change the order of mapPositions and put the wellID coordinate system first? This would break most of our code, since we do not directly use the mapPositions class variable when we're assembling the map output tuple, so the order of the coordinate systems in the returned tuple is hard-coded and *static,* that is, it does not change even if we change the order in mapPositions.

How could we make our code more robust by also using the mapPositions class variable to configure the values returned by the map method?

We could also have returned a dictionary like mapPositions with the same three keys (position1D, position2D, wellID) as mapPositions, but with the actual values of the mapped positions corresponding to each coordinate system, like this:

```
{'position1D':9,'position2D':(2,3),'wellID':'B03'}
```

Or in true OOP style, we could even create a mapped coordinate class with each of the three coordinate systems corresponding to a field in an object. Furthermore, we could then embed the entire map method into our new class and allow our __init__ constructor method to accept any one of the three coordinate types as an argument. The only issue with this approach is that you now have separate classes for the plate and for the coordinates, which nonetheless are dependent upon one another. This is an issue that can be easily remedied however.

Here's another little *Gedankenexperiment* for the reader...

How would you use separate but co-dependent plate and coordinate classes together in a robust OOP approach to coding this problem? For inspiration, you could review the introduction to OOP in Chapter 7.

Now back to our regularly scheduled programming (pun intended)...

We've added the code for the map function, so let's run a little test by creating a classic 96-well plate of 8 rows and 12 columns and running some map tests.

```
p = Plate('Assay 42',8,12)
print(p.map(1))
(1, (1, 1), 'A01')
print(p.map((1,1)))
(1, (1, 1), 'A01')
print(p.map('A01'))
(1, (1, 1), 'A01')
print(p.map(96))
(96, (8, 12), 'H12')
```

```
print(p.map((8,12)))
(96, (8, 12), 'H12')
print(p.map('H12'))
(96, (8, 12), 'H12')
result = p.map('B01')
print(result[Plate.mapPositions['wellID']])
```
B01

The last little piece of code shows how we can use the class variable `mapPositions` to "remember" which position each coordinate mapping occupies in the output tuple, so we never have to explicitly enter the position in the tuple in order to reference the coordinate type we want.

Before we get fully into the code of the `map` function, having seen a "black box" example of how it works at the level of inputs and outputs, we can now understand how the `__init__` constructor method builds the `validate` dictionary that is used to validate (or reject) any coordinates that are supplied as input to any of the plate class methods. The `validate` dictionary has three keys taken directly from the `mapPositions` dictionary that we created as a class variable, one for each coordinate system. The value of each key is just a list of all the valid coordinates for the plate, as expressed in that coordinate system.

So for a 96-well plate of 8 rows and 12 columns, the valid values for each coordinate system are as follows:

- Coordinate system `position1D`: **1, 2, 3, ... 94, 95, 96**

- Coordinate system `position2D`: **(1,1), (1,2), (1,3), ... (8,10), (8,11), (8,12)**

- Coordinate system `wellID`: **'A01', 'A02', 'A03', ... 'H10', 'H11', 'H12'**

If we look at the following code segment in the constructor from Listing 9-1 that actually populates the `validate` dictionary

```
for n in range(1,self.size+1):
    self.data[n] = {}
    m = self.map(n,check=False)
    for key in Plate.mapPositions:
        self.validate[key].append(m[Plate.mapPositions[key]])
```

we can see that it loops over all of the position1D coordinates for the plate, which is just the integer sequence from **1** to **n** where **n** is the number of wells and, for each position, generates a tuple that contains the three coordinate mappings. Each of these mapping values is then added to the list of valid coordinates for the corresponding coordinate type in the validate dictionary.

A couple of notes on this: firstly, you will see that the range over which the loop is done runs from 1 to the plate's size field + 1.

```
for n in range(1,self.size+1):
```

Why is this?

It is important to keep in mind that all Python sequences (like strings) and lists are indexed from zero. In keeping with this convention therefore, the Python range() method[2] always generates values **up to but not including** the second range parameter. For example, range(0,100) would generate the values 0 to 99 – in other words, the 100 values which would be the correct indexes of a Python sequence or list containing 100 elements.

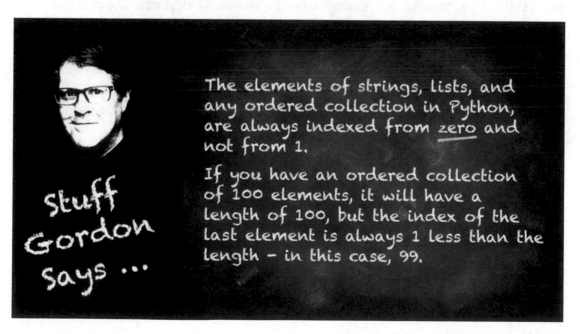

Stuff Gordon Says ...

The elements of strings, lists, and any ordered collection in Python, are always indexed from zero and not from 1.

If you have an ordered collection of 100 elements, it will have a length of 100, but the index of the last element is always 1 less than the length – in this case, 99.

---

[2]https://docs.python.org/2/library/functions.html#range

Don't worry too much about the whys and wherefores of this right now, just remember these very important Python facts that are worth repeating here:

- The elements of all ordered Python sequences and lists are **indexed from 0**.

- The highest index in an ordered Python sequence or list of length **n** is **n – 1**.

- A Python `range(m,n)` call generates all integer values from **m** to **n – 1**.

For a multi-well plate, we are normally used to numbering the wells from **1** to **n**, rather than from zero, so if we are starting with 1 instead, we need to adjust the `range()` method to **n + 1** (i.e., `self.size+1`) in the code.

Secondly, what's with the mysterious `check=False` in the call to the `map` method?

```
m = self.map(n,check=False)
```

The reason for this is that the `map` method has a dual function. Not only does it provide the set of coordinate mappings for an input coordinate, but it also checks whether the supplied input coordinate is valid for the current `Plate` instance. Now the first time we run through the `map` method to generate the lists of valid coordinates, we need to disable this secondary coordinate checking function, since we are actually in the process of generating the coordinate lists that will be used to do the checking. In other words, we can't check the input coordinate against the list of valid coordinates until we have generated the list of valid coordinates!

This is a nice segue into looking at the `map` method code in more detail.

So now that we know what the `check=False` statement in the `map` method signature is for, let's see how `map` works.

If we look at the `map` method, we can see that it is divided into four sections by an **if**-elif-else-style conditional statement that tests the `type` of the input coordinate passed to the method in the `loc` method argument.

```
if type(loc) == type(15):
        ... do this
elif type(loc) == type((3,2)):
        ... do that
elif type(loc) == type('A07'):
        ... do the other
```

```
else:
```

>   *... do something else altogether*

The Python type method,[3] as its name implies, returns the type of the object that is passed to it. For example, if you type in the Python console

```
a = 9
print type(a)
```

you will see this:

‹type 'int'›

or even simpler, you could type this:

```
print type(9)
```
‹type 'int'›

So in the first test, for example, where we have written

```
if type(loc) == type(15):
```

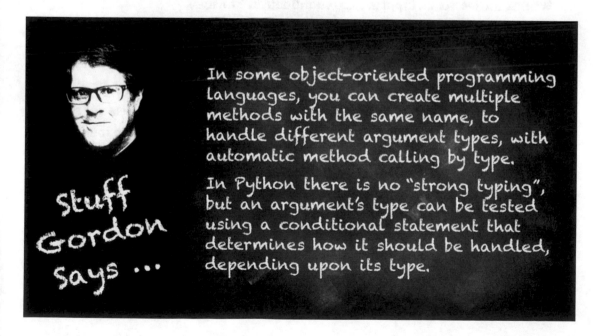

In some object-oriented programming languages, you can create multiple methods with the same name, to handle different argument types, with automatic method calling by type.

In Python there is no "strong typing", but an argument's type can be tested using a conditional statement that determines how it should be handled, depending upon its type.

Stuff Gordon Says ...

---

[3]https://docs.python.org/2/library/functions.html#type

we are testing to see if `loc` is a `position1D` coordinate, and since these are just integers, we could instead have written the test like this:

```
if type(loc) == int:
```

In fact for all three of the coordinate type tests, we could have written

```
if type(loc) == int:
elif type(loc) == tuple:
elif type(loc) == str:
```

where `int`, `tuple`, and `str` are the Python types that correspond to the coordinates in each of the three supported coordinate systems for the plate. This would work equally as well as the way we have chosen to implement the `type` tests, but then we also need to remember when we're looking at the code, not only which `type` corresponds to which coordinate system but also the expected format of each one. For example, the fact that the `wellID` coordinate type must be a `str` type does not tell us, or perhaps more importantly, does not tell anybody else reading our code, the fact that this needs to consist of a single row letter followed by a two-digit column number.

Writing the test for an input `wellID` coordinate like this:

```
elif type(loc) == type('A07'):
```

Imparts more information and makes the code easier to understand.

So the `map` method is divided by a block of conditional statements, each of which is for handling one specific coordinate type. Looking at the code for each case, we can see that the very first statement utilizes the `check` method argument to see whether to run the validation test on the input coordinate.

```
if check:
        if not loc in self.validate['position1D']:
            raise Exception('Invalid 1D Plate Position: %s' %
            str(loc))
```

You might be a little surprised by the initial `check` statement. Don't we need to say

```
if check == True?
```

Actually, no. This demonstrates a convenient shortcut in Python and merits a little explanation. It's important (and illuminating) to realize that this method evaluates whatever follows it in order to determine whether it is True or False. This is often some kind of comparison statement such as

```
if a > b:
```

or something more complicated like:

```
if (gene.length > 1000 and gene.hasBRE()):
```

Either way, once the statement is evaluated, you can imagine the whole statement after the if being substituted with True or False, like this:

```
if True:
```

and the subsequent code block being executed or not, depending upon the result.

In our case, we have a variable check that is set to either True or False, so simply evaluating the variable is enough, and we don't need to add the == True comparison.

Before we move on, this next piece of code illustrates other ways you can use this if shortcut.

```
def testA(a):
    if a:
        return "a seems to be True"
    else:
        return "a seems to be False"
print(testA(1))
```
a seems to be True
```
print(testA(0))
```
a seems to be False
```
print(testA(-1))
```
a seems to be True
```
print(testA(0.0))
```
a seems to be False
```
print(testA(0.00001))
```
a seems to be True
```
print(testA([]))
```
a seems to be False
```
print(testA([1,2,3]))
```
a seems to be True

```
print(testA(""))
```
a seems to be False
```
print(testA("a"))
```
a seems to be True

Interesting! Python gives you a convenient shortcut for testing whether numerical variables have non-zero values, or whether ordered collections like strings and lists are empty or not (in other words, whether or not they are of zero length). But getting back to our multi-well plate code...

```
if check:
        if not loc in self.validate['position1D']:
                raise Exception('Invalid 1D Plate Position: %s' %
                str(loc))
```

If the check is set to True, the input coordinate loc is searched for in the appropriate list in the validate dictionary that we created in the Plate class constructor, and if it's not there, we raise an Exception, terminating the program with an appropriate error message.

Let's assume that loc checks out as valid and look at what happens in that case. In the next two lines of code, we calculate the row and column indexes corresponding to the input coordinate.

```
row = int(math.ceil(float(loc)/float(self.columns))) - 1
col = loc - (row * self.columns) - 1
```

This looks a little complicated but it's really very simple. Let's work through an example for a 96-well plate of 8 rows and 12 columns. Let's say we want to map the coordinates for the 15th well. The input value of loc in position1D format would be simply the integer 15.

To calculate which row it's on, we divide by the number of columns. But 12.0/15.0 is 1.25. There is no row 1.25, but we know that 1.25 is kind of liking saying "row 1 plus 0.25 of the next row." This is where we use the imported Python math module.[4] The math.ceil method rounds up the value 1.25 to the next highest whole (floating point) number, which is 2.0, which is the row number we are looking for. Since we needed to do this arithmetic in floating point numbers but we want our row number as an integer, we need to cast the

---

[4]https://docs.python.org/2/library/math.html

whole result back to an int. This gives us our integer row number as we would label it on the plate, but remember that **Python collections are indexed from zero, not 1,** so row 1 on the plate is indexed internally in our Plate class as row 0; hence, we have to complete the calculation by subtracting 1 for now, so that we can work consistently with our internal representation of the plate.

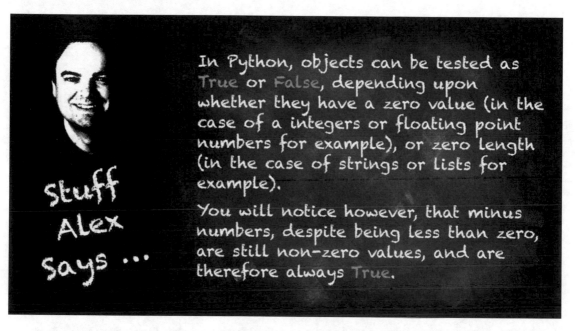

Stuff Alex Says …

In Python, objects can be tested as True or False, depending upon whether they have a zero value (in the case of a integers or floating point numbers for example), or zero length (in the case of strings or lists for example).

You will notice however, that minus numbers, despite being less than zero, are still non-zero values, and are therefore always True.

Later on, when we're ready to output the mapped coordinates, we will transition from the internal plate representation indexed from 0 back to the external coordinate system that we use for plates in the real world, with rows and columns indexed from 1. Note: this is why we said that these two lines of code calculate the row and column *indexes* and not the actual row and column *numbers*, which we will convert back to later.

That might have seemed like a long explanation of the code block to handle the loc input coordinates, but if you look at the map method, you will see that each of the three input coordinate types is handled essentially identically. The input coordinate is checked against the validate dictionary and is then converted into row and a column indexes, since this is a very easy place from which to compute any of the three coordinate formats, as we will see in a moment.

Before we get to the final calculation of the returned tuple with the three mappings, we should just mention that we also have an else clause that's there to catch any kind of input that does not conform to one of the three coordinate types – if somebody were to input a Python dictionary as a coordinate, for example. The `else` clause just handles "any other stuff" that might be passed to the `map` method, that it does not recognize as one of the three coordinate types.

So now we're ready to finish up the `map` method and output the coordinate mappings like this:

```
pos = self.columns * row + col + 1
id = "%s%02d" % (Plate.rowLabels[row],col+1)
return (pos,(row+1,col+1),id)
```

We calculate the `position1D` coordinate `pos` and add 1 back to the result so that we're expressing it in external plate coordinates. We have the `position2D` coordinate since we already calculated row and column indexes, and all we need to do with those is to remember to add 1 back to each of them to express them in plate coordinates, which we do in the (`row+1,col+1`) segment of the `return` statement. Finally, we need to calculate the `wellID` coordinate in the form of a well label with a row letter and column number.

Now we can clearly see the difference between the internal (indexed from zero) coordinates and the external (indexed from 1) plate coordinates if we work through a 96-well example.

Let's say that our input coordinate was **5**. This corresponds to row **1**, column **5**, and we have calculated row and column indices of **0** and **4**, respectively. To convert to a `wellID` coordinate, we use some more advanced Python string formatting[5] (we first introduced string formatting in Chapter 4):

```
id = "%s%02d" % (Plate.rowLabels[row],col+1)
```

The `%s` format should be familiar to you by now, it converts to a simple string, which is what we want for the row label. The `%02d` format converts to an integer string representation of length 2, front-padded with zeros as needed. In other words, an integer such as 12 would be formatted "12," whereas an integer like 5 would be formatted "05."

Now all we have to do is use our row index of 0 with the `rowLabels` class variable to get the row label – the `rowLabels[0]` evaluates to `"A"` – and the real (plate) column number is just the column index plus 1, giving us **5**.

---

[5]https://docs.python.org/2/library/string.html#format-string-syntax

So our input coordinate **5** maps to the string `"A05"` in the `wellID` coordinate system. All that remains is for the `map` method to assemble the tuple with the three coordinate mappings and return it, like this:

```
return (pos,(row+1,col+1),id)
```

Phew!

That was a lot of ground to cover just for one class method, but the beauty of creating a chapter around this `Plate` class is that in addition to giving you, the reader, a useful foundation for using Python to handle multi-well plates, it affords us, the authors, an opportunity to demonstrate the features of Python and the "Pythonic" way of doing things, which aside from the biology is what this book is all about.

Before we finally move on from the `map` method. The more observant of you might have noticed that once we had generated the `validate` dictionary with its list of valid coordinates for each of the coordinate systems, we could have subsequently used those lists to provide the mappings for any coordinate input to the `map` method, instead of recalculating the mappings each time. We would still need the code in the `map` method as written, in order to calculate those initial lists in the validate dictionary, but yes – we could definitely use those lists from that point onward instead of recalculating the mappings each time.

If you find yourself wondering how this would be implemented, why not take a few moments to figure it out and even to implement it for yourself. In the spirit of those textbooks that encourage the reader to go beyond the book's contents and pursue additional exploration around the subject matter, we will leave implementing a more efficient `map` method using the generated coordinate lists in the `validate` dictionary as an exercise for the reader!

Assigning and Retrieving Plate Data

Now that we have established the coordinate systems necessary for defining which location (well) on the plate we're talking about, let's write some code for adding data to wells and retrieving it. To do this, we will create a couple of new `Plate` methods, the very aptly and obviously named `set` and `get`.

The first `Plate` method `set` is shown in Listing 9-3.

Listing 9-3. set method for Plate class

```
def set(self,loc,propertyName,value):
    m = self.map(loc)
    pos = m[Plate.mapPositions['position1D']]
    self.data[pos][key] = value
```

Having waded through the code for the map method, the code for the set method should seem pretty self-explanatory at this point. The method takes a plate location (in one of our three supported coordinate formats), a property name, and a value. It then generates the mapping for the supplied location and uses the position1D coordinate to add the property and its value as a **key-value** pair into the plate's data dictionary that we created in the class constructor.

You will remember that in the Plate __init__ method, we created an empty dictionary for data and then iterated over all of the position1D positions on the plate, creating **key-value** pairs consisting of the position1D coordinate and an empty dictionary in which to hold the data for that well, like this: 5:{}. If, for example, we used the set method like this:

```
myPlate.set(5,'concentration',27.4)
```

and then examined the data dictionary like this:

```
print(myPlate.data[5])
```

we would see

```
{'concentration': 27.4}
```

Just from looking at this example, it's now pretty obvious how the get method should work to retrieve data by well and by property. A valid well coordinate and a property would be passed to the method, and it would return the property value for the specified well, just as in Listing 9-4.

Listing 9-4. get method for Plate class

```
def get(self,loc,propertyName):
    m = self.map(loc)
    pos = m[Plate.mapPositions['position1D']]
```

```
if propertyName in self.data[pos]:
    return self.data[pos][propertyName]
else:
    return
```

We have added one little wrinkle here, insofar as we don't just directly return the property value for the specified well, but rather, we check first to see if the specified well actually has the property that was referenced. If we did not do this and the well dictionary did not contain a key for the specified property, our code would crash with an error. Instead, we handle this gracefully with a `return` from the method if the property does not exist in the well's dictionary.

Let's check out our `set` and `get` methods just to make sure they work before we move on.

```
p = Plate('myPlate',8,12)
p.set('B01', 'conc', 0.87)
print(p.get(13, 'conc'))
0.87
print(p.get((2,1), 'conc'))
0.87
print(p.get('B01', 'conc'))
0.87
```

Reading and Writing From CSV Files

Well that's all fine and dandy, but you're probably not going want to manually enter all the data points from your plate assay experiments in the lab. In any case, these days the chances are that a lot of your plate assay data is being automagically generated by instruments and/or robots that write the data for each well to some kind of structured file whose layout broadly mirrors that of the plate itself. There's also a pretty good chance that you have a lot of your plate assay data stored in Excel spreadsheets. Either way, we're going to add some code to our `Plate` class for reading plate assay data from one of the most common and universal file formats for storing tabular data that is widely used by lab instruments, robots, and humans – the comma-separated values format or CSV.

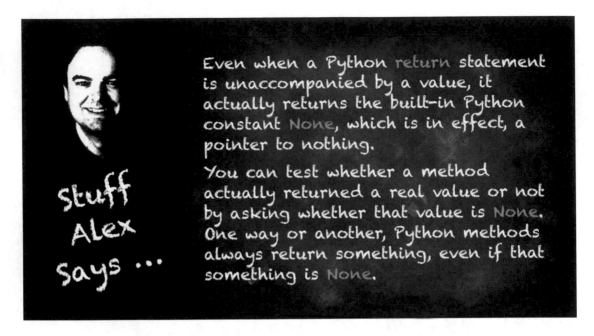

Even when a Python return statement is unaccompanied by a value, it actually returns the built-in Python constant None, which is in effect, a pointer to nothing.

You can test whether a method actually returned a real value or not by asking whether that value is None. One way or another, Python methods always return something, even if that something is None.

Stuff Alex Says …

CSV is a plain text format that simply arranges tabular data such that each row of the table is represented by a single line in the file (ending with a carriage return <CR> character), with the columns along each row being separated by commas, like this:

```
3.2, 4.8, 4.1, 2.0, 0.9, 3.5, ...
1.1, 2.4, 3.7, 3.1, 1.1, 4.6, ...
...
```

Incidentally, you probably already know that you can export in CSV format tabular data from spreadsheet applications like Microsoft Excel. This is particularly useful if you want to have your table data in a more human-readable format or to input it into another application that does not handle Excel's own internal data format.

Before we go any further, we will pause to observe that CSV is such a universal and commonly used format, that the Python standard library even includes a csv module,[6] especially for handling data that is formatted this way. And since we've already shown you in Chapter 5 how to write your own code to handle input file data, we will use the Python csv module here, particularly since it is a part of the Python standard library.

So let's take the absolute simplest case and assume that we have a lab instrument that writes multi-well data in a simple CSV format consisting only of rows and columns

---

[6]https://docs.python.org/2/library/csv.html

of data. Sometimes you will encounter more complex CSV files that also include additional data such as row and column axis labels for the table. These are often included as additional fields in the file ahead of the actual row and column data, like this:

Concentration, Incubation Time (Hrs)
3.2, 4.8, 4.1, 2.0, 0.9, 3.5, ...
1.1, 2.4, 3.7, 3.1, 1.1, 4.6, ...
...

Or even individual row and column labels embedded within the tabular data like this:

1, 2, 3, 4, 5, 6, ...
A, 3.2, 4.8, 4.1, 2.0, 0.9, 3.5, ...
B, 1.1, 2.4, 3.7, 3.1, 1.1, 4.6, ...
C, ...

And so on...

Handling these more complex CSV formats is something that the Python **csv** module does very elegantly, but for now, we're going to assume that the instrument creating the file just writes out the very simplest format of rows and columns of well data from the plate.

Let's create a method within our **Plate** class to read in the plate data from a simple CSV file in Listing 9-5.

Listing 9-5. readCSV method for Plate class

```python
def readCSV(self,filePath,propertyName):
    try:
        nWell = 1
        with open(filePath, mode="r") as csvFile:
            csvReader = csv.reader(csvFile)
            for row in csvReader:
                for wellData in row:
                    self.set(nWell, propertyName,float(wellData))
                    nWell += 1
```

```
    except:
        print("CSV data could not be correctly read from: %s" %
        filePath)
        return
    return
```

First thing to notice is that we've wrapped up all the code that deals with the file handling, data reading, and data conversion inside the `try ... except` clause that we introduced in Chapter 5, in order to trap and gracefully exit from any errors that might occur opening or reading data from our CSV file. We are also trapping any errors that might occur from converting the data which is read as strings into floating point numbers. Such an error might occur, for example, at a position in the file where for some reason the lab instrument was unable to read a valid value for the well and skipped that position, marking it as unread in the CSV file with a string value that cannot be cast to a floating point value.

Within the `try ... except` clause, we define the open file handle `csvFile` whose scope is limited to a new code block we create using the `with` statement. We then instantiate a class called `reader` that is defined for us within the `csv` module using the statement

```
    csvReader = csv.reader(csvFile)
```

This `reader` class turns out to be one of those very useful Python iterators[7] that we have encountered previously in various forms such as strings and lists. An iterator is basically any Python object type that supports the **for <element> in <collection>** syntax. In the case of the `reader` class, the elements it stores are the rows of data from the CSV file, each of which is itself a list over which an additional layer of iteration can be performed. With this in mind, we can now see that our method iterates over the rows at the top level

```
for row in csvReader:
```

and then, for each row, iterates over the list of values that comprise it

```
    for wellData in row:
```

casting each value it encounters to a floating point number and using our previously written `set` method to assign to the corresponding well. You will also notice that with

---

[7]https://docs.python.org/2.7/library/stdtypes.html#iterator-types

each pass through the values in the current row, we increment the variable nWell by 1, so that we're updating our position in the plate as we write the values for each well.

If any errors occur during all of this file reading and data conversion, the method will jump to the code in the except clause and raise a Python exception with an error message. We have used a single "one size traps all" approach here in which an error due to any of the following:

- Opening the CSV file

- Reading data from the CSV file

- Converting data from the CSV file

triggers our except clause. You will notice that as a result of this approach, we get the same generic error message no matter which of the preceding errors occurs. For simple situations, this approach might be fine. It probably wouldn't be a lot of work to figure out where the error actually occurred while reading a small CSV file in our current scenario – but where a lot of data or a more complex workflow for handling it is involved, it would almost certainly be worth using separate try … except clauses for each stage of the process, along with more specific and informative error messages for each one.

So let's test our readCSV method with an actual CSV file, and as they always say on those cooking shows, "here's one that we made earlier." The following table shows a set of data for a 96-well plate of 8 rows and 12 columns, formatted as comma-separated values (by the way, in case you were wondering, this data is completely made up just for the purposes of testing our Plate class). We also added a little extra whitespace in front of some of the shorter numbers, so that all of the numbers line up vertically and are easier to read.

It is important to note that if we are designating the comma as the separator between data points in a row of data values, it normally doesn't matter what other whitespace characters (such as spaces and tabs) are present in a line of data values, since the software that parses CSV files normally defaults to ignoring these characters, and stripping them out during the parsing process (though this default behavior can also be overridden when needed). It's also important to keep in mind that although this table appears to contain 96 floating point values, when they're read from a file, they will be read as strings, since the CSV format is not specific to files containing numerical data.

You might, for example, have a file of personal contact details, wherein the fields such as first name, last name, address, phone number, and so on are comma-separated values on a row that represents one contact. It's important to remember that the CSV format is intended only to separate the individual data values in a file or a table and not to provide any rules for how each data value should be interpreted or used. That part is up to you, the end user of the data.

To test our new CSV functionality, we store the following data in text file called 96plateCSV.txt:

0.32, 1.13, 2.72, 4.85, 5.79, 6.51, 7.43, 7.65, 8.06, 8.11, v8.28, 9.49
1.37, 0.86, 8.02, 9.47, 10.03, 12.13, 13.97, 13.78, 14.53, 15.22, 18.50, 19.88
1.01, 0.22, 19.32, 20.64, 24.93, 25.41, 26.15, 26.33, 30.40, 34.48, 35.93, 37.22
0.29, 0.65, 31.35, 31.75, 40.04, 41.18, 42.21, 44.90, 46.16, 46.49, 48.41, 53.10
1.10, 1.36, 54.68, 55.09, 57.47, 57.62, 57.42, 61.82, 64.15, 65.97, 70.95, 72.55
0.78, 0.33, 74.53, 78.97, 79.34, 80.01, 80.94, 81.55, 83.88, 83.49, 84.37, 86.49
0.12, 0.72, 86.40, 86.42, 87.13, 87.57, 88.02, 88.47, 89.25, 89.05, 89.61, 90.76
0.24, 0.21, 90.29, 93.49, 93.53, 95.18, 95.34, 95.96, 96.77, 97.73, 98.08, 98.72

We then instantiate a new 96-well Plate and use the readCSV method to read it in like this:

```
p = Plate('My 96-Well Plate',8,12)
p.readCSV('96plateCSV.txt','concentration')
```

You can see from the code that we're going to read in the table of CSV data and assign it to the well property concentration. Since the readCSV method uses the set method to assign each data value to a well, the CSV data are successfully placed into the data dictionary that the Plate class defines for holding a plate's data. We can use the get method to see what value(s) has been assigned to each well.

```
print(p.get(1,'concentration'))
0.32
print(p.get(12,'concentration'))
9.49
print(p.get(96,'concentration'))
98.72
```

So far, so good. We can navigate around our multi-well plate using any of our three coordinate systems; we can read multi-well plate data in the widely used CSV format; we can assign named data values to individual wells; and we can retrieve them by specifying a well and a property name. This is already a solid, basic foundation for a multi-well plate class, but let's consider some further functionality that we might want to add.

If we were coding a real `Plate` class for use in our work, there is a wealth of functionality that you could imagine wanting to add. We might, for example, even make each well an instance of a `Well` class, complete with a bunch of fields and methods for handling well data in all manner of sophisticated ways. So before we finish with multi-well plates, let's extend the functionality of our `Plate` class a little further with a few basic examples of the kind of things we would like it to do. As we promised at the beginning of this chapter, this should include some basic functionality for dealing with the kind of laboratory automation that is becoming ever more prevalent in the handling of plate data.

Writing code for lab automation could be (and is) the subject of whole books in and of itself. So while it is beyond the scope of this book to present a detailed description of how to write drivers for robots and automated instruments, we will show you how to write high-level code that would enable you to interface your Python software with the kind of low-level driver software that is used for machine control (and is more typically written in a programming languages like C).

Well, Well, Well: Some Math on a Plate

The grid layout of multi-well plates lends itself naturally to the organization of plate assay experiments using the plate's rows and columns – for example, by placing each sample and its controls on a single row, or assaying successive dilutions of a given sample horizontally across a row, or vertically down a column of wells. For this reason, data from a multi-well plate can often be usefully organized and/or analyzed by rows and columns. With this in mind, let's add some further functionality to our `Plate` class to be able to quickly and conveniently retrieve data by rows and columns on the plate.

We will add two methods to the `Plate` class – `getRow` and `getColumn` – which take a single plate location in any one of our three supported coordinate systems, and return a list of the positions for the row or column on which that location sits. This will be relatively quick and easy to do, since we will use our nice `map` method that we already implemented to do most of the heavy lifting. First the `getRow` method shown in Listing 9-6.

Listing 9-6. getRow method for Plate class

```
def getRow(self,loc):
    here = self.map(loc)
    row = []
    for n in range(0,self.size):
        there = self.map(n+1)
        if there[1][0] == here[1][0]:
            row.append(there)
    return row
```

This method is easy to deconstruct. First we check the supplied location using our map method which also provides us with the tuple containing the location's mapping to the three supported coordinate systems.

```
here = self.map(loc)
```

Once we have created an empty list called row to hold the row positions that our method is going to return, we then iterate over all of the positions on the plate, generating the coordinates for each and using the position2D **(row, column)** coordinate to test whether or not the row index at each position matches the row index of our input location. One nice side effect of this approach is that the positions that sit on the same row as our input location are added to the row list in the order that they occur on the plate.

As always, let's test our new code:

```
p = Plate('My 96-Well Plate',8,12)
p.readCSV('96plateCSV.txt','concentration')
print(p.getRow('B01'))
[(13, (2, 1), 'B01'), (14, (2, 2), 'B02'), (15, (2, 3), 'B03'),
(16, (2, 4), 'B04'), ...
print(p.getRow(27))
[(25, (3, 1), 'C01'), (26, (3, 2), 'C02'), (27, (3, 3), 'C03'),
(28, (3, 4), 'C04'), ...
print(p.getRow((4,7)))
[(37, (4, 1), 'D01'), (38, (4, 2), 'D02'), (39, (4, 3), 'D03'), (40, (4,
4), 'D04'), ...
```

We've truncated the outputs from the print statements, but you get the idea. The getRow method returns the mapped coordinates for all plate location that sit on the same row as the input plate location. Let's create a similar getColumn method in Listing 9-7.

Listing 9-7. getColumn method for Plate class

```
def getColumn(self,loc):
    here = self.map(loc)
    col = []
    for n in range(0,self.size):
        there = self.map(n+1)
        if there[1][1] == here[1][1]:
            col.append(there)
    return col
```

This works in a practically identical way to the getRow method, except that it uses the column index of the position2D coordinate to match the positions.

These two methods are so similar in fact that we could easily combine them into a single getRowAndColumn method that fills both the row and the col list as it iterates over the plate positions and returns them as two lists. We will leave this as an exercise for the reader.

Analyzing data from multi-well plates often involves making calculations based upon rows and columns of wells on the plate, or even over the entire plate. This includes mathematical operations such as subtracting the control well values from a row of well data or calculating the average values over a row or column. There is a wealth of calculations that one could imagine wanting to perform on multi-well plate data, and armed with the methods we have written for identifying row and column positions on the plate, and for retrieving data from specific wells, we are well-placed to implement such methods. By way of example, let's look at the simple, but universal problem of calculating mean values over multiple wells. We will build directly on our get, getRow, and getColumn methods to demonstrate how this basic infrastructure for the Plate class can be used to extend its functionality.

In Listing 9-8 we show the code for a method that accepts a property name and (optionally) single location as input and calculates the mean value for that property over a row or column of wells or even over the entire plate.

Listing 9-8. Computing the average across a feature in the Plate class

```
def average(self,propertyName,loc=None):
    if loc == None:
        total = 0.0
        for pos in range(0,self.size):
            total += self.get(pos+1, propertyName)
        return total/self.size
    row = self.getRow(loc)
    col = self.getColumn(loc)
    rowTotal = 0.0
    colTotal = 0.0
    for pos in row:
        rowTotal += self.get(pos[1],propertyName)
    rowMean = rowTotal / self.columns
    for pos in col:
        colTotal += self.get(pos[1],propertyName)
    colMean = colTotal / self.rows
    return (rowMean,colMean)
```

Here we can see that the loc argument to the method is optional, since a default value loc=None is supplied that will be used in the event that no value for loc is passed to the average method. Passing no specific location is effectively a way for the method user to have the method calculate the average over the entire plate, which you can see it doing in the code block that follows if loc == None:. The total over all the wells is initialized at zero, and we iterate over every position on the plate, summing the values for the specified property and finally dividing them by the number of positions.

In the event that a value is supplied for the loc argument, the average method uses the getRow and getColumn methods to generate lists of the row and column positions, respectively, and then iterates over the positions in these lists to calculate row and column averages, returning both values in the tuple (rowMean,colMean).

Let's test this with a 96-well plate that uses the table of test data we introduced earlier, read from a CSV file, and labeled with the property name concentration:

```
p = Plate('My 96-Well Plate',8,12)
p.readCSV('96plateCSV.txt','concentration')
```

First, a test of row and column averages for a specified well position:

```
print(p.average('concentration','B03'))
```
(11.479999999999999, 45.91375)

Next, a test of averaging over the whole plate by not specifying a well position:

```
print(p.average('concentration'))
```
43.6519791667

If you're the kind of person that needs to check this for yourself, by all means have at it with the data table provided ealier. Spoiler alert though – we checked it already if you're happy just to take our word for it!

Next up: we take our virtual plate code on the road, and put it through its paces in the real (physical) world of automation and visualization in Chapter 10.

References and Further Exploration

- Everything you ever wanted to know about microtiter plates, but were afraid to ask

CHAPTER 10

Well on the Way

Microtiter Plate Assays II: Automation and Visualization

"Where did you two come from?" asked Alice.

"Over there," said one of the twins pointing at a spot on the ground some 10 feet away.

"No, I meant before that," said Alice.

"Over there," said the other twin pointing at a spot on the ground about 10 feet further away than the first spot.

"I can see that you guys take a very literal interpretation of things," said Alice, amused.

"Oh yes," said the first twin. "My brother once used some shampoo that said 'Lather, rinse, and repeat' on the bottle, and he was in the shower for days before it ran out."

 Classes, `matplotlib`, `pyplot`, *colormaps, RGB color model, plot resolution, plot size, iterators, SWIG,* `round()`

 Microtiter plate layouts and physical dimensions, 2D coordinate systems, stepper motors, robots, heat maps, optical density

---

A. Lancaster and G. Webster, *Python for the Life Sciences*, https://doi.org/10.1007/978-1-4842-4523-1_10

Now that we have looked at handling the plate as a virtual object, let's look at handling as a physical (and visual) object. Laboratory plate assays are a popular target for anyone looking to create a high-throughput pipeline using lab automation and robotics, and there are already a wealth of laboratory instruments and robots that can automatically set up experiments in multi-well plates, monitor them, and read data from them. In order for any of this to occur, the computer-driven machinery being used requires some kind of physical map of the plate.

Mapping a Plate Physically

The simple schema that we will use for physically mapping a multi-well plate is shown in the following diagram and makes the following assumptions. The first well, that we are calling **1**, **(1,1)** or '**A01**' in our three coordinate systems, is the top-left well on the plate. We will choose the top, left corner of our plate to be the origin of our two-dimensional, physical coordinate system that we will use to navigate around on our plate. The plate has a defined width along a left-to-right axis **x** and height along a top-to-bottom axis **y** that define its edges. You will notice that since we have defined the origin of our physical coordinate system as the top, left corner of the plate, as advance in row number, we are descending in **y**. The position of the leftmost column of wells relative to the left edge of the plate can be defined by **xb**, an offset in **x**. Similarly the position of the topmost row of wells relative to the top edge of the plate can be defined by **yb**, an offset in **y**. The internal diameter of each well is defined by a parameter **d**. The spacing of the wells is assumed to be equal horizontally and vertically and is represented by a single parameter **p**.

Some of these assumptions need not necessarily true for a real plate, but for the purposes of demonstrating the physical mapping of a plate, this very simple schema will suffice. If the physical layout of a real plate is more complex, for example, if the horizontal and vertical spacing of the wells is not equal, then more parameters would be needed to describe it. The calculations needed for physically navigating around on the plate would also be more complicated.

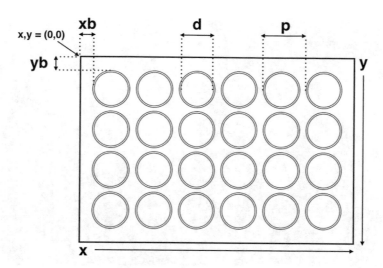

Figure 10-1. *Physical layout of 96-well plate*

In essence though, the principles would be the same as we're describing for our simple schema. We identify one or more reference points on the plate and describe the layout of the wells with respect to this (or these) reference point(s).

Before we move on, it's probably worth taking the time to examine the diagram of our simple, physical plate schema shown in Figure 10-1, since it explains a lot of the code that we will use in this section.

Let's add a method `definePhysicalMap` to our `Plate` class that defines the physical layout of the plate that we will need for the purposes of automation and visualization. You can guess from looking at this schema that our method is going to accept each of the parameters in the schema as an argument. We will have our `definePhysicalMap` method use these parameters to calculate and store the physical positions of all the wells on the plate for use later on. We will also use this method to initialize our automation code by generating a starting position on the plate that would correspond to the default initialization position of a robot arm or instrument read head. We will set this initialization position (arbitrarily) at the coordinate (0,0) corresponding to the top left corner of the plate, and all subsequent movements of our robot or instrument will be made with reference to this starting position.

But what about the units of our physical coordinate system?

The way we will write the code, we will not actually need to specify a set of distance units in `definePhysicalMap`. This is because we will work exclusively in whatever set of units the robot or instrument uses for its movements. For the kind of computer-controlled stepper motor that typically drives a robot or a moving sensor on an instrument, the step size of the motor is typically defined with significant precision as some fraction of a degree of rotation.

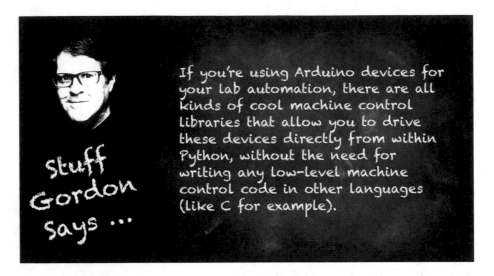

If you're using Arduino devices for your lab automation, there are all kinds of cool machine control libraries that allow you to drive these devices directly from within Python, without the need for writing any low-level machine control code in other languages (like C for example).

stuff Gordon says ...

Once this rotation has been transmitted through the linkages and gearing of the instrument, this fractional rotation will result in a correspondingly tiny linear movement. In other words, a single rotational **step** of the motor can be mapped to a linear movement, typically measured in millimeters or micrometers, depending upon the precision of the motor and the gearing of the instrument or robot. For our definePhysicalMap method therefore, all we need to do is to make sure that we enter all of our physical plate parameters in the same units (e.g., millimeters) and that we specify a step size for the instrument in those same units.

Again, for the purposes of demonstration and to keep things simple, we will assume that the step sizes along the x and y dimensions of the instrument's motion are equal. If this were not the case, we would need to add additional parameters and make separate calculations for movements in different dimensions.

So here's the code for the definePhysicalMap method in our Plate class in Listing 10-1 (remember these code listings for defining the Plate class are cumulative and are intended to be added after all the other methods already introduced in the code listings in Chapter 9).

Listing 10-1. Defining a physical map for Plate class

```
def definePhysicalMap(self,width,height,xBorder,yBorder, \
                      diameter,pitch,stepsize):
    self.width = width
    self.height = height
    self.xBorder = xBorder
    self.yBorder = yBorder
```

```
self.diameter = diameter
self.pitch = pitch
self.stepSize = stepsize
self.xwells = []
self.ywells = []
xpos = self.xBorder

for nx in range(0,self.columns):
    self.xwells.append(xpos)
    xpos += self.pitch
ypos = -self.yBorder
for ny in range(0,self.rows):
    self.ywells.append(ypos)
    ypos -= self.pitch
self.initializePlateHead()
self.setPlotCurrentPosition()
```

If you look again at the physical plate schema shown in Figure 10-1, you will see that each of the parameters that we use to define our physical plate is passed to the definePhysicalMap method as arguments. The arguments width and height correspond to the dimensions of the plate in **x** and **y** in our schema. xBorder and yBorder correspond to **xb** and **yb**, diameter corresponds to **d**, and pitch to **p**. You will notice that we also have a stepSize argument that defines the size of a single unit of linear motion in the **x** and **y** dimensions of the plate. The stepSize argument must be in the same units as the other arguments and would typically be some fraction of those units – for example, if the plate dimensions are supplied in millimeters, stepSize might be 0.01 which would correspond to a step size of a hundredth of a millimeter. For this configuration, we would therefore need the machine control system to send 100 steps to the robot or instrument drive motor in order to achieve one linear millimeter of movement in our chosen dimension.

Having stored the supplied arguments as instance variables, the definePhysicalMap method then creates two instance variables xwells and ywells, which are lists that contain the horizontal positions of the plate's columns and rows, respectively. Here's the code that generates the xwells list:

```
xpos = self.xBorder + self.diameter/2.0
for nx in range(0,self.columns):
    self.xwells.append(xpos)
    xpos += self.pitch
```

The horizontal well position xpos is initialized to the instance variable xBorder plus half of a well diameter, so that we are in effect defining the **x** position of the leftmost column as the center of the leftmost well. Then we iterate over the number of columns on the plate, each time appending the current column position to the xwells list, before adding the well spacing pitch to the current position to calculate the next position. Starting at the center of the leftmost well therefore, this means that all subsequent well positions will also correspond to the center of their respective wells. This will be important for the automation code, since we will probably want our robots and instruments to be pipetting and/or sampling from the **centers** of the wells, rather than their edges.

We perform a similar operation to generate the ywells list of vertical row positions, but due to the fact that the plate's y axis runs in reverse order to the row numbers, we must use *decrements* of **y** as we iterate through the vertical row positions – in other words, we start at zero **y** and move down the plate in *negative* increments of **y**. The reason for this is immediately apparent if you refer once more to the plate schema.

```
ypos = -self.yBorder - self.diameter/2.0
for ny in range(0,self.rows):
    self.ywells.append(ypos)
    ypos -= self.pitch
```

Now that we have the horizontal and vertical positions of every row and column on the plate, we can easily calculate the physical position of any well on the plate, simply by using its position in the plate's grid layout, to look up its horizontal and vertical positions on the plate.

Having extended our Plate class to enable it to be mapped physically, all that remains to do is to provide our Plate instance with a method initializePlatePosition that handles a couple of new instance variables **x** and **y** that we will use to store a current physical position on the plate. Once these variables have been created, the main job of the initializePlatePosition method will be to initialize them to (0,0), our coordinate system origin. This is somewhat arbitrary – we could have started out at the first well, or the last one, or even some other physical location that might be more amenable to a robot or an instrument, such as the geographic center of the plate.

At the end of our definePhysicalMap method, you will see that there is also a call to another method called setPlotCurrentPlatePosition that we will introduce as well. This is simply a method that sets a flag True or False to determine whether or not to visually represent the current plate position when we are visualizing the plate. We haven't talked yet about visualization of the plate, but this will be the very last topic of this chapter, in which we will introduce the very powerful, but easy to use `matplotlib`[49] library. In our plate visualization methods, we wish to have the option to show the current plate position (corresponding, for example, to the position of a robotic pipetting device or an instrument read head). This will be very useful for testing purposes, showing us where the current position is relative to the layout of the plate, as we use our physical mapping code to move around the plate. As shown in Listing 10-2, all we need this simple `setPlotCurrentPlatePosition` method to do is to flag whether or not to include the current plate position in any visualizations and to provide the option to assign a color to it. The reason for wanting to be able to choose the color will become more evident when we get into the visualization topic and learn about using colormaps to visualize the plate's data.

Listing 10-2. Initializing methods for `Plate` class

```
def initializePlatePosition(self):
    self.x = 0
    self.y = 0

def setPlotCurrentPosition(self,status=False,color='yellow'):
    self.plotCurrentPosition = status
    self.currentPositionColor = color
```

You will notice that the plate's current position represented by the **x** and **y** variables is in **integer** units. When we start navigating around the plate physically using robots and instruments, we are assuming that the motion of these devices will be driven by stepper motors and that the units of movement must therefore be expressed in integer steps.

You will also notice that the default status for `plotCurrentPlatePosition` is `False`, but later on, when we want to fully test our code for navigating physically around the plate, we will switch it on. More to come on that very soon.

The physical locations we are primarily concerned with on the plate are the locations of the wells, so now let's use our generated lists of the plate's row and column positions `xwells` and `ywells`, and add a method to the `Plate` class, to physically map the position of any well in Listing 10-3.

Listing 10-3. `mapWell` method for `Plate` class

```
def mapWell(self,loc):
    m = self.map(loc)[Plate.mapPositions['position2D']]
    xpos = self.xwells[m[1]-1]
    ypos = self.ywells[m[0]-1]
    return (xpos,ypos)
```

The `mapWell` method uses our `map` method that generates the tuple of coordinates for the input well location, but instead of assigning the entire tuple of three values to `m`, we are extracting from the tuple only the `position2D` coordinate.

```
m = self.map(loc)[Plate.mapPositions['position2D']]
```

Syntactically, this might look a little strange, since we're kind of tacking on a dictionary key lookup to a method call, but this is perfectly legal in Python. A helpful way to think about this is that whenever you see a method call that returns an object (be it an integer, a list, a dictionary, a user-defined class for simulating the breeding habits of *Tyrannosaurus rex,* or whatever), you can mentally substitute that object in place of the method call, and whatever syntax you would use to access that object's elements or fields is perfectly legal. In a sense, this is just a kind of shorthand that saves some additional code. In our example, we could have assigned the tuple returned from `map` to `m` and then extracted the `position2D` coordinate from it subsequently.

```
m = self.map(loc)
m = m[Plate.mapPositions['position2D']]
```

The result would have been the same, but the code a little longer.

Now that we have our coordinate in the form (row,column), we can use our `xwells` and `ywells` lists of row and column locations to look up the well's physical position on the plate. You will notice that in keeping with the fact that Python lists are indexed from zero, we need to subtract 1 from both the row and the column, since we are indexing both of these from 1 in our plate coordinate system.

```
xpos = self.xwells[m[1]-1]
ypos = self.ywells[m[0]-1]
```

Before moving on, let's create a 96-well plate, apply a physical mapping to it, and do a quick test drive of our new `mapWell` method.

```
p = Plate('My 96-well plate',8,12)
p.definePhysicalMap(127.71,85.43,14.36,10.0,3.47,9.0,0.1)

print(p.mapWell(1))
```
(16.095, -11.735)
```
print(p.mapWell(2))
```
(25.095, -11.735)
```
print(p.mapWell(12))
```
(115.095, -11.735)
```
print(p.mapWell(85))
```
(16.095, -74.735)
```
print(p.mapWell(96))
```
(115.095, -74.735)

Our mapped 96-well plate is 85.43mm wide by 127.71 high. Measure from the top left corner of the plate, the horizontal offset of the first column is 14.36mm and the vertical offset of the first row is 10.0mm. The wells have a diameter of 3.47mm and a spacing of 9.0mm. Finally, the step size for the automated device we are using is 0.1mm.

Based upon these parameters and referring to our plate schema diagram once more, the x position of the first well should be

$$\mathbf{xb} + \mathbf{d}/2 = 14.36 + 3.47/2 = 16.095$$

Similarly, the y position of the first well should be

$$\mathbf{yb} + \mathbf{d}/2 = 10.0 + 3.47/2 = 11.735$$

So the `mapWell` calculation for the first well is correct. For the second well on the plate, the y position of the well should remain the same since it is in the same row, and the x position should advance by the well spacing p, which it does $16.095 + 9.00 = 25.095$. You will also notice that as we advance down the rows, the values for a well's y position are increasingly negative in keeping with our coordinate origin at the top, left of the plate. As before, if you wish to check the remaining calculations, have at it.

Programming Movement Around the Plate

Now that we can define the physical location of any well on a plate, it's a small step to defining the x and y axis movements that we would need to send to an instrument or a robot, in order to physically move a pipetting robot or a sensor around a plate. All we need to know is where we are and where we want to go next, and then we can use our stepSize parameter to calculate the number of steps in x and y needed to get us there.

Listing 10-4. moveTo method for Plate class

```
def moveTo(self,loc):
    pos = self.mapWell(loc)
    stepsPerUnit = 1.0 / self.stepSize
    newx = int(round(pos[0] * stepsPerUnit))
    newy = int(round(pos[1] * stepsPerUnit))
    xshift = newx - self.x
    yshift = newy - self.y
    self.x += xshift
    self.y += yshift
    return (xshift,yshift)
```

The moveTo method in Listing 10-4 does exactly this, accepting a well location as a destination, calculating the number of steps required in x and y to get from the plate's current position (self.x, self.y) to the destination, and updating the plate's current position to this new position in the process. Now that we are working in physical coordinates, you will notice that we always have to work in integer values for both the current x and y position on the plate and the shifts required to move from the current position to the new position. Because the xxx parameter is a fraction of the units that we are using to define the physical layout of the plate, it will not necessarily yield an integer number of steps per unit, so we need to do some rounding to the nearest integer when we're calculating our new position. This is what the Python built-in function round[1] does – for example:

```
print(round(5.4))
```
5.0
```
print(round(5.6))
```
6.0

---

[1]https://docs.python.org/2/library/functions.html#round

Even though `round` returns the nearest whole number, it is still a floating point number, which must be converted to a Python integer (`int`) if it's an integer that you need, like this:

```
print(int(round(5.6)))
6
```

It's important to remember that all of the physical coordinates on our plate must be expressed in **integer values**, since we're defining the two-dimensional, physical motion across the plate in terms of integer steps.

Time to test our `moveTo` method. We'll start with a move to well 1, then advance a single place along the first row to well 2, then we'll go down a row and back to column 1, where well 13 is located, and finally we'll skip all the way to the last well on the plate, number 96. For each move we will print out the x and y shifts required, the new physical position we have moved to, and the physical location of the well at the current position, for comparison. You will immediately see that the current physical position and the exact position of the well determined by the `mapWell` method are not exactly the same, due to the fact that we are working in integer steps for the physical movements. The differences we see will always be tiny and never a problem for our robot or automated instrument, so long as we're using stepper motors whose step size is small relative to the physical dimensions of the plate. In our case, we have supplied the plate dimensions in millimeters and defined `stepSize` to be 0.1, or 1/10 of a millimeter. This linear unit is indeed pretty small compared to the dimensions of our plate, so there is little danger of our automated machinery ever failing to locate a well with sufficient accuracy.

So to the test:

```
print(p.moveTo(1))
(161, -117)
print(p.x, p.y)
161 -117
print(p.mapWell(1))
(16.095, -11.735)

print(p.moveTo(2))
(90, 0)
print(p.x, p.y)
251 -117
```

```
print(p.mapWell(2))
```
(25.095, -11.735)

```
print(p.moveTo(13))
```
(-90, -90)
```
print(p.x, p.y)
```
161 -207
```
print(p.mapWell(13))
```
(16.095, -20.735)

```
print(p.moveTo(96))
```
(990, -540)
```
print(p.x, p.y)
```
1151 -747
```
print(p.mapWell(96))
```
(115.095, -74.735)

Great! You can see from the test results that the final position (p.x, p.y) that results from the application of the shifts output by the moveTo method are in each case the nearest integer values to the actual floating point well positions calculated by the mapWell method.

In a real-world laboratory automation project that one of us undertook for a client, this kind of high-level Python code produced two-dimensional movements in exactly the way that we've shown here and subsequently passed them to a low-level machine control library written in C that actually drove the stepper motors on the laboratory robot. This required a little code wrangling with the help the previously mentioned platform called SWIG (Simplified Wrapper and Interface Generator) that enables code libraries written in languages like C to interface with your Python code in a way that allows its subroutines and functions be callable from Python, as if they were Python methods. Most laboratory automation hardware comes supplied with these kinds of low-level machine control libraries that the user can incorporate into their own applications, either directly or through the use of interface software like SWIG.

It is beyond the scope and purpose of this book to get into all the details of how to set up, program, and use this kind of automation hardware, but we do refer you to some of the excellent resources that cover the topic of laboratory automation in more depth at the end of this chapter.

Visualizing Multi-well Plates with matplotlib

So finally we come to the last topic in our long odyssey with multi-well plates – visualizing plate assay data. We've dedicated a lot of time to handling plate assay data in Python, partly because plate assays have become such a universal feature of life science research, but also because this topic gives us so many excellent Python learning opportunities.

The matplotlib library[2] is a powerful, but easy to use, extension to Python that provides cool graphical and plotting functionality. If you look at the matplotlib documentation, you will see that pyplot,[3] which we will discuss extensively in this chapter, is a kind of MATLAB-like[4] plotting framework within matplotlib. The environment and setup of matplotlib in general and pyplot specifically will seem quite familiar to you if you have ever used MATLAB.[5] matplotlib is normally found in most Python distributions available on Windows or macOS and is also available in most Linux distributions as an add-on package (e.g., in both Ubuntu and Fedora the package is called `python-matplotlib`). See Chapter 1 for more details on installing matplotlib via `pip` if matplotlib is not already included in your main Python installation.

With that brief introduction out of the way, let's start with simple example of the library in action! We will develop some code for plotting the layout of a plate, with the wells color-coded by some chosen property.

We will also make use of the `currentPlatePosition` flag and plot color that we implemented in our `setPlotCurrentPlatePosition` method to plot the current position on the plate.

Working with matplotlib Colormaps

First, let's consider how we might color-code our wells by a certain property. Let's say that we want to represent the `concentration` data that we read in from a CSV file in an earlier example. Each well on the plate has an associated value for the `concentration` property, and we want to be able to represent the range of concentration values on the

---

[2]`http://matplotlib.org/`
[3]`http://matplotlib.org/api/pyplot_api.html`
[4]`www.mathworks.com/products/matlab.html`
[5]MATLAB is a trademark of MathWorks Inc.

plate using a colormap. You've probably seen colormaps used before in many other applications. The obvious one that springs to mind in biology is the use of colored heat maps to represent differential levels of gene expression in cells as in Figure 10-2.

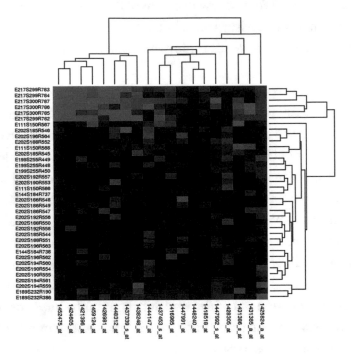

Figure 10-2. *Heat map representing differential gene expression*

We are going to develop some Python code to create a kind of heat map of the wells on a plate, colored by some specified property for which we have assigned a value to each well. Per the old maxim that a picture is worth a thousand words, we will exploit the power of visualization to represent plate assay data in a way that is intuitive and which shows, at a glance, the trends (if any) that exist in the data.

To do this, we will make use of a method by which colors can be represented on computers using the RGB color model. In Python's matplotlib library, the red, green, and blue components of a color can be represented using tuples of three values, one for each of the color's red, blue, and green components. In matplotlib, these components have floating point values between 0.0 corresponding to zero intensity and 1.0 corresponding to full intensity. On many computers that used a fixed number of bits to represent colors on the screen, you will often see values that are integers in a range that reflects the numerical limits for the number of bits used to define each color (e.g., from 0 to 255 for 8-bit color).

Python matplotlib's use of floating point numbers to represent a color range effectively decouples its RGB color model from any specific fixed bit color model, since it is always translated to the nearest bit value appropriate for the display or printer being used for the visualization. Naturally however, a system with a higher number of bits per color will always be able to display a larger number of shades of a particular color.

To illustrate how our colormap will work, let's imagine that we want to color-code each well by the concentration of one of its contents, with white corresponding to our minimum concentration and red corresponding to our maximum concentration.

- The color white in our matplotlib RGB color model is (1.0, 1.0, 1.0) corresponding to maximum intensities of all three component colors.

- The color red is (1.0, 0.0, 0.0) – maximum red and no green or blue at all.

To generate the color of a concentration that is exactly halfway between these two extremes, we simply take the differences between each individual color component, divide those differences by 2.0, and add the result to the lower concentration color.

The math would look like this:

$R = 1.0 + ((1.0 - 1.0) / 2.0)$, $G = 1.0 + ((0.0 - 1.0) / 2.0)$, $B = 1.0 + ((0.0 - 1.0) / 2.0)$

$RGB = (1.0, 0.5, 0.5)$

To see what this color-mapping algorithm looks like in action, in Figure 10-3 we show what the minimum, halfway, and maximum concentration colors look like plotted as circles.

Figure 10-3. *Concentration colors of red color*

So this is the basis for how our color-mapping system will work. The user will specify the well property to be color-coded, a "minimum" property color, and a "maximum" property color. The color-mapping method will then scan all of the wells on the plate for the specified property and assign a color to each well that corresponds to the value of the chosen property for that well. Since we're very thoughtful coders with the best interests of our end users at heart, let's also allow the user to choose the minimum and maximum values of the property to be color-coded. This will mean that all values at or less than this chosen minimum property value will have the "minimum" color applied and all values at or above the "maximum" property value will have the "maximum" color applied. Allowing the user to choose the range of property values over which to apply the colormap gives them a greater degree of control over the final visualization.

So before we jump in to plotting our plate with the option to color-code the wells by their property values, let's implement the method that generates the colormap. In Listing 10-5 is the new createColorMap method for our Plate class.

Listing 10-5. Creating the colormap for the Plate class

```
def createColorMap(self, propertyName, loColor=(1.0,1.0,1.0), \
                   hiColor=(1.0,0.0,0.0), propertyRange=(0.0, 100.0)):
    self.colorMap = []
    pRange = propertyRange[1] - propertyRange[0]
    rRange = hiColor[0] - loColor[0]
    gRange = hiColor[1] - loColor[1]
    bRange = hiColor[2] - loColor[2]
    for n in range(0,self.size):
        p = self.get(n+1,propertyName)
        scaledP = (p - propertyRange[0]) / pRange
        r = loColor[0] + (scaledP * rRange)
        if r < 0.0: r = 0.0
        if r > 1.0: r = 1.0
        g = loColor[1] + (scaledP * gRange)
        if g < 0.0: g = 0.0
        if g > 1.0: g = 1.0
        b = loColor[2] + (scaledP * bRange)
```

```
    if b < 0.0: b = 0.0
    if b > 1.0: b = 1.0
    self.colorMap.append((r,g,b))
return
```

You can see that we have provided default colors – white for the minimum value and red for the maximum, as well as a default range for the property, which is supplied to the method as a tuple containing the minimum and maximum property values.

Once the method has calculated the range of property values, and a color range for each color component, we're off to the races, iterating over every well on the plate and calculating a color that corresponds to the property value for each well. These values are stored in a new instance variable colorMap that we will need later on for plotting the plate, assuming that we decide to exercise the option to plot by color. The instance variable colorMap is simply a list of color tuples, one for each position (well) on the plate.

So here's another small exercise for the reader: an instance of our Plate class could have multiple properties for the wells – a concentration for each separate well constituent, for example, an optical density measurement, a cell line ID, etc., etc. How would you implement the feature that allowed colormaps for all of these properties to be stored simultaneously and any one of them selected for plotting with a colormap? *Hint: Python dictionaries are your friend.*

Now that we are allowing the user to set their own minimum and maximum property values for the colormap, we need a way to deal with property values that fall outside of the specified range. As we said previously, we need to set any values that fall below the property range to the minimum color and any values that fall above the property range to the maximum color value. That's what these code blocks for each color component are taking care of.

```
r = loColor[0] + (scaledP * rRange)
if r < 0.0: r = 0.0
if r > 1.0: r = 1.0
```

Here's the calculation of the *red* color component, for example. The scaled color value must lie between 0.0 and 1.0, and values that are calculated outside the range must be reset.

Once a suitably scaled value has been calculated for each color component, the RGB tuple is appended to the colorMap list.

matplotlib Plotting Commands

Now that we can generate colormaps for well properties, we're finally ready to plot our plate using matplotlib. For example, you can define the size and resolution of the output figure, which can be very useful if you are generating figures that are to be used in a print publication such as a scientific journal. We will use the physical map of the plate that we defined earlier to define the coordinate system for the plot and the layout of all the wells, but we will switch off the scaled and marked axes that would normally be present if we were plotting a graph, for example, since these are not relevant for our purposes.

We will plot the plate as a grid layout of circles (we're assuming that the wells are circular), and we will also use matplotlib's text features to label the rows and columns of the plate. If a colormap has been generated for the plate instance, we will use it to color-code the wells, and finally, if the instance's plotCurrentPlatePosition flag is True, we will add a small circle to show the plate's currentPlatePosition. In Listing 10-6, we see the code for the new plotPlate method for our Plate class.

Listing 10-6. Creating an image: plotPlate method in Plate class

```
def plotPlate(self,figWidth=4.0,figHeight=3.0,dpi=200, \
              rowlabelOffset=3.0,columnLabelOffset=2.0, fontSize=None):
    if self.width == None:
        return
    wellColor = 'w'
    plt.figure(figsize=(figWidth,figHeight),dpi=dpi)
    plt.axes()
    plt.axis('off')
    if fontSize == None:
        fontSize = figHeight * 3
    #outline = plt.Rectangle((0, 0), self.width, -self.height, fc="gray")
    #plt.gca().add_patch(outline)
    npos = -1
    leftText = self.xwells[0] - (self.diameter * rowlabelOffset)
    topText = self.ywells[0] + (self.diameter * columnLabelOffset)
    for yw in self.ywells:
        ymap = self.map(npos+2)
        letter = ymap[2][0]
```

```
        plt.text(leftText, yw - (self.diameter / 2.0), letter,
        color="black", \
                  fontsize=fontSize)
        for xw in self.xwells:
            npos += 1
            if npos <= self.columns:
                xmap = self.map(npos+1)
                col = str(int(xmap[2][1:]))
                plt.text(xw - (self.diameter / 2.0), topText, col,
                color="black", \
                          fontsize=fontSize)
            if not self.colorMap == None:
                wellColor = self.colorMap[npos]
            circle = plt.Circle((xw, yw), radius=self.diameter,
            fc=wellColor)
            plt.gca().add_patch(circle)
    if self.plotCurrentPosition:
        circle = plt.Circle((self.x * self.stepSize, self.y * self.
        stepSize), \
                            radius=self.diameter / 3.0, fc=self.
                            currentPositionColor)
        plt.gca().add_patch(circle)
    plt.axis('scaled')
    plt.show()
```

Before we jump into the dissection of the code, let's take a quick look at its output, so that we have some additional context for our discussion. We'll create a 96-well plate, read in the data from the CSV file that we used previously, apply a physical map and a colormap to color-code the data, and then plot the result.

```
p = Plate('My 96-well plate', 8, 12)
p.definePhysicalMap(127.71, 85.43, 14.36, 10.0, 3.47, 9.0, 0.1)
p.readCSV('96plateCSV.txt', 'concentration')
p.createColorMap('concentration', propertyRange=[0.0, 100.0])
p.setPlotCurrentPosition(True, color="orange")
print(p.moveTo(15))
p.plotPlate(figWidth=8.0, figHeight=5.0, dpi=200)
```

You can see that we define a colormap using the default white-red color scheme, with a range from 0.0 to 100.0, we set the plate's plotCurrentPlatePosition flag to True, and assign the color "orange" for plotting the plate's currentPlatePosition. Finally, we also perform a moveTo operation to set the plate's currentPlatePosition to position 15 before actually plotting the result. And here it is shown in Figure 10-4.

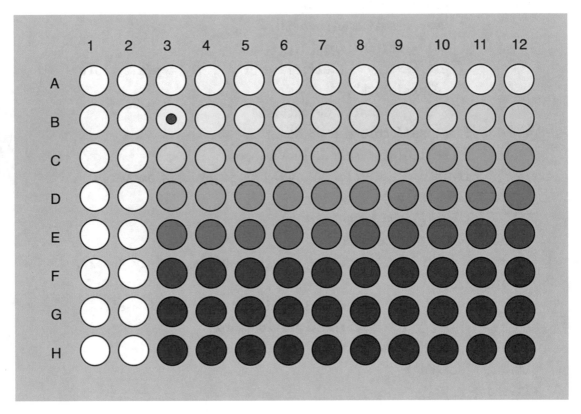

Figure 10-4. *Plotting the output of plate levels*

In the totally made-up dataset for this plate, you can see that the first two wells on each row are meant to be the controls, with the subsequent wells on each row showing a clear trend toward higher concentrations. You could imagine, for example, a successive dilution experiment in which each row of the plate represents a particular dilution of a set of conditions. In any case, this fictitious dataset was created to nicely illustrate the color-mapping algorithm (which it does). You will also notice the small orange circle on position 15 of the plate, corresponding to the currentPlatePosition that resulted from our moveTo operation. This visualization is a very convenient way of simulating the movements over the plate of a robot arm or instrument sensor. We could, for example, program a whole series of movements and visualize them on the plate, as shown in Figure 10-5.

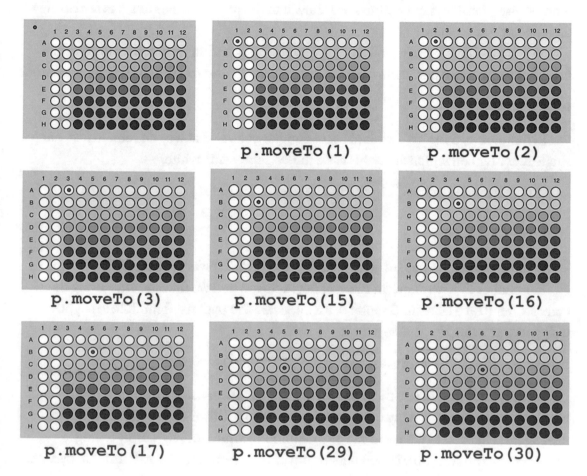

Figure 10-5. *Possible programmed set of movements on plate by a robot or sensor*

So, to the code... As we move through the code for plotPlate, we recommend that you also refer to the documentation for pyplot,[6] since our aim here is not to offer an exhaustive tutorial on matplotlib or pyplot.

```
if self.width == None:
    return
```

The first thing to do in our new `plotPlate` method is to check that the current plate instance even has a physical mapping assigned to it, since we are unable to plot it otherwise. If `width` is not defined, we know that the physical mapping has not been assigned and so we bail.

Next we assign a default well color to handle the situation where no colormap has been defined and we just want to plot the plate's layout and (optionally) current position.

```
wellColor = 'w'
```

In matplotlib, there's a standard set of popular colors[7] that we can refer to just using a single letter for convenience. In this case, the 'w' represents white.

```
plt.figure(figsize=(figWidth,figHeight),dpi=dpi)
plt.axes()
plt.axis('off')
```

Next we initialize a `pyplot` figure. Where does the `plt` symbol come from?

Remember that way back in the very beginning, when we first started writing the code for our `Plate` class, in Chapter 9, we imported the pyplot submodule in slightly different way using the "as" keyword:

```
import matplotlib.pyplot as plt
```

It's very common to use the "`import ... as ..`" form using an abbreviation like "plt" which saves having to type `mathplotlib.pyplot` or even `pyplot` over and over again. This makes it easy to call any matplotlib command, by simply typing `plt.<command>` name. So `plt` becomes a convenient shorthand for `matplotlib.pyplot`.

```
plt.figure(figsize=(figWidth,figHeight),dpi=dpi)
```

We initialize our new `plt` figure using the `figWidth`, `figHeight`, and `dpi` arguments that we passed to the `plotPlate` method. This allows the user to specify the width and height of the figure in inches and also the resolution of the figure in dots per inch. We added this feature to the plate visualization code, because this degree of control over the size and resolution of your matplotlib graphical output can be extremely important when you are using Python to generate any kind of graphs or figures that are destined for publication in a print journal. It is very common for these scientific journals to have fairly

---

[7]http://matplotlib.org/api/colors_api.html

rigorous requirements for figure sizes and resolutions, so as a life scientist, it's very useful to know how to tailor your graphs and figures to their specifications. Similarly, whether you're producing oversize graphics for a poster at a conference or figures for your laboratory's web site, Python is a great way to generate graphics for all kinds of media.

In the next section of code, we add a set of (invisible) axes to our plot, which essentially defines its coordinate system

```
plt.axes()
```

but we switch off the visible axes

```
plt.axis('off')
```

since we're not plotting a graph and therefore don't need them.

In addition to offering the user some control over the size and resolution of the output figure, we also provide the option to set the font size for the plate labels while also providing the option to let the method itself choose a sensible default font size, based upon the size of the figure.

```
if fontSize == None:
    fontSize = figHeight * 3
```

The next task is to calculate the positions in the plot for the horizontal line of column labels (A through H for a 96-well plate with 12 columns) and the vertical line of row labels (1 through 8 for a 96-well plate with 8 rows). In keeping with our philosophy to provide the user some degree of control over the aesthetic details of the plot, we also provide two method arguments rowLabelOffset and columnLabelOffset with which the user can control how far from the edge of the wells the row and column labels will appear. To keep these offsets scaled proportionally with the layout of the plate itself, they are actually used as multiples of a single well diameter, so, for example, a rowLabelOffset of 3.0 (which is the default) will position the row labels three well diameters from the edge of the leftmost well. For different plate layouts in which the wells themselves may start closer or further from the edge of the plate than is typical, it's easy to imagine that the user might wish to have some degree of control over the position of the row and column labels.

Next comes the main body of the method in which we use nested loops in y and x to iterate over all of the plate positions by row and by column, adding the row and column labels where necessary and actually plotting the color-coded wells.

The structure of this code looks like this:

Iterate over each row:

Plot the row label for the current row

Iterate over each column in the current row:

    If we're on the top row of the plate:

        Plot the current column label

        Plot the current well

    Otherwise:

        Plot the current well

If the `plotCurrentPlatePosition` flag is set:

  Plot the plate's current position

You will notice in the actual code that when we're at the point of actually plotting a well, we will use a colormap if one is available; otherwise, we just use the default (white) well color.

The very last line in the `plotPlate` method

```
plt.show()
```

actually generates the plot and voila!

Different Plate Layouts

Just before we end our long odyssey with multi-well plates, you might notice that we've only been plotting 96-well plates so far, so let's just satisfy ourselves that the plotPlate method works for other layouts as well. We'll take the standard 24-well plate with four rows and six columns, as an example. You can see the results in Figure 10-6.

```
p = Plate('My 24-well plate', 4, 6)
p.readCSV('24plateCSV.txt','concentration')
p.definePhysicalMap(140.71, 100.43, 14.36, 10, 7.0, 18.0, 0.1)
p.createColorMap('concentration', propertyRange=[0.0, 100.0])
p.moveTo(24)
p.setPlotCurrentPosition(True, color="orange")
p.plotPlate(figWidth=8.0, figHeight=5.0, dpi=200)
```

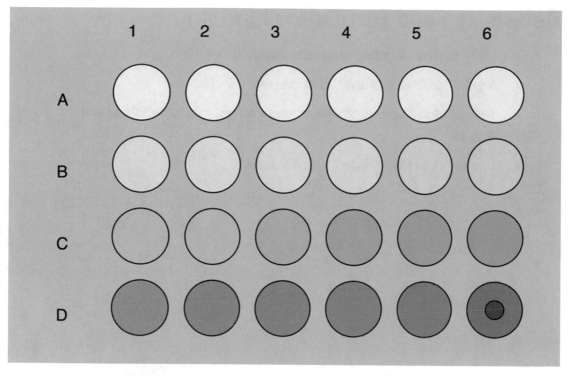

Figure 10-6. *Output plate levels in a 24-well configuration*

Let's put away the lab equipment for the time being. In the next chapter, we'll continue our journey of representing biology in code by looking at very smallest of "biological" systems: a single molecule. At the molecular scale, we're really much more in the realm of physics and chemistry than in biology, but much of modern biology is the study of biological systems at these very small scales, so our book would not be complete without it.

References and Further Exploration

- More about laboratory automation from Wikipedia

- A guide[8] to the use of Python to program robots

- The Arduino Playground's page[9] about programming Arduinos with Python

- You can even run Python on an Arduino[10]!

[8]www.amazon.com/Learning-Robotics-Python-Lentin-Joseph/dp/1783287535/ref=sr_1_2?s=books&ie=UTF8&qid=1475251026&sr=1-2

[9]http://playground.arduino.cc/Interfacing/Python

[10]http://playground.arduino.cc/CommonTopics/PyMite

## CHAPTER 11

Molecules in 3D

Mathematics and Linear Algebra for Structural Biology

"*Goodness gracious! A talking chess piece,*" *said Alice.*

"*Not just any chess piece,*" *said the chess piece angrily.* "*I'm the queen and you are an impertinent little girl.*"

"*I'm sorry,*" *said Alice,* "*but you made me jump.*"

"*Made you jump?*" *said the chess piece.* "*Ah, yes – do please remind me again how wonderful it is in your three-dimensional world, while I and all my fellow chess pieces have only a two-dimensional grid to move around on. There's nothing like having an extra dimension to give one an air of entitlement!*"

"*I'm sorry,*" *said Alice.* "*I had no idea.*"

"*Trust me, there's no upside to being a chess piece,*" *said the chess piece,* "*mainly because there's no 'up' to begin with. Between you and me, I would like to tell you that sometimes I get pretty down about it, except that there's no 'down' for us either.*"

"*Maybe you could just be beside yourself about it,*" *said Alice trying to be helpful.*

"*Nobody likes a smartass,*" *replied the chess piece, stony faced.*

Matplotlib, sciPy, numPy, classes, **unittest**

Molecular structure, covalent bond rotation, linear algebra, Protein Data Bank (PDB), protein structure, electrostatics, semi-empirical energy calculations, molecular mechanics/dynamics, erythropoietin, atomic charge, Avogadro constant, Coulomb, vectors

© Alexander Lancaster and Gordon Webster 2019

A. Lancaster and G. Webster, *Python for the Life Sciences*, https://doi.org/10.1007/978-1-4842-4523-1_11

One of the great ironies of modern biology is that it has become more and more a study of the "dead stuff" from which biological systems are built. This chapter is all about that "dead stuff." It is all about biology at the smallest scales at which living systems are studied from a "biological" perspective.

Biology has always been the study of living systems, but the phenomena of interest to earlier biologists were largely macroscopic and more purely "biological" in the sense that they were the very phenomena that distinguish living organisms from all of the other "dead stuff" of which our universe is composed – adaptation, growth, reproduction, and so on. Our science and technology has now advanced to the point at which the modern biologist can study living organisms at the molecular level, that is, the level at which living systems are essentially governed by the same laws of physics and chemistry as all of the "dead stuff" that isn't normally considered the subject matter of biology.

This seeming contradiction is actually a consistent approach from a purely materialistic perspective, since it treats biological systems as complex and highly organized assemblies of regular matter that are governed by the same universal laws of physics and chemistry. It is an approach that does not require postulating the existence of some special animus or vital principle that animates life and sets organisms apart conceptually from nonliving matter. Under the optic of this approach, life is seen as the emergent property of these universal laws of physics and chemistry in staggeringly complex assemblies of matter – but manifest at much more macroscopic scales – the kind of scales at which the phenomena we would label as "biology" are evident. Life at the molecular level looks more chemical than biological.

All of which is a rather long-winded way of saying that much of what appears in this chapter will probably seem more like pure physics and chemistry to the reader, since it deals with the application of Python to biology at the atomic and molecular level.

Rotating Molecular Bonds

The example that we're going to consider in this chapter illustrates how Python can be used to manipulate and analyze ***three-dimensional molecular structures*** – specifically, we will look at the rotation around a chemical bond of an amino acid side chain in a protein. This example will illustrate how to implement basic linear algebra to perform three-dimensional transformations using vectors and matrices, as well as some elementary molecular energy calculations using molecular mechanics. As with all of the examples in this book, we've tried to keep the example as simple as possible so that the complexity of the example itself does not become an impediment to understanding the Python implementation.

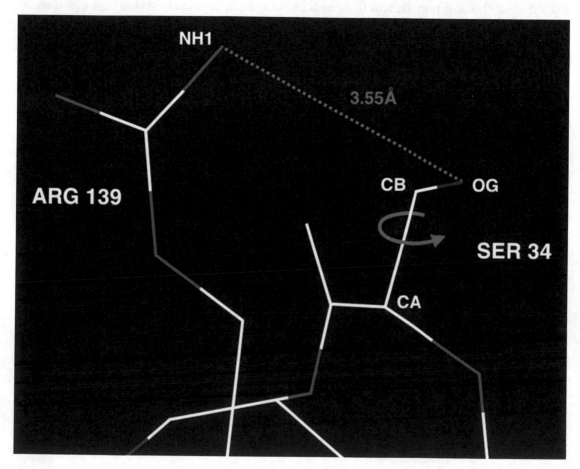

Figure 11-1. *Three-dimensional structure of the human erythropoietin protein*

So without any further ado, here is the example we are going to consider. The diagram in Figure 11-1 shows some of the amino acids adjacent to serine 34 in the three-dimensional structure of the **human erythropoietin** protein (Protein Data Bank accession ID 1EER[1]) that was solved by X-ray crystallography. In the diagram, we have removed all of the hydrogen atoms for additional clarity. The amino acid serine has one of the simplest side chains that can exist in different rotameric forms (conformational variants that differ only in the rotation angles of their freely rotatable bonds). In the case of serine, as shown by the rotational arrow in the diagram, rotation of the side chain's terminal oxygen (OG) is possible around the carbon-carbon single bond between the serine's backbone alpha carbon (CA) and its side chain beta carbon (CB). As can also be seen from the diagram, the serine oxygen is a little over 3 Å away from a nitrogen (NH1) on the side chain of arginine 139 which, despite its distance in the polypeptide sequence from serine 34, ends up being adjacent to it as a result of the protein's three-dimensional fold.

Both the serine oxygen and the arginine nitrogen will possess a net negative charge when the protein is in an environment at roughly neutral pH, meaning that there will be a repulsive electrostatic force between these two atoms. There are, of course, a whole slew of other forces at work in the protein environment of these two atoms that will determine the conformations that these side chains will adopt with respect to one another – and while we will *not* be implementing algorithms to calculate all of these forces, it wouldn't hurt to take a quick look at the general form of the semi-empirical force field function that is generally used for molecular energy calculations.

$$u\left(r^{N}\right) = \sum_{\text{bonds}} k_i \left(l_i - l_{i,0}\right)^2 + \sum_{\text{angles}} k_i \left(\theta_i - \theta_{i,0}\right)^2$$

$$+ \sum_{\text{torsions}} \frac{V_n}{2}(1 + \cos(n\omega - \gamma))$$

$$+ \sum_{i=1}^{N} \sum_{j=i+1}^{N} \left(4\varepsilon_{ij} \left[\left(\frac{\sigma_{ij}}{r_{ij}}\right)^{12} - \left(\frac{\sigma_{ij}}{r_{ij}}\right)^{6} \right] + \frac{q_i q_j}{r_{ij}} \right)$$

Figure 11-2. *Semi-empirical force field function*

Barring our ability to solve the Schrödinger equation for anything more complex than a diatomic molecule, chemists and biologists use the kind of semi-empirical force field function shown in Figure 11-2 to model the behavior of molecules. This function is an essentially mechanical model of the covalent and non-bonded forces within and between the molecules in the system under consideration. We can consider the terms in the function as belonging to three groups:

1. The ***bonds*** and ***angles*** terms in the *first line* treat bond length and angle vibration, respectively, as spring-like forces that act to restore equilibrium bond lengths and angles.

2. The *second line* (**torsions**) is a term that describes torsion angle energy for rotations around a bond. This term depends upon the geometry of the rotated group, for example, a methyl group has a threefold symmetry about the axis of rotation, so the cosine term will include an $n = 3$ value to reflect the symmetrical, threefold arrangement of energy maxima and minima around the rotated bond.

3. The *last line* represents what are referred to as the *non-bonded* or *non-covalent* energy terms which include van der Waals forces, dipole moments, and the previously mentioned electrostatic force.

(The three terms that make up the first and second lines are collectively referred to as *bonded* or *covalent* energy terms, since they all apply to ensembles of atoms that include one or more covalent bonds between them.)

Molecular Mechanics or Dynamics?

Like all the chapters in this book, the aim here is not to provide a tutorial on molecular modeling but rather to demonstrate with simple examples how one might go about implementing this approach in Python. That said however, we will pause to consider a couple more points before throwing ourselves into the examples.

The force field function shown here can be used in two distinct ways. For molecular mechanics, it can be used to calculate the molecular energy components and their force vectors for the system under consideration. These can then be summed and an energy minimization landscape calculated for each atom in the system. Each atom is then fractionally adjusted in the direction of the strongest local energy minima and we rinse and repeat. This process of energy minimization can of course converge once all of the atoms have reached their accessible, local energy minima, which may or may not (most likely) correspond to any kind of global minimum for the system as a whole.

A second, more powerful but computationally more expensive approach is molecular dynamics simulation, in which each atom in the system is assigned a velocity and direction, based upon a Boltzmann distribution of energies corresponding to the temperature of the system being simulated. In this scenario, the atomic energies and their vectors are calculated as before, but this time, they are applied in each case to an atom moving according to its preassigned velocity by solving Newton's laws of motion.

A new velocity is computed, and the atom's new position based upon its motion with that velocity over a suitable timestep is calculated.

The extremely short femtosecond (*femto* = 10^{-18}) vibrational timescales for the bond and angle terms in the force field function essentially determine the length of a suitable timestep for molecular dynamics simulations, which must therefore be of the order of a femtosecond. **In other words, these energies and velocities must be recomputed over every atom in the system being studied, for each femtosecond timestep.** Even a million such cycles of computation only corresponds to a molecular dynamics simulation of one picosecond (*pico* = 10^{-12}) of the system's dynamic behavior.

Do It Yourself to Appreciate the Need for Efficiency

It's not difficult therefore to see why the efficiency of your code can be a big deal here. We'll have more to say on this in a moment.

One further issue that impacts the performance of your simulation code is the number of non-bonded interactions that must be considered. These are typically orders of magnitude *larger* than the number of covalent terms since they must be computed over a much larger range. It is typical, for example, to consider the electrostatic interactions of all other atoms within a 10 Å sphere of a given atom. In a large protein, or any molecular system in which an aqueous environment is being simulated by placing the ensemble within a volume of water molecules, the number of these non-bonded interactions that must be computed can be vast. Again, the performance of your code can make a huge difference here.

So why are we dwelling so heavily on this issue of code performance?

Because the example we are going to give you in this chapter is purely for the purposes of demonstrating how these kinds of three-dimensional energy calculations can be implemented in Python – but in real life, you would use one of the highly optimized and speedy math libraries that have been written in C and compiled for use with Python. These are the libraries like SciPy[2] and NumPy[3] that we have already mentioned in this book – libraries that can efficiently do all of the linear algebra and energy calculations that you need to implement molecular modeling in Python – there

---

[2]www.scipy.org/

[3]www.numpy.org/

are even specific, custom-made Python molecular modeling libraries[4] that you can use as well (most of which actually use SciPy and NumPy).

We could have just told you about these libraries and shown you to plug them into your (higher level) Python code to implement your molecular modeling approach, but then you would never have seen how to implement three-dimensional vectors and rotation matrices, as well as the actual energy calculations themselves. You would not have seen how to use object-oriented programming to create these kinds of mathematical libraries in a clear and consistent way that makes your code easy to write, use, and maintain. Furthermore, in our experience, there always comes a day when that awesome favorite library you love to use just does not have the critical piece that you need for your project and, horror of horrors, you might have to code it yourself!

We are **fully aware** that the algorithms in this chapter could be more easily and efficiently implemented in NumPy and SciPy. But our aim here is to teach you how to code in Python, not how to use Python's numerical and scientific libraries. At the end of this chapter you will find a further reading and resources section that will point you to such libraries and all of the documentation.

Entering the 3D Math Matrix

As a very simple demonstration of some low-level Python code for doing the kind of three-dimensional math that is needed for molecular modeling, we will implement an algorithm for performing a rotation around a covalent bond, for calculating the distances between two atoms, and for calculating the electrostatic energy between those two atoms. We will also use the object-oriented programming approach that we introduced in earlier chapters to implement a simple math library for handling three-dimensional vectors and rotation matrices.

Let's first look at rotation around a bond. A generally useful form for a matrix, R, that defines a rotation about an arbitrary three-dimensional axis is shown in Figure 11-3.

$$R = \begin{bmatrix} \cos\theta + u_x^2(1-\cos\theta) & u_x u_y(1-\cos\theta) - u_z\sin\theta & u_x u_z(1-\cos\theta) + u_y\sin\theta \\ u_y u_x(1-\cos\theta) + u_z\sin\theta & \cos\theta + u_y^2(1-\cos\theta) & u_y u_z(1-\cos\theta) - u_x\sin\theta \\ u_z u_x(1-\cos\theta) - u_y\sin\theta & u_z u_y(1-\cos\theta) + u_x\sin\theta & \cos\theta + u_z^2(1-\cos\theta) \end{bmatrix}$$

Figure 11-3. *Matrix that defines a rotation around a three-dimensional axis*

---

[4]`http://dirac.cnrs-orleans.fr/MMTK/`

This is a normalized rotation matrix for a rotation of θ (radians) about the unit vector. If you're interested in the derivation of this matrix, you will find more information in the source materials listed at the end of the chapter. The rotation axis in our example corresponds to the bond that we are going to rotate about. The vector for this axis is therefore the difference vector between the positions of the atoms at each end of the bond. If you look at the preceding structural diagram, you can see that we will be rotating the serine oxygen atom around the serine CA to CB bond, so the rotation axis itself will therefore be defined by the vector between the serine CA and CB atoms.

So let's deal with the bond rotation component first.

Let's use the object-oriented programming (OOP) approach that we learned earlier in the book to define objects to represent three-dimensional vectors and matrices, along with corresponding object methods that implement the linear algebra we will need to manipulate them. In keeping with our philosophy in this book, to keep the examples simple enough that their complexity doesn't become an impediment to understanding the Python implementation, we will assume that this library will only handle vectors and matrices in three dimensions and we won't generalize it to spaces of higher or lower dimension.

In Listing 11-1 is the class definition for 3D matrices.

Listing 11-1. Class definition of a three-dimensional matrix

```python
class Matrix3D:
    def __init__(self,a,b,c,d,e,f,g,h,i):
        self.a = a
        self.b = b
        self.c = c
        self.d = d
        self.e = e
        self.f = f
        self.g = g
        self.h = h
        self.i = i

    def transform3DVector(self,vector):
        tx = self.a * vector.x + self.b * vector.y + self.c * vector.z
        ty = self.d * vector.x + self.e * vector.y + self.f * vector.z
        tz = self.g * vector.x + self.h * vector.y + self.i * vector.z
        return Vector3D(tx,ty,tz)
```

Pretty obvious right? We are representing the matrix as a 3 x 3 array of values that can be applied to a column vector (x,y,z) to yield a transformed vector, as shown in Figure 11-4.

```
| a, b, c |    | x |    |a.x + b.y + c.z |
| d, e, f | .  | y | =  |d.x + e.y + f.z |
| g, h, i |    | z |    |g.x + h.y + i.z |
```

Figure 11-4. *Vector transformation equation*

You will notice that the transform3DVector method returns an instance of the Vector3D class that we have yet to define, so in Listing 11-2, we add the code for that class (running this code requires having previously executed the code in Listing 11-1).

Listing 11-2. Vector3D class definition

```python
import math

class Vector3D:
    def __init__(self,x,y,z):
        self.x = x
        self.y = y
        self.z = z

    def magnitude(self):
        return math.sqrt(self.x * self.x + self.y * self.y + self.z * self.z)

    def unitVector(self):
        m = self.magnitude()
        xu = self.x / m
        yu = self.y / m
        zu = self.z / m
        return Vector3D(xu,yu,zu)

    def rotationMatrix(self,degrees):
        radians = math.radians(degrees)
        u = self.unitVector()
        sa = math.sin(radians)
```

```
ca = math.cos(radians)
a = ca + u.x * u.x * (1 - ca)
b = u.x * u.y * (1 - ca) - u.z * sa
c = u.x * u.z * (1 - ca) + u.y * sa
d = u.y * u.x * (1 - ca) + u.z * sa
e = ca + u.y * u.y * (1 - ca)
f = u.y * u.z * (1 - ca) - u.x * sa
g = u.z * u.x * (1 - ca) - u.y * sa
h = u.z * u.y * (1 - ca) + u.x * sa
i = ca + u.z * u.z * (1 - ca)
return Matrix3D(a,b,c,d,e,f,g,h,i)
```

Since we are going to be using some of the methods from the Python math[5] module (e.g., to convert from degrees to radians in the rotationMatrix method), we obviously need to import this module. The definition of the vector itself in the __init__ method is pretty self-explanatory. We have also included in the Vector3D class a method magnitude for calculating the vector's magnitude, since we need this for calculating the unit vector which is done (surprise, surprise) by the unitVector method. Finally, the rotationMatrix method calculates a matrix for a rotation of degrees degrees around the current vector. We could have implemented this function to accept the rotation angle directly in radians, but since it is conceptually simpler to handle small, incremental rotations in degrees (rather than in fractions of a radian), we made the decision to accept the rotation angle in degrees and then convert to radians inside the method itself. You will notice that this method does not perform any transformations. It simply generates the necessary rotation matrix that can subsequently be applied to a vector using the transform3DVector method in the Vector3D class, which takes this rotation matrix as an input.

A Python Representation of our Molecular System

Before we can test our rotation-around-a-bond code, we need some actual atoms, so let's encode in Python our example molecular system – the small segment of the human erythropoietin protein structure that is illustrated in the structural diagram at the beginning of this chapter. We'll again use an OOP approach and create a very simple

---

[5]https://docs.python.org/2/library/math.html

Atom class with a couple of the basic methods that we will need for the purposes of this chapter in Listing 11-3.

Listing 11-3. Class definition for an atom

```
class Atom:

    def __init__(self,name,x,y,z,q):
        self.name = name
        self.x = x
        self.y = y
        self.z = z
        self.q = q

    def distance(self,other):
        xd = self.x - other.x
        yd = self.y - other.y
        zd = self.z - other.z
        return math.sqrt(xd * xd + yd * yd + zd * zd)

    def electrostatic(self,other):
        r = self.distance(other) * 1.0e-10
        q1 = self.q * 1.6e-19
        q2 = other.q * 1.6e-19
        return 0.000239 * (9.0e9 * 6.02e23 * q1 * q2) / (4.0 * r)
```

So the first thing to notice is that we need four parameters to define an atom in order to be able to run the Python demonstrations in this chapter – three spatial parameters (obviously) x, y, and z and a value for the partial or net atomic charge q.

This electrostatic charge value arises from the asymmetric distribution of electrons in the atom as a result of their participation in the atom's chemical bonds and is expressed in units of elementary charge ($e = 1.602\times10^{-19}$ coulombs, the charge on an electron). We will need q when it comes to do our electrostatic energy calculations later in this chapter.

The second thing to notice is that we have a couple of class methods – a simple (Pythagoras) method distance for determining the distance between the current atom and another atom (provided as an additional argument to the method) and electrostatic, a method for calculating an electrostatic energy arising from the proximity of the current atom to another atom. You will notice that we actually use the `distance` method within the `electrostatic` method, since the `electrostatic` energy term is distance-dependent.

A couple of brief remarks about the `electrostatic` method: you will see that the distance is scaled to Ångstroms (10^{-10} m) since these are the units of scale used for spatial coordinates in a PDB file. We have also scaled the energy term so that it is calculated in units of *kcal per mole*. This is not a strict SI unit (its SI equivalent would be 4.184 *kilojoules* per mole), but *kcal per mole* has historically been widely used for thermodynamic quantities in chemistry.

Let's break down the numbers in the `electrostatic` method.

```
r = self.distance(other) * 1.0e-10
```

(This scales our units of distance to Ångstroms.)

```
q1 = self.q * 1.6e-19
```

(This scales charges relative to e, the charge on a single electron) and in the line

```
return 0.000239 * (9.0e9 * 6.02e23 * q1 * q2) / (4.0 * r)
```

the term `0.000239` scales the energy from kilojoules to kilocalories (kcal); `9.0e9` is the electric force or Coulomb's constant; and `6.02e23` is Avogadro's constant for scaling the calculation to 1 mole. In summary then, the `electrostatic` method will return the energy equivalent to 1 mole of the interacting atoms in units of *kilocalories per mole*.

Now that we have an `Atom` class that can store the spatial and charge parameters that we need and can compute the distances and electrostatic energies between two atoms, let's use it to encode the atoms we will need for our demonstration (after first executing the code in Listing 11-3).

```
serCA = Atom('CA',-44.104,2.133,-16.495,0.07)
serCB = Atom('CB',-45.239,1.307,-17.044,0.05)
serOG = Atom('OG',-44.722,0.368,-18.048,-0.66)
argNH1 = Atom('NH1',-45.692,1.823,-20.906,-0.8)
```

The atom positions we have used here are taken directly from the previously mentioned Protein Data Bank (PDB) file for human erythropoietin, and the net atomic charges were obtained from the online repositories of force field parameters created by the research groups who write and maintain the popular molecular modeling packages. You can find a list of these web sites at the end of the chapter. Strictly speaking, it was hardly necessary to create an `Atom` class for the very simple examples in this chapter, but in a real molecular modeling application, each atom would likely have a host of different properties that would need to be stored and manipulated, far beyond the four parameters shown here. There would also almost certainly be far (far) more than four atoms in the typical molecular ensemble that you would be interested in modeling, so an OOP approach would probably be the easiest way for keeping track of everything in a Python implementation.

Visualizing our 3D Math by Using Matplotlib

Armed with the atoms we need to run our demonstration, we can now test our new three-dimensional math routines by applying them to the rotation of a point around an axis in increments of 30 degrees and plotting the result using the matplotlib library which we first encountered in Chapter 10. We'll do a very simple two-dimensional plot of the rotated atom position x and y values, which is equivalent to viewing the rotated atoms along the z axis. We can also use the simple trick of shading the atoms by a given property, in this case, their position on the z axis. What we should see then is the circle of atoms in projection (since we're not viewing them directly along the axis of rotation) shaded according to their z axis position.

As an additional test, we will calculate the distance from each rotated serine OG atom to the serine CB atom about which it was rotated. If our rotation matrix is correct, **the distance from each rotated OG atom to the CB atom should be invariant under this transformation**, give or take any tiny rounding errors that arise from the math. These are two very simple tests that we can easily do to satisfy ourselves that our bond rotation code works as it should. When we first wrote this code, we actually saved the rotated atoms into a Protein Data Bank (PDB) file that could be read into the Swiss PDB Viewer molecular graphics program that we used to make the structural diagram that appears near the beginning of this chapter (it is beyond the scope of this book to provide a tutorial on how to use any particular molecular graphics software, but you can find details of how to download this free molecular graphics program and its documentation at the end of this chapter). That way, we were able to view the rotated atoms dynamically in three dimensions to ensure that their positions were correct.

OK, now we're ready to start plotting! In Listing 11-4 is the Python code for our simple test (code for the Vector3D class in Listing 11-2 should be executed first).

Listing 11-4. Visualizing three-dimensional mathematics

```python
import math
import matplotlib.pyplot as plt

serCA = Atom('CA',-44.104,2.133,-16.495,0.07)
serCB = Atom('CB',-45.239,1.307,-17.044,0.05)
serOG = Atom('OG',-44.722,0.368,-18.048,-0.66)
argNH1 = Atom('NH1',-45.692,1.823,-20.906,-0.8)

posx = []
posy = []
posz = []
dist = []
rotationAxis = Vector3D(serCA.x - serCB.x,serCA.y - serCB.y,serCA.z -
serCB.z)
positionOG = Vector3D(serOG.x-serCB.x,serOG.y-serCB.y,serOG.z-serCB.z)

for angle in range(0,360,30):
    rotMat = rotationAxis.rotationMatrix(float(angle))
    xyzOG = rotMat.transform3DVector(positionOG)
    px = xyzOG.x+serCB.x
    py = xyzOG.y+serCB.y
    pz = xyzOG.z+serCB.z
    posx.append(px)
    posy.append(py)
    posz.append(pz)
    dist.append(math.sqrt((px-serCB.x)**2 + (py-serCB.y)**2 +
    (pz-serCB.z)**2))

for d in dist:
    print("%.5f" % d, end=' ')
print()
plt.scatter(posx, posy, c=posz, s=100)
plt.gray()
plt.show()
```

This code outputs some numbers followed by a plot, before getting to the description of the output and showing you the plot, we first break down the code. Looking at the code in more detail, you can see that we are including the required `import` statements here, just to remind ourselves which Python modules are needed – even though in reality, we would already have imported these modules when we wrote the code for our classes and methods.

As we first described in Chapter 10, we use the "`import matplotlib.pyplot as plt`" form to access `pyplot` commands. Let's move on to the code body. We start out by declaring four empty lists to store the *x, y,* and *z* coordinates respectively of the rotated atoms' positions and also their distances from the static CB atom around which they are being rotated. If all goes well, these will all be the same. We next define the rotation axis as the vector between the CA and CB atoms (notice that we create an instance of the `Vector3D` class, so that we can then use its `rotationMatrix` method to compute the rotation matrix that we need).

Next, we need the three-dimensional vector that we're going to transform, in this case, the vector corresponding to the CB-OG bond. Now that we've got our rotation axis and the vector to be rotated, we set up a `for` loop to iterate from 0 to 360 degrees of rotation in 30-degree increments, and for each rotation, we calculate the axial rotation matrix `rotmat` for the corresponding rotation around the CA-CB bond vector.

The distance invariance test toward the end of the block

```
for d in dist:
    print("%.5f" % d, end=' ')
print()
```

outputs the following:

**1.46868 1.46868 1.46868 1.46868 1.46868 1.46868 1.46868 1.46868 1.46868
1.46868 1.46868 1.46868**

Looks good. All of the OG atoms whose positions have been transformed using our rotation matrix derived from the CA-CB axis are (to five decimal places) the same distance as the original OG atom from the static CB atom around which they were rotated. One thing worthy of note before we move on: the rotation matrix we calculate from the axis vector for the CA-CB bond does not take into account the actual position of the rotation axis in the three-dimensional space. It is in effect a rotation around our bond axis displaced such that it passes through the origin. This is why we must add the coordinates of the CB atom around which the OG atom was rotated back to the computed coordinates of the rotated OG atoms.

This last part of the code in Listing 11-4

```
plt.scatter(posx, posy, c=posz, s=100)
plt.gray()
plt.show()
```

does a quick visual test to see if the rotated atoms are distributed in a circle as we expect them to be. The plot is shown in Figure 11-5.

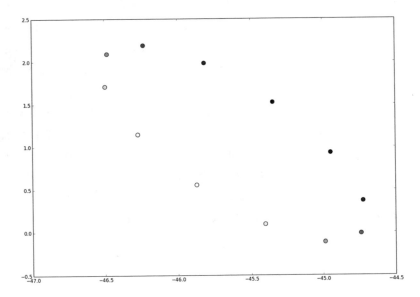

Figure 11-5. *Position of rotated atoms*

As we said before, this is a very crude visual test, but along with the distance invariance test, it gives us confidence that our algorithm for performing rotations around a bond is working correctly. The c=posz term in our plot setup tells matplotlib to color each point (using shades of gray) by its position on the z axis – allowing us to visualize in a very rudimentary way a third dimension in our two-dimensional plot.

Testing, Testing, One-Two-Three...

Before we move on and finish up the chapter by computing the changes in electrostatic energy that arise when we rotate the OG atom around the CA-CB bond, let's just take a few moments to talk about testing code and why it's pretty much always a good idea to do this incrementally.

The advice we're about to give you might sound somewhat obvious, but you would be amazed how many programmers forget it or fail to heed it in the first place. Imagine that after writing our code, we had just jumped forward and tested the effect of rotating the serine OG atom on the electrostatic component of its interaction energy with the NH1 atom of the adjacent arginine. If the computed energies came out all screwy and nonsensical, where would we start looking in the code to isolate the problem? If the positions of the rotated atoms are wrong, the computed electrostatic energies will make no sense, but this would also be true if the rotation algorithm was working correctly but there was an error in the electrostatic energy calculation. This might seem somewhat trivial for a small, toy problem like the one presented here, but once your code starts to get more complex and has many moving parts, tracking down these bugs can be like trying to find the proverbial needle in the haystack.

In the interests of full disclosure, when we wrote the code presented in this chapter, we wrote detailed tests for every class and method as we went along, in order to avoid this problem and they appear in the associated file. In the software world, this is known as unit testing, and there is even a special Python module called (not surprisingly) `unittest` that contains all the tools that you need for creating such tests. Although a detailed discussion of Python unit testing is beyond our book's scope, we would strongly urge you to consider learning and using `unittest` for any Python project that requires more than just a few lines of code. Check out the unittest section[6] of the documentation for the standard Python library.

---

[6]`https://docs.python.org/2/library/unittest.html`

Testing is a critical part of software development, that is all too often short-changed. We used the Python unittest framework to test the code in this book, but we didn't include it in the book because you really only develop a true appreciation for the importance of testing through actual experience, writing code.

After a few "needle in the haystack" experiences of debugging your code, you start to see the value of testing incrementally and testing often.

Stuff Gordon Says ...

Calculating an Electrostatic Interaction

So where were we? Oh yes, we are now ready to test our electrostatic energy calculation.

What we're going to do is to rotate the serine OG atom around the CA-CB bond as previously, but this time, for each incremental rotation position, we're going to compute the distance and the electrostatic energy and store them in lists, along with the rotation angle itself, so that we can graph these quantities using matplotlib. In Listing 11-5, we won't repeat the import statements in the code here, since we're assuming at this point that you already have executed the previous code preceding this segment (from Listings 11-1, 11-2, and 11-3).

Listing 11-5. Calculating an electrostatic interaction

```
angleData = []
distData = []
eData = []
incRot = 10
for angle in range(0,360,incRot):
    rotMat = rotationAxis.rotationMatrix(float(angle))
    xyzOG = rotMat.transform3DVector(positionOG)
    rotOG = Atom('OG',xyzOG.x+serCB.x,xyzOG.y+serCB.y,xyzOG.
    z+serCB.z,-0.66)
    dist = rotOG.distance(argNH1)
```

```
    elec = rotOG.electrostatic(argNH1)
    angleData.append(angle)
    distData.append(dist)
    eData.append(elec)
    print(angle,dist,elec)

plt.title('Distance/Electrostatic Energy vs. Bond Rotation')
plt.plot(angleData,eData,"red",angleData,distData,'blue')
plt.axis([0,360,0,20])
plt.xlabel('Rotation Angle (Degrees)')
plt.ylabel('Distance (A)                              E (kCal/mol)')
plt.show()
```

Having already dissected the code for the bond rotation and the energy calculation, most of this new code should be pretty self-explanatory. We are going to rotate the serine OG atom around the serine CA-CB bond in increments of 10 degrees and store both the computed distance to the adjacent arginine NH1 atom and the electrostatic energy component.

You will notice that we are also plotting both sets of data on the same axes with the matplotlib code – the x axis of our plot will be the rotation angle in degrees, the y axis will be used to plot both the OG-NH1 distance (in blue) and the electrostatic energy component (*kcal/mol* in red), since the magnitudes of both quantities are conveniently similar. You can see the resulting matplotlib plot in Figure 11-6.

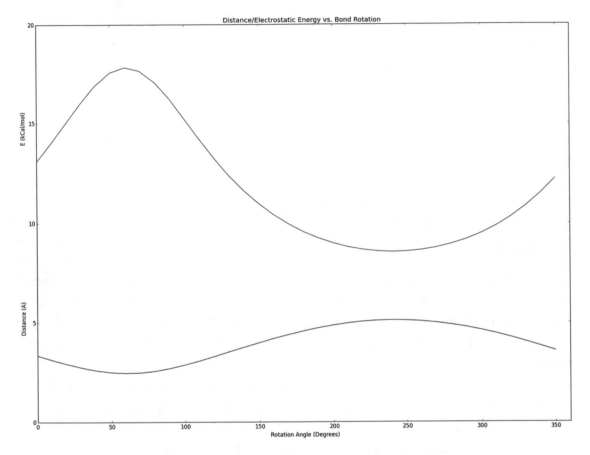

Figure 11-6. *Plot of distance and electrostatic energy vs. bond rotation*

We can see from Figure 11-6 that the electrostatic energy component varies from about 13 to 18 kcal/mol as the interatomic distance between the serine OG and the arginine NH1 varies over a range of about 2 Å as the bond rotates. We can also see that the variation in the electrostatic energy component with distance is greater per unit distance at smaller distances. In a real-world molecular modeling application, we would of course be calculating and summing all of the energy terms in the semi-empirical force field function and doing so over all of the atoms in the molecular ensemble we are considering. For the purposes of simplicity and clarity in this example, we are calculating only a single energy term between two atoms.

Again, just to be clear, there are excellent, efficient, and highly optimized Python libraries both for the kind of linear algebra featured in this chapter and for molecular modeling and simulation. You will find pointers to these resources in the resources and further reading section at the end of the chapter.

In the next chapter, we're going to move away from pure biophysics and look at the biochemical kinetics of gene promoters, and this time we'll use the NumPy library to assist with the visualization.

References and Further Exploration

References

- Arthur Lesk, *Introduction to Protein Science*[7] (Oxford University Press, 2016). Newer edition of Lesk's *Introduction to Protein Architecture* (Oxford, 2001) which featured great three-dimensional visualizations. This new and expanded edition also focuses on bioinformatics and genomics approaches.

- Andrew Leach, *Molecular Modelling: Principles and Applications*[8] (Pearson, 2001) (2nd Edition)

- Tamar Schlick, *Molecular Modeling and Simulation: An Interdisciplinary Guide*[9] (Springer, 2010) (2nd Edition)

- Jenny Gu and Philip E. Bourne (editors), *Structural Bioinformatics*[10] (Wiley-Blackwell, 2009) (2nd Edition)

- The aforementioned awesome NumPy and SciPy libraries, for virtually every kind of quantitative scientific computation you could ever imagine doing.

Molecular modeling software

- The Python Molecular Modeling Toolkit,[11] a complete Python framework for simulating molecules and molecular ensembles.

---

[7] https://global.oup.com/ukhe/product/introduction-to-protein-science-9780198716846
[8] www.pearsonhighered.com/program/Leach-Molecular-Modelling-Principles-and-Applications-2nd-Edition/PGM251961.html
[9] www.springer.com/us/book/9781441963505
[10] www.wiley.com/WileyCDA/WileyTitle/productCd-0470181052.html
[11] https://pypi.python.org/pypi/MMTK

- The Swiss PDB Viewer,[12] a free molecular modeling and visualization package available for download as convenient, precompiled, and ready-to-run binaries for Mac, Linux, and Windows.

- The excellent, open source PyMOL[13] program that extends and is extensible by the Python language. PyMOL was written by Warren DeLano, a gifted scientist and programmer who was an energetic and effective advocate for the increased adoption of open source practices in the life sciences, but who very sadly passed away unexpectedly and before his time.

Molecular force field parameters

These are listed primarily as online repositories of force field parameters for molecular simulation, but in each case, these platforms may also include suites of software tools for molecular simulation and analysis, along with more specialized libraries of force field parameters for different applications (e.g., for simulating glycans or complex lipids):

- The CHARMM[14] platform

- The AMBER[15] platform

- The NAMD[16] platform

- The GROMACS[17] platform

Online structural databases and structure analysis tools

- RCSB Protein Data Bank[18]

- SCOPe (Structural Classification of Proteins)[19]

---

[12]http://spdbv.vital-it.ch/

[13]www.pymol.org/

[14]www.charmm.org

[15]http://ambermd.org/

[16]www.ks.uiuc.edu/Research/namd/

[17]www.gromacs.org/

[18]www.rcsb.org/pdb/home/home.do

[19]http://scop.berkeley.edu/

CHAPTER 12

Turning Genes On and Off

Visualizing Biochemical Kinetics using Matplotlib

"Well," said Alice tightening the saucepan on the twin's head and stepping back, "that just about does it. Now that you're all ready, do you think you might allow me to pass along the path this time?"

"Only if my other brother says so," said the twin in a muffled voice that sounded like he was inside a vast echo chamber. "What my other brother said," boomed the second twin, sounding like he was in an underwater cavern.

"Oh dear," said Alice, rolling her eyes, "not another one of these confounding logical impasses?"

Tired of these silly antics, Alice walked up and pushed them both over. As they toppled, the twins both exclaimed: "Well, that was bound to happen sooner or later." Alice just stepped over them gingerly and was on her way.

---

  numpy *library, arrays,* `numpy.arange()`, `matplot loglog()`, `annotation()`, `legend()`

Gene transcription, kinetics, cooperative binding, transcription factors, promoter, operator, repressor, Lac operon

---

A. Lancaster and G. Webster, *Python for the Life Sciences*, https://doi.org/10.1007/978-1-4842-4523-1_12

In Chapter 11 we explored the world of three-dimensional structural biology using Python. We showed you how to use Python to explore the effect of a rotated bond on the structure of the molecule. We now move up the rungs of complexity away from almost pure physics and chemistry toward things that are more recognizably *biological*. What happens when all those molecules get together in large or small numbers is the subject of biochemical kinetics. But what's even more interesting is when molecules get together to perform some biological function in the cell. In this chapter we'll show you how to use some more advanced Python matplotlib functions to help you visualize the relationship between the *concentration* of a transcription factor protein and its primary biological function in the cell: the initiation of transcription from DNA to messenger RNA, that is, *turning the gene **on** or **off***.

We start with one of the most basic forms of transcriptional regulation: a **repressor regulatory motif**. Repressor-type motifs consist of DNA **binding sites** present in the promoter region downstream of a gene, such that when that transcription factor (most often referred to as a TF) is bound to that site, it blocks access to the RNA polymerase that to turn the gene on. The blocking of those RNA polymerases acts to *repress* gene expression or *turn a gene off*. Like much in biology, the reality is more complicated than this highly simplified picture, but it roughly describes what happens in bacteria like *E. coli*.

Simple Transcriptional Repression: Lac Operon

Let's take a look at the most simplest form of repression, where a ***single binding site*** (sometimes called an operator) overlaps with a core promoter as shown in Figure 12-1 (this is a stylized version of the Lac operon in *E. coli*).

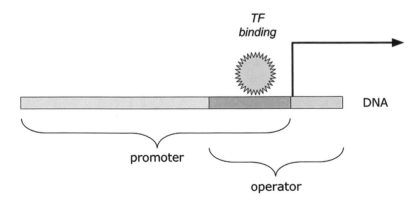

Figure 12-1. *Lac operon*

The portion of the promoter (in **blue**) that overlaps with the operator site (in **pink**) is **orange**. When a transcription factor binds to this site, as described previously, it blocks the RNA polymerases' access to the promoter. Intuitively as the concentration of the *free* TF increases, the *greater* the chance of a TF binding to that site. This, in turn, dials *down* the rate at which the gene is expressed. Let's call the resulting rate of **gene expression**, or **s**.

The exact relationship between the TF concentration and the amount of gene repression can be derived from thermodynamic and statistical mechanical models of occupancy, but luckily for you dear reader, we're not going to go down that rabbit hole here! (For a good treatment, which we draw on in our examples here, check out the Bintu et al. (2005) reference listed at the end of the chapter).

Out of this derivation comes a simple and fairly intuitive equation that describes this relationship in the simple repressor case shown in Figure 12-2.

$$s = (1 + \frac{[TF]}{K_D})^{-1}$$

Figure 12-2. *Rate of gene expression for a simple repressor*

In the preceding equation, [*TF*] is the ***transcription factor concentration*** and K_D is the ***dissociation constant*** of the *bound* TF-operator molecular complex. Let's "kick the tires" on this equation, so to speak, before we start codifying it into Python to ensure it passes the basic "smell test" of biological plausibility.

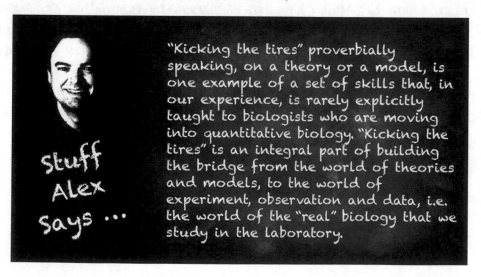

"Kicking the tires" proverbially speaking, on a theory or a model, is one example of a set of skills that, in our experience, is rarely explicitly taught to biologists who are moving into quantitative biology. "Kicking the tires" is an integral part of building the bridge from the world of theories and models, to the world of experiment, observation and data, i.e. the world of the "real" biology that we study in the laboratory.

stuff Alex Says ...

One particularly useful skill is to consider the limiting cases.

Firstly, you can see that if the transcription factor concentration is zero (i.e., $[TF] = 0$), the degree of repression is $s=1$. This should be intuitive: if there are no TFs floating around binding to the operator site and gumming up the works, the RNA polymerase can access the gene. In fact, s can never be larger than one: $s=1$ is the base case of *no repression at all*. It's all downhill from here; however, once you start *increasing* the TF concentration, s will *decrease*: repression has begun!

Secondly, how does K_D affect things? Well, if you remember from your basic enzyme kinetics, a dissociation constant measures the rate at which a chemical complex comes apart. You can see from the equation in Figure 12-2 that as you *increase* K_D, this will have the tendency to *increase s*. Again this makes sense, if the TF is more easily dissociated from the DNA, the greater the access to those RNA polymerases and the more gene expression. Yay!

Introducing NumPy and From ... Import

Enough background, let's take a look at using a combination of two external Python libraries to visualize this relationship. Here we will use the NumPy[1] ("**Num**eric **Py**thon") library as well as matplotlib. NumPy, which we mentioned briefly in the **Prologue** and Chapter 11, is a library of data structures and libraries that is optimized for scientific and mathematical purposes (if you have not yet installed numpy, please review the installation procedures in Chapter 1). Although we have largely avoided external libraries to keep things manageable, NumPy is a special case since it is widely available, well-maintained, and contains many efficient data structures as well as features that are widely used in conjunction with matplotlib. Listing 12-1 shows the code.

Listing 12-1. Using NumPy and matplotlib to visualize simple gene repression

```
from numpy import arange
import matplotlib.pyplot as plt

# transcription activation function for a single repressor
def single_repressor(TF_concentration_1, K_D1):
    F = 1/(1 + TF_concentration_1/K_D1)
    return F
```

---

[1]www.numpy.org/

```
fig1 = plt.figure()
K_D1 = 7.9E-10 # dissociation constants
TF_concentration_1  = arange(0.001, 1000, 0.001) * K_D1
plt.loglog(TF_concentration_1 / K_D1,
            single_repressor(TF_concentration_1, K_D1),
            basex=10, color="blue")
plt.xlabel("[TF]/$K_D$")
plt.ylabel("repression, $F$")
plt.title('Transcriptional repression')
plt.show()
```

The first thing you'll notice is that the format of the import statement is a little different: from NumPy arange. What's up with that? Well, arange is a function contained with the external module numpy so we could have simply imported the module, but then when you use the arange function, you also have to include that module name as well:

```
import numpy
numpy.arange(0.001, 1000, 0.001)
```

This will work fine, but typing numpy.arange can quickly get old, especially if you want to use it over and over in a Python program, and you'll probably find yourself wondering why you couldn't just import the function just *once*. This is exactly what using the from statement in conjunction with import does:

```
from numpy import arange
```

We have imported the string function into our *local* namespace, so we no longer need to qualify each use with the extra numpy. This is an example of the use of namespace shorthands that we first met in Chapter 7. We can now use arange on its own with abandon! Yippee!

We next define the function simple_repression() which implements the repression equation we introduced previously: given a TF_concentration and K_D1 (dissociation constant), it computes the output repression level, F. (Note: we use "1" in the variable name of K_D1 because we will later introduce a dual repressor.) It is useful to define this as a function, rather than simply inline, because we will reuse it later for future computations. We then use matplotlib's `figure()`[2] function to initialize the figure, then we define the dissociation constant `K_D1`.

Next we use `arange(0.001, 1000, 0.001)` to create points for plotting: starting at 0.001 up to 1000 in increments of 0.001. The arange[3] function is modeled on the `range` function in base Python, but allows more fine-grained control and returns a new data type: an `array`.[4] When using a large number of numeric values, NumPy's arrays are more efficient than an equivalent standard Python list. In addition, matplotlib (which we introduced and discussed in Chapter 10) already "understands" NumPy arrays. We also multiply the resulting array by `K_D1` to get the `TF_concentration` – this is because we will be plotting the *ratio* of $[TF]/K_D$ rather than the absolute value of $[TF]$, and we want the plot to show nice round orders of magnitude (10^{-3} to 10^3). Round orders of magnitude are good!

We now are now ready for the plot itself: matplotlib's `loglog()`[5] function creates log-log plots, so that we can easily visualize the degree of repression over a wide range of TF concentration levels. The first argument to the `loglog` function is the *x* axis, the NumPy array we created before, the second is the *y* axis. For this second argument, we use the simple_repression function to transform the array into the output. Note the use of the `simple_repression` function ***inline*** within the `loglog` call, this avoids the need to create a separate variable just for the *y* axis. We also specify that we want the log-log plot to use base 10 (`basex=10`) and the color (`color="blue"`).

The last few lines are mostly self-explanatory: we set the axis and title labels using `xlabel`, `ylabel`, and `title`, followed by `show()`. A nice feature of matplotlib is that any text in labels enclosed within dollar signs is treated as LaTeX math.[6] Matplotlib will convert these expressions to a nicely formatted version, for example, the axis labels `$K_D$` and `$s$` are rendered as K_D and s, respectively (see documentation for more details[7]). (If you don't know what LaTeX is, don't stress, you don't need to worry about it, but it's worth checking out the beautiful typography that LaTeX[8] produces).

---

[2]http://matplotlib.org/api/figure_api.html
[3]http://docs.scipy.org/doc/numpy/reference/generated/numpy.arange.html
[4]http://docs.scipy.org/doc/numpy/reference/arrays.html
[5]http://matplotlib.org/examples/pylab_examples/log_demo.html
[6]http://web.ift.uib.no/Teori/KURS/WRK/TeX/symALL.html
[7]http://matplotlib.org/users/mathtext.html
[8]http://tex.stackexchange.com/questions/1319/
showcase-of-beautiful-typography-done-in-tex-friends

In Figure 12-3 we show our plot!

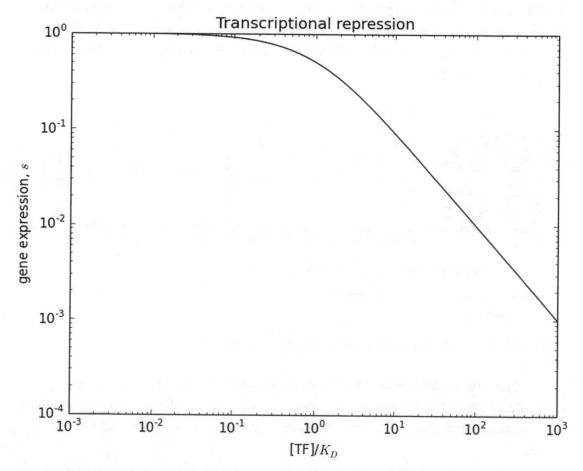

Figure 12-3. *Plot of gene expression repression as a function of transcription factor concentration*

Now we can see how the transcription repression plays out in practice we increase the concentration of TF molecules. You'll notice that the plot ranges over six orders of magnitude and repression doesn't really get going in any meaningful way until the ratio is between 0.1 and 1.

Dual Interacting Repressors: Two is Better than One

But biological systems are nothing if not crafty. In prokaryotes and some eukaryotes (like yeast), a relatively simple tweak of the DNA, say through a mutation (we model evolution in Chapter 19, but let's not get ahead of ourselves), can introduce another binding site in close proximity to the original binding site. The presence of a new repressor motif introduces a new regulatory possibility: an operator in which the transcription factors that bind to the site interact to increase the amount of repression for the same relative number of TFs. More bang for the TF buck. How does this quantitatively compare with the simple repressor case?

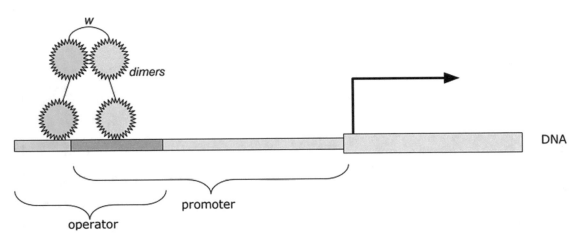

Figure 12-4. *Promoter with dual interacting repressors*

Let's go back to the molecular biology. Shown in Figure 12-4 is our promoter controlling a gene. Again we have an operator (pink) that partially overlaps the promoter (blue) in the orange region. Except in this case there are now *two* adjacent binding motifs.

A common occurrence is that TFs **dimerize** (*two* copies of the same kind of molecule that form a *single* complex) before the TF **binds** to the DNA operator site, depicted in the preceding cartoon. Further, these two pairs of dimers, since they stick out from the DNA even more, are now more likely to interact with *each other*. This interaction between two sets of molecules is known as cooperative binding and *increases* the probability that when both binding sites are occupied by TFs, they *stay* bound to the promoter as compared to the situation when only one of the two sites are occupied. So now we have *two* TFs that can be bound *separately*, as well as *together*. Let's also say that the strength of interaction between the TFs is *w* (as shown in the preceding diagram). This is known as a **dual interacting repressor**. How much repression of transcription do we now get from the same TF concentration?

Again the formula can be derived from first principles along the same lines as for the simple repressor (see Bintu et al. (2005) for details), but to cut to the chase, in Figure 12-5 we show the formula.

$$s = \left(1 + \frac{[TF_1]}{K_{D1}} + \frac{[TF_2]}{K_{D2}} + w\frac{[TF_1][TF_2]}{K_{D1}K_{D2}}\right)^{-1}$$

Figure 12-5. *Rate of gene expression for two interacting repressors*

Here we have two transcription factors with separate concentrations ($[TF_1]$, $[TF_2]$) and dissociation constants (K_{D1}, K_{D2}). Again even without deriving or explaining the formula in any detail, the structure of the formula should make some intuitive sense. It's almost the same as the previous formula, except that in addition to the ***first*** term, we now have a ***second*** term for the second TF concentration (representing the repression due to that second TF alone), as well as a ***third*** term, which, given the presence of both TF concentrations and the repression *w*, clearly represents the additional repression represented by the *cooperative* interaction *between* the TFs.

So how does this compare to the simple repressor case? Let's start by assuming that both TFs are the same, so are their concentrations $[TF_1] = [TF_2] (= [TF])$. We can then easily encode the formula into Python and plot the repression factor *F* on the same axis as for the simple repressor case. In Listing 12-2 we show the code.

Listing 12-2. Superimposing the two gene expression relationships on single plot

```
from numpy import arange
import matplotlib.pyplot as plt

# transcription activation function for a single repressor
def single_repressor(TF_concentration_1, K_D1):
  F = 1/(1 + TF_concentration_1/K_D1 )
  return F

# transcription activation function for a dual repressor
# where repressors interact with strength w
def dual_repressor(TF_concentration_1, TF_concentration_2, K_D1, K_D2, w):
  F = 1/(1 + TF_concentration_1/K_D1 + TF_concentration_2/K_D2 +
  ((TF_concentration_1/K_D1) * (TF_concentration_2/K_D2))* w)
  return F
```

```python
fig1 = plt.figure()
K_D1 = 7.9E-10      # dissociation constants
K_D2 = 25 * K_D1  # dissociation constants

# single repressor
TF_concentration_1 = arange(0.001, 1000, 0.001) * K_D1
plt.loglog(TF_concentration_1 / K_D1,
           single_repressor(TF_concentration_1, K_D1),
           basex=10, color="blue", label="single")
plt.xlabel("[TF]/$K_D$")
plt.ylabel("repression, $F$")

# dual repressor
w = 200
TF_concentration_2 = arange(0.001, 1000, 0.001) * K_D2
plt.loglog(TF_concentration_2 / K_D2,
           dual_repressor(TF_concentration_2, TF_concentration_2, K_D1,
           K_D2, w),
           basex=10, color="green", label="dual")

plt.title('Transcriptional repression')
plt.legend(loc='lower left')
plt.show()
```

This is almost identical in structure to the previous code and should be fairly self-explanatory at this point. We have created another function dual_repressor() that encodes the preceding formula. We further set the K_D2 to be 25 times the K_D1 dissociation constant (see Bintu et al. (2005b) for details). In the loglog calls, we additionally supply a label argument. This is then used by the legend[9] matplotlib call to create a legend for the colored lines. We also place the legend in the left hand corner (loc='lower left') so it is out of the way. Note also that we only need to create the *x* and *y* axis labels *once*.

OK, so now we're ready to compare repressors in Figure 12-6!

---

[9]http://matplotlib.org/users/legend_guide.html

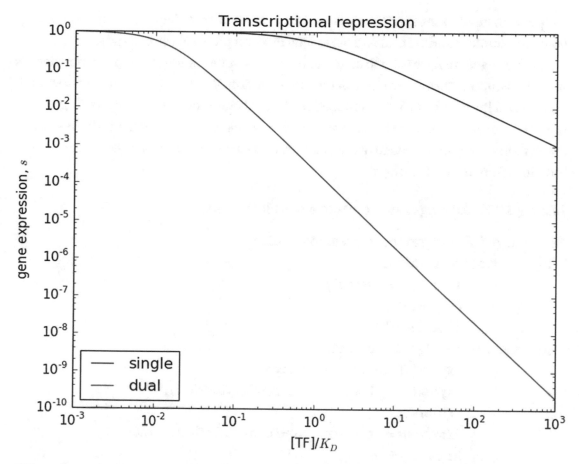

Figure 12-6. *Comparing the effect of single and dual repression on gene expression*

Clearly the dual repressor is more efficient at turning a gene off. For the same concentration of TF, you get a lot more transcriptional repression. This plot really helps the biologist get a feel for the variation in regulation over a wide range of transcription factors.

Same Concentration, more Repression: Annotating Plots

OK, all well and good, but let's say you were presenting this to a skeptical audience. For some folks, log-log plots just aren't as intuitive as they may be for others. Let's say you really wanted to drive home the point that dual repression really makes a difference to people who need to see *specific numbers*. This is where a combination of superimposing text annotations[10] and vertical and horizontal lines on plots comes in handy.

Let's imagine that we want to compare how the *absolute* amount of repression changes when you double the transcription factor concentration. We start by overlaying horizontal and vertical lines at the two different levels of TF concentration, followed by adding text boxes with arrows pointing to the repression levels in each case. In Listing 12-3 we show the Python code (you'll need to define the `single_repressor` and `dual_repressor` functions from the early listings).

Listing 12-3. Adding annotations to a matplotlib plot

```python
def draw_points(TF_ratio, repression, color):
  plt.axhline(repression,
              linestyle='dashed',
              color=color,
              linewidth=2)
  plt.annotate("%.1g" % repression,
               xy = (TF_ratio, repression),
               xytext = (TF_ratio*0.1, repression*0.1),
               color=color,
             arrowprops=dict(facecolor=color, width=2, frac=0.2,
             shrink=0.05))

for TF_ratio in [0.5, 1.0]:
  plt.axvline(x=TF_ratio, linestyle="dashed", color="pink", linewidth=3)
  TF_value = TF_ratio * K_D1   # convert ratio into TF concentration
  repression = single_repressor(TF_value, K_D1)
  draw_points(TF_ratio, repression, "blue")
  TF_value = TF_ratio * K_D2
  repression = dual_repressor(TF_value, TF_value, K_D1, K_D2, w)
  draw_points(TF_ratio, repression, "green")
```

---

[10]http://matplotlib.org/1.5.1/users/annotations_intro.html

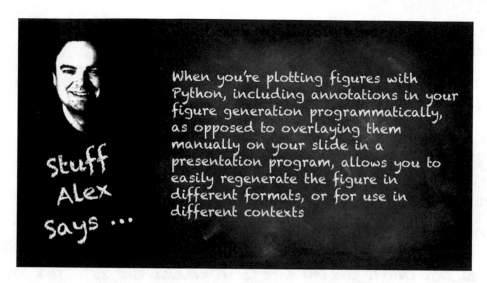

We start with a function `draw_points()`, this function first uses the `axhline()`[11] matplotlib function to draw a dashed horizontal line with the color `color` at the given `repression` level. It then uses the `annotate` function to draw the repression level with an arrow to the exact point on the plot. The xy keyword is the location of the *actual point on the figure*, and xytext is the *location of the text box*. The `arrowprops`[12] keyword creates an arrow from the label to the point also in the color `color`. Note that in xytext we multiply the coordinates supplied to xy by 0.1, this has the effect of offsetting the label slightly from the end of the arrow.

We next add a for loop for the `TF_ratio`: 0.5 and 1.0 (double the concentration). In each loop iteration, we first use `axvline`[13] to draw a vertical line at the specified `TF_ratio`. We then convert the `TF_ratio` to an actual `TF_value` and call `single_repressor` to get the `repression` level which we can then supply to the `draw_points()` function. We then repeat the same procedure for the `dual_repressor()`. Note that we also match the colors of the original curves, ***blue*** for single repressor and ***green*** for the dual repressor.

Now let's put the whole program together and generate the figure. The complete code is in Listing 12-4.

Listing 12-4. Complete code to generate annotated plot of gene expression repression

```python
from numpy import arange
import matplotlib.pyplot as plt

# transcription activation function for a single repressor
def single_repressor(TF_concentration_1, K_D1):
  F = 1/(1 + TF_concentration_1/K_D1 )
  return F

# transcription activation function for a dual repressor
# where repressors interact with strength w
def dual_repressor(TF_concentration_1, TF_concentration_2, K_D1, K_D2, w):
  F = 1/(1 + TF_concentration_1/K_D1 + TF_concentration_2/K_D2 + ((TF_
concentration_1/K_D1) * (TF_concentration_2/K_D2))* w)
      return F

def draw_points(TF_ratio, repression, color):
  plt.axhline(repression,
              linestyle='dashed',
              color=color,
              linewidth=2)
  plt.annotate("%.1g" % repression,
                xy = (TF_ratio, repression),
                xytext = (TF_ratio*0.1, repression*0.1),
                color=color,
                arrowprops=dict(facecolor=color, width=2, frac=0.2,
                shrink=0.05))

fig1 = plt.figure()

# dissociation constants
K_D1 = 7.9E-10
K_D2 = 25 * K_D1
```

```python
# single repressor
TF_concentration_1  = arange(0.001, 1000, 0.001) * K_D1
plt.loglog(TF_concentration_1 / K_D1,
           single_repressor(TF_concentration_1, K_D1),
           basex=10, color="blue", label="single")
plt.xlabel("[TF]/$K_D$")
plt.ylabel("repression, $F$")

# dual repressor
w = 200
TF_concentration_2  = arange(0.001, 1000, 0.001) * K_D2
plt.loglog(TF_concentration_2 / K_D2,
           dual_repressor(TF_concentration_2, TF_concentration_2, K_D1,
K_D2, w),
           basex=10, color="green", label="dual")

for TF_ratio in [0.5, 1.0]:
        plt.axvline(x=TF_ratio, linestyle="dashed", color="pink",
linewidth=3)
        TF_value = TF_ratio * K_D1  # convert ratio into TF concentration
        repression = single_repressor(TF_value, K_D1)
        draw_points(TF_ratio, repression, "blue")
        TF_value = TF_ratio * K_D2
        repression = dual_repressor(TF_value, TF_value, K_D1, K_D2, w)
        draw_points(TF_ratio, repression, "green")

plt.title('Transcriptional repression')
plt.legend(loc='lower left')
plt.show()
```

And in Figure 12-7, we show the plot!

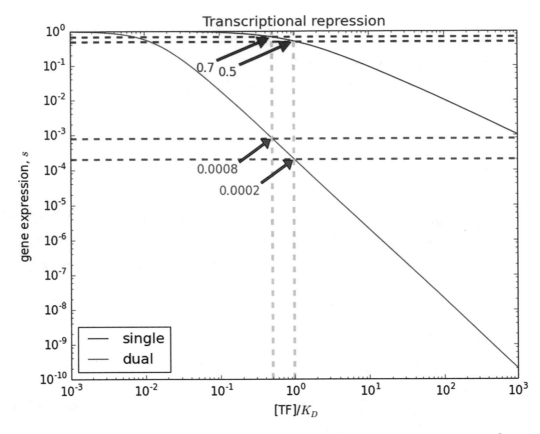

Figure 12-7. *Annotated figure with figure legend showing gene repression for single and dual repressors*

You can clearly see that a single repressor motif represses gene expression only 1.4-fold (=0.7/0.5) as compared with the fourfold reduction for the dual repressor motif (=0.0008/0.0002). It's useful to keep these matplotlib annotation features in your back pocket as they make for highly effective additions to a plot.

So visualizing the kinetics of transcription factor binding is starting to feel more like real biology. Next up in Chapter 13, we go further up the ladder of biological complexity and use Python to mine a dataset consisting of all the transcription factors "wired" up to the genes they control within the cell of a simple unicellular organism: brewer's yeast. Then in Chapter 14, we put it all together to create a simple Python-based **simulation model** to explore the dynamics where the interacting genes are "wired" up to regulate each other via the dual interacting repressor motif introduced in this chapter.

References and Further Exploration

- James A. Goodrich and Jennifer F. Kugel, *Binding and Kinetics of Molecular Biologists*[14] (Cold Spring Harbor Press, 2007)

- Bintu, Buchler, Garcia, Gerland, Hwa, Kondev, and Phillips (2005a). Transcriptional regulation by the numbers: models.[15] *Current Opinion in Genetics & Development*, **15**, 116–124

- Bintu, Buchler, Garcia, Gerland, Hwa, Kondev, Kuhlman, *et al.* (2005b). Transcriptional regulation by the numbers: applications.[16] *Current Opinion in Genetics & Development*, **15**, 125–135

[14]http://kinetics.cshl.edu/
[15]www.ncbi.nlm.nih.gov/pmc/articles/PMC3482385/
[16]www.ncbi.nlm.nih.gov/pmc/articles/PMC3462814/

CHAPTER 13

Taming the Network Hairball

Using Python Sets to Mine Systems Biology Data

The Cheshire Cat was trapped; he tried to move left and then he tried to move right. It was no use. The thick tangled branches of the tree proved unyielding even to such an ethereal and ghostly presence as the Cat.

"Will no one rescue me from this infernal mess?" meowed the Cat.

Alice who was watching the Cat from the ground looked up with some amusement. She was beginning to understand the topsy-turviness of this world where nothing was what it seemed.

"Cat," she shouted, "You should be used to dealing with such tangled knots. After all, you invented the hairball!"

And with that the Cat went "poof" and disappeared.

---

 set(), *set functions* **union**, **intersection**, *list comprehensions*

 Systems biology, gene networks, transcription networks, gene regulation

---

© Alexander Lancaster and Gordon Webster 2019
A. Lancaster and G. Webster, *Python for the Life Sciences*, https://doi.org/10.1007/978-1-4842-4523-1_13

As we've already seen in several previous chapters, not all work in computational biology revolves around analyzing sequences. Sequences, although very important, are in a sense just the ground floor for understanding complex biological systems. They represent a kind of "database" of solutions that evolution has crafted over millennia. What makes biological systems so fascinating to study is seeing how these sequences help construct the networks that underlie the traits that we see in biology. The growing area of biology that studies such networks, particularly within cells, has come to be known as "systems biology."

Systems biology is a huge field and ranges from the experimental study of the interactions of proteins, messenger RNA, DNA, through to the mathematical modeling and simulation of the interaction networks. In this chapter, we'll be rolling up our sleeves and working on some real biological datasets, using skills such as parsing data files, data structures, and regular expressions that we've developed in previous chapters. We've already met a building block of systems biology in Chapter 12.

Python has an excellent set of tried and tested tools that can help you navigate the huge and growing resource of network datasets in systems biology. So for starters, let's imagine that you are interested in tackling just one kind of network: genes and the network of transcription factors that regulate how these genes are turned on or off in **yeast** cells. Yeast are interesting organisms to study for many different reasons: they have short generation times, ideal for experimental evolution; and although they mostly live as single cells, they are also eukaryotes, so many genes are conserved between yeast and humans. But one big advantage that yeast have in the context of systems biology is that there are very comprehensive experimentally validated databases of interactions between their cellular components. The number of interactions between all these components can be huge, with many connecting edges overlapping, which has led many to dub this kind of data the ***network hairball***.

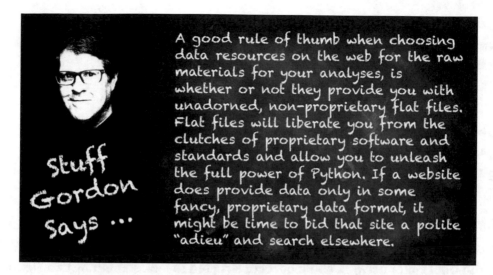

A good rule of thumb when choosing data resources on the web for the raw materials for your analyses, is whether or not they provide you with unadorned, non-proprietary flat files. Flat files will liberate you from the clutches of proprietary software and standards and allow you to unleash the full power of Python. If a website does provide data only in some fancy, proprietary data format, it might be time to bid that site a polite "adieu" and search elsewhere.

There are many different databases we could explore. Let's start by looking at just one: YEASTRACT,[1] which stands for **Yea**st **S**earch for **T**ranscriptional **R**egulators **A**nd **C**onsensus **T**racking. It's a *manually curated* site (meaning that real human beings look at the entries and make periodic corrections), and you can do a lot of interactive visualizations from the site. For example, you can view all the genes that a particular transcription factor regulates. However, at some point you'll want to start off on your own quantitative explorations of the network, beyond what the programmers of the web site could imagine.

The first thing to do is to look around for "flat files." These are plain text files in formats like **CSV** (comma-separated values) or **TSV** (tab-separated values).

A quick look at the YEASTRACT and you'll find the download page

`www.yeastract.com/download.php`

Grab the flat file

`RegulationTwoColumnTable_Documented_2013927.tsv.gz`

and unzip it using an archiving program such as `gunzip`, you will find it contains two columns in the following format:

```
ABF1;ABF1
ABF1;ACS1
ABF1;ADE5,7
```

---

[1] www.yeastract.com/

ABF1;ADH1
ABF1;ALD3
ABF1;AMS1
ABF1;ARN2
ABF1;ARO3
ABF1;ARP5
ABF1;BAP3
ABF1;BNA2
• • •

The *first column* contains a transcription factor, and the *second column* contains the name of the gene that is regulated by that transcription factor. Visually the underlying transcriptional factor network could be reconstructed to look something like Figure 13-1, which shows a single transcription factor regulating multiple genes.

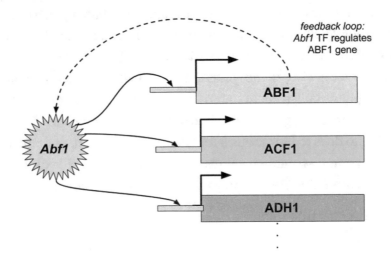

Figure 13-1. *Single transcription factor Abf1 regulating multiple genes*

Setting the Table with Set

A set, as you might recall from distantly remembered introductory maths[2] classes, contains only *unique* members. In the context of the data structures for transcription networks, this means for each transcription factor, we only need to record that particular gene *once*.

---

[2]Alex notes: As an Australian I still maintain that it's "maths," not "math", because we study *mathematics* not *mathematic*.

Let's create an empty set of genes:

```
genes = set()
```

So that was easy! Let's start adding genes to our set:

```
genes.add("ABF1")
genes.add("ACS1")
print(genes)
{'ABF1', 'ACS1'}
```

Great, so we now have a set of genes. Sets, however, really come into their own because they will refuse to add duplicates. This is really handy, because instead of having to check whether a set contains an element (as we would with a list), we can just keep adding genes, and the set will magically ensure that there is only one entry. To continue with the example:

```
genes.add("ABF1")
print(genes)
{'ABF1', 'ACS1'}
```

So note that there is still only one copy of the **ABF1** gene! Pretty cool, eh? This turns out to come into its own when adding large numbers of genes to your dataset, because sometimes (and this will come as shocking fact to biologists), there may be *errors* or *duplicates* in your input data! I know, I know, wonders will never cease.

Now you've automatically guarded against one of the problems that often bedevil budding computational biologists, the presence of missing or duplicate data!

Sets have some other cool features. You can easily check whether an element is contained within the set:

```
'ABF1' in genes
True
'FakeGene' in genes
False
```

Or you can check whether a set is a subset of another (note that you can initialize the set using a list), in this case, note that the set `smaller` containing just the gene **ABF1** is a subset of the original genes set:

```
smaller=set(['ABF1'])
print(smaller)
{'ABF1'}
smaller < genes
True
smaller > genes
False
```

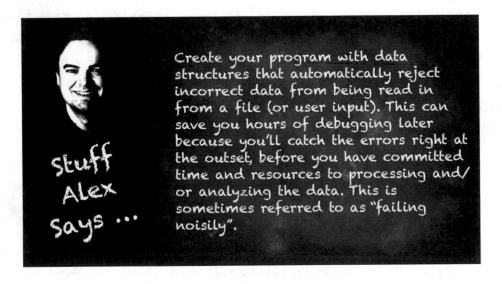

You can also perform all kinds of standard set operations, such as `intersection` (A & B), union (A | B), and many more (for a full list, see the Python language documentation on sets[3]).

You can now begin to see how sets might be very useful indeed when interrogating biological data that consists of discrete objects like transcription factors and genes. For example, given two different transcription factors, which genes are regulated by *both* transcription factors, which genes are only regulated by only one of them? So let's start seeing some `set` action using our YEASTRACT example!

---

[3]https://docs.python.org/2/library/stdtypes.html#set-types-set-frozenset

A Tale of Two Dictionaries: Data Structures for Networks

Let's start creating the data structures for the network. We first start by reading in the file using the with statement approach that we introduced in Chapter 8:

```
with open("RegulationTwoColumnTable_Documented_2013927.tsv") as file:
    lines = file.readlines()
```

We'll start by creating *two* dictionary data structures. The reason for this is that we will often want to look up information from the point of view of the TFs, that is, given a TF, what genes does *it* control? But also the reverse: given a gene, what TFs is it controlled *by*? (Note that we're leaving aside third-party packages for creating networks such as **NetworkX** – see the references section at the end of the chapter for pointers – for the moment we're just focusing on the core Python language.)

The two data structures and the underlying biology are depicted graphically in Figure 13-2.

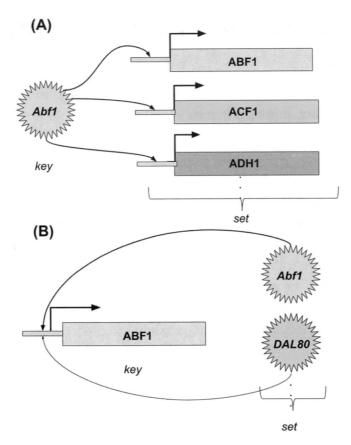

Figure 13-2. *Two data structures: (A) TFs regulating a set of genes, (B) genes being regulated by a set of TFs*

Figure 13-2 is a visual representation of sets – in part (A) of the figure, the key is the TF, in part (B) of the figure, the key is the gene.

A. `alltfs`: A dictionary indexed by TFs, each *key* is a TF, each *value* is a `set` of genes it regulates (**A** shows a single *key*: the TF *Abf1* regulating several genes; note only the first few are shown).

B. `allgenes`: A dictionary indexed by genes, each *key* is a gene, each *value* is a `set` of TFs regulated by that gene (**B** shows a single *key*, the ABF1 *gene,* and all the TFs that are regulating it – again only the first few are shown).

Let's start by initializing the dictionaries and looping through and parsing the lines that we've already retrieved data from

```
alltfs = {}
allgenes = {}
for line in lines:
  items = line.split(';') # split line into elements using ';' as separator
  items = [item.lower() for item in items]    # lowercase each item
  tf = items[0].strip()    # first column  = TF  (element 0)
  gene = items[1].strip() # second column = gene that TF regulates (element 1)
```

Let's pause here and review before creating the data structures themselves. We are doing *quite* a lot in these few short lines, and we will require a couple of short detours into new language features that we haven't yet described.

First, we use split on the string contained within the line variable into a **list** of string items (we specify that split should use the semicolon as the character that separates each variable – this is often called a **delimiter**). (For users of Python 2.7, please note that in Python 3 the split and strip functions are no longer part of the string module, we just use those functions directly on the strings).

List Comprehensions

Second, the next line in the loop introduces another new feature: a **list comprehension**. A list comprehension allows you to take a list and

1. Loop through that list (this is the inner "for item in items")

2. Modify each item in the list by applying the lower() function to lowercase each item

3. Return a *new* list in between the new brackets [   ] (overwriting the old one)

All that in one line! Pretty cool, right? Python is nothing if not concise. List comprehensions are very handy for these kinds of jobs. For more details than you could poke a stick at, see Python tutorial on list comprehensions.[4]

---

[4]https://docs.python.org/2/tutorial/datastructures.html#list-comprehensions

We've now successfully lowercased each element in the input data in one line. We do this so that minor typographical differences in the font case in the input file don't get counted as being different, for example, the TF "**Pma1**" should really be treated the same as the TF "**pma1**" (this is yet another case of our general principle of building in robustness by ensuring that we clean the data *up-front*). This leads us to…

Third, these last two lines extract the tf (the first column in the original file, and therefore the zeroth item in items) and the regulating gene (the second column, and therefore the first item in items, remembering that all lists start at the zero position). Also before we assign tf and gene, however, we first strip the strings of extraneous characters, in particular the dreaded end-of-line characters that have "come along for the ride" in the original line. (This is yet another example of the defensive programming that we mentioned before.)

Finally, we now have the actual information from the file and are in a position to actually *do* something with that data, using our dictionary muscles (see Chapter 2) and the set features we just introduced previously. So here's the next stanza after reading the data file:

```
# genes keyed by TF
if tf in alltfs:
  (alltfs[tf]).add(gene)   # TF already added, we just add the gene
else:
  alltfs[tf] = set()       # otherwise, we create an empty set
  (alltfs[tf]).add(gene)   # then add it
```

Let's briefly unpack this. We first check to see if the tf key exists. If it does, we add the gene to the set of genes that this particular TF regulates by using the add() function. Otherwise we just *create* a new *empty* set, then add the gene as before. One thing that might be puzzling at first is the extra set of brackets around (alltfs[tf]). Although these are not strictly necessary, they remind us that when we add() the gene, **we are adding to the set** at that particular dictionary entry. They also make it easier to keep track of what goes with what if the example becomes more complicated.

The next stanza is basically of the same format as the preceding one, but instead of adding genes to a set, we are adding TFs to a set, with those sets having genes as keys:

```
# TFs keyed by gene
if gene in allgenes:
  (allgenes[gene]).add(tf) # if gene already exists, we just add the TF
```

```
  else:
    allgenes[gene] = set()    # otherwise create empty set
    (allgenes[gene]).add(tf) # then add it
```

Phew! Let's put it together and see what we have in Listing 13-1.

Listing 13-1. Parsing the network data from a file into the two data structures

```python
#!/usr/bin/env python3

with open("RegulationTwoColumnTable_Documented_2013927.tsv") as file:
 lines = file.readlines()

alltfs = {}
allgenes = {}
for line in lines:
  items = line.split()         # split each line into elements
  items = [item.lower() for item in items] # lowercase each item
  tf = items[0]                # first column = TF (element 0)
  gene = items[1]              # second column = gene regulated by TF (element 1)

  # genes keyed by TF
  if tf in alltfs:
    (alltfs[tf]).add(gene)     # TF already added, we just add the gene
  else:
    alltfs[tf] = set()         # otherwise, we create an empty set
    (alltfs[tf]).add(gene)     # then add it

  # TFs keyed by genes
  if gene in allgenes:
    (allgenes[gene]).add(tf) # gene already exists, we just add the TF
  else:
    allgenes[gene] = set()     # otherwise, we create an empty set
    (allgenes[gene]).add(tf)   # then add it

print("total TFs:", len(alltfs))
print("total genes:", len(allgenes))
```

If you run the preceding program, it should read in the file and give you some summary statistics that should look something like this:

total TFs: 183
total genes: 6403

The len() function, who we first met back in Chapter 3, prints out the *length* of the data structure, and what this means varies depending on the *kind* of data structure. In the case of our *dictionaries*, this is the number of *keys*.

Congratulations you've now successfully created the data structures you can use to start asking some actual biological questions!

Who Regulates Whom?

One kind of question that often comes up in analyzing these kinds of interaction network data is: given, say, two different transcription factors, what are the *common* genes that they regulate? Now with a lot of the hard work done for us, this turns out to be ridiculously easy to answer by using the set intersection function (using shortcut "&"):

print("genes regulated by both abf1 & cyc8:", alltfs['abf1'] & alltfs['cyc8'])
genes regulated by both abf1 and cyc8: {'hxt2', 'hxt4'}

This turns out to be a quite small set: just two genes. We can also ask for the full superset, that is, *all* the genes that *both* of them regulate, and by using the **set** functionality, we can be sure – without needing any additional code – that our set will only contain unique elements by using the union (shortcut "|") function:

print("genes regulated by abf1 or cyc8:", alltfs['abf1'] | alltfs['cyc8'])
genes regulated by abf1 or cyc8: {'ycr064c', 'ugx2', 'ydr095c', 'spp2',
'mtq1', ...

We have truncated the output of the preceding set, because it would take up a whole chapter! Note also that **hxt2** and **hxt4** will only occur *once* in the resulting set despite being in both original sets. Excellent.

You now have the tools to start exploring the network data in many ways by using all the rich possibilities enabled via the set function and limited only by your imagination. You can also use the allgenes data structure to ask similar questions, such as which TFs regulate a specific gene. We'll leave those functions for you to discover!

All Together Now: Using Python __main__

We can now put it all together, by putting the file reading and data structure creation into one function get_tf_yeastract and the functions that get the intersection and union into their own separate functions, get_common_genes and get_all_genes (using the def keyword and appropriate indentation as we covered in Chapter 2). This is very handy because it means we can then *reuse* these functions with different variables. We can then make the actual *main* program very short. Here's what the main program looks like (note that we also use sorted, which we first encountered all the way back in Chapter 3, to alphabetically sort the genes and transcription factors in the output):

```python
if __name__ == "__main__":

    # get TF regulation data
    alltfs, allgenes = get_tf_yeastract()

    # remember we lowercased the gene names!
    common_genes = get_common_genes(alltfs, 'abf1', 'cyc8')
    print("genes regulated by both abf1 & cyc8", sorted(common_genes))

    all_genes = get_all_genes(alltfs, 'abf1', 'cyc8')
    print("genes regulated by abf1 or cyc8", sorted(all_genes))
```

This shows off another nifty feature of namespaces; we can put all the functions into one file and then include the *main* program at the bottom in the *same* file without having to move it into separate file. This is very handy when you want to keep all the functions, variables, and test cases in one place. This is magically enabled by the use of

```python
if __name__ == "__main__"
```

By using "__main__" the Python interpreter notices that the file is being executed directly, and only runs them in when the file is executed directly, but not when importing the file (see the Python tutorial on modules and scripts[5] for more gory details).

So finally we have our complete program in Listing 13-2, and notice it's pretty short (even more so if we stripped out some of the comments).

---

[5]https://docs.python.org/2/tutorial/modules.html#executing-modules-as-scripts

Listing 13-2. Complete program for reading and parsing transcription network data

```python
#!/usr/bin/env python

# get the TF regulation data from yeastract
def get_tf_yeastract():

  with open("RegulationTwoColumnTable_Documented_2013927.tsv") as file:
   lines = file.readlines()

  # create a dictionary indexed by transcription factors (TF)
  # each key is a TF, each value is a *list* of genes it regulates
  alltfs = {}

  # create a dictionary of indexed by genes
  # each key is a gene, each value is a *list* of TFs regulated by that gene
  allgenes = {}

  for line in lines:

    items = line.strip(';') # split line into elements using ';' as separator
    # lowercase each item, so that minor differences in casing don't confuse
    items = [item.lower() for item in items]
    tf = items[0].strip()  # first col  = TF   (element 0)
    gene = items[1].strip() # second col = gene that TF regulates (element 1)

    # genes keyed by TF
    if tf in alltfs:
     (alltfs[tf]).add(gene)  # TF already added, we just add the gene
    else:
      alltfs[tf] = set()      # otherwise, we create an empty set
      (alltfs[tf]).add(gene) # then add it

    # TFs keyed by gene
    if gene in allgenes:
      (allgenes[gene]).add(tf) # if gene already exists, we just add the TF
    else:
      allgenes[gene] = set()   # otherwise create empty set
      (allgenes[gene]).add(tf) # then add it
```

```
    print("total TFs:", len(alltfs))
    print("total genes:", len(allgenes))
    return alltfs, allgenes

def get_common_genes(alltfs, tf1, tf2):
  return alltfs[tf1] & alltfs[tf2]

def get_all_genes(alltfs, tf1, tf2):
  return alltfs[tf1] | alltfs[tf2]

if __name__ == "__main__":
  # get TF regulation data
  alltfs, allgenes = get_tf_yeastract()

  # remember we lowercased the gene names!
  common_genes = get_common_genes(alltfs, 'abf1', 'cyc8')
  print("genes regulated by both abf1 and cyc8", sorted(common_genes))

  all_genes = get_all_genes(alltfs, 'abf1', 'cyc8')
  print("all genes regulated by either abf1 OR cyc8", sorted(all_genes))
```

So go forth and plunder yon interaction network data, budding Pythonistas! Even more systems biology awaits in Chapter 14, where we create an actual dynamic simulation model of a network of genes and transcription factors interacting with each other.

References and Further Exploration

- NetworkX[6]: a Python library for network data structures

- Hive Plots[7]: visualization approaches to complex biological networks that go beyond the "hairball"; associated Python package: pyveplot[8]

---

[6]https://networkx.github.io/

[7]www.hiveplot.net/

[8]https://pypi.python.org/pypi/pyveplot/

- Teixeira *et al.* (2014). The YEASTRACT database: an upgraded information system for the analysis of gene and genomic transcription regulation in Saccharomyces cerevisiae.[9] *Nucleic Acids Res*, **42**, D161-D166

- Monteiro *et al.* (2008). YEASTRACT-DISCOVERER: new tools to improve the analysis of transcriptional regulatory associations in Saccharomyces cerevisiae.[10] *Nucleic Acids Res*, **36**, D132–D136

---

[9]www.ncbi.nlm.nih.gov/pmc/articles/PMC3965121/
[10]www.ncbi.nlm.nih.gov/pmc/articles/PMC2238916/

CHAPTER 14

Genetic Feedback Loops

Modeling Gene Networks with the Gillespie Algorithm

"Oh, dear," cried Alice as she rushed along the path. "All these cards keep flying over me at a constant rate, it seems one every second! I can't possibly collect them all."

She looked toward the white rabbit at her feet, who was barely able to stay out Alice's way as she ran, dodging cards left and right.

"Is it really necessary to be sending these messages so frequently?" she exclaimed with exasperation to Rabbit. "After all we only need to get a singal if there's something new to be done!"

"Pish posh," said Rabbit, "you've never had to do any **real** simulation, have you? All my life I've been collecting cards, one every second, it's just the way of the world, dearie."

"Oh Rabbit, you are a most vexing animal," huffed Alice, who was becoming very cross indeed, because she was always in danger of stepping on the furry creature as it dashed hither and yon collecting cards to the left and right.

"I shall pretend I never heard that. I am going to talk to the card master and ask him to only send cards when something important changes." And with that, Alice stomped off angrily.

 `sum()`, `numpy.random` *module*, `exponential()`, `uniform()`

 Gene regulatory networks, systems biology, chemical master equation, dimerization, feedback loops, transcription factors, mRNA, translation, protein degradation

---

A. Lancaster and G. Webster, *Python for the Life Sciences*, https://doi.org/10.1007/978-1-4842-4523-1_14

Biology, in case you hadn't already noticed, can be kind of messy. Physics has its frictionless surfaces, its point charges, and its ideal gases. The real versions of those systems are often not quite so far away from their abstractions, and nice clean simple solvable equations can actually describe the results of experiments reasonably accurately. This is often not the case in biology. There is a standing joke about mathematics in biology that has a cartoon of a scientist standing in front of a slide with the title "consider a spherical cow." The joke, of course, is that although obviously cows are not spherical, but only if we assume that cows actually *are* spherical, can the equations actually be solved!

Modeling cellular networks such as gene regulatory networks or **metabolic networks** can be complicated: the cell can be **noisy** place! With molecules bumping around left, right, and center, or being synthesized or degraded, it can get pretty messy. Sometimes these individual events: the bumps, creations, and destructions all "average out." This is true of, say, a large number of proteins of a particular kind; if the concentration is high enough, we can ignore the individual events and focus on the macro behavior. So when modeling metabolic networks ordinary differential equation are sufficient to model their dynamics. In other cases, for example, transcription factor networks, just a few individual transcription factor molecules binding to a promoter can make the difference between a gene turning on or off. Then the *individual* events start to seem very important indeed: small changes in the number of copies can make a big difference. In this case noise, or more technically, **stochasticity**, matters!

As mentioned in the Prologue, our approach throughout the book is a little different from most: we believe it's useful to build intuition by modeling from the "bottom-up." Later, you can come back and study the mathematics. It's often more interesting – and fun – to start by building a direct simulation. Simulations are a great way to learn by doing, in line with our overall philosophy that "playing around" with simple models builds that intuition. You also never know where you'll end up! And, as it happens, simulation is also a handy tool to use to model cellular noise.

One of the most well-used techniques for simulating biochemical networks is called the Gillespie algorithm, first published back in the 1970s by Daniel Gillespie. Although it is based on underlying mathematical formalism called the chemical master equation, the essence of the algorithm can be easily grasped without mathematics. The core idea is that any simulation involving a number of different kinds of molecules consists of a prespecified series of *possible events*: it may be a binding or unbinding of transcription factor, or creation or degradation of an mRNA molecules. Each of these events has a certain *probability* of occurring based on the number of copies of the molecules involved in the event.

Cutting to the chase: In other kinds of algorithms, time advances in a steady manner by a prespecified timestep and we check at each one what we need to do. Not so with Gillespie. With Gillespie we need to ask just two questions: when is the next event and which event is it? We then update the time and do the event by updating our number of molecules, and rinse and repeat. No need to waste time, hah! on all the intervening timesteps when nothing interesting is happening anyway.

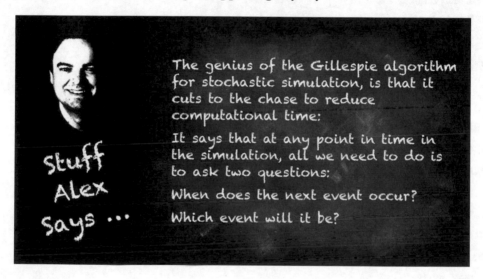

It Takes Two to Tango

One of the simplest cases to model is that of **dimerization** *where two molecules*, say A and B, become *one dimer* (AB). There are only two possible events, dimerization as just described and **dissociation** where a dimer again becomes two separate molecules. As shown in Figure 14-1, we can represent this by the two chemical equations which occur at rates k_D and k_U.

$$A + B \rightarrow AB \qquad (k_D)$$
$$AB \rightarrow A + B \qquad (k_U)$$

Figure 14-1. *Chemical equations for dimerization*

Obviously having a very small number of each of the kinds of molecules can have a major effect on the number of each kind of the three species. Let's live dangerously and dive straight into the Python code in Listing 14-1.

Listing 14-1. Setting up

```python
from numpy.random import exponential, uniform
import matplotlib.pyplot as plt
# Model 1: dimerization: just two reactions
# A + B -> AB   (k_D)
# AB -> A + B   (k_U)
k_D = 2.0
k_U = 1.0
time_points = []
A_counts  = []
B_counts  = []
AB_counts = []
t = 0.0
max_time = 10.0
# maximum number of molecules
max_molecules = 100
n_A = max_molecules
n_B = max_molecules
n_AB = 0
```

We start with the import of NumPy and matplotlib (already discussed in Chapter 12 and Chapter 10, respectively). Then we set up the parameters, followed by the lists that will hold the outputs of the simulation the number of copies of each kind of chemical species (A_counts, B_counts, AB_counts). We also store the list of times (time_points) as floating point numbers in the simulation. This is in contrast to previous simulations we have discussed, we are not simply incrementing, say, an integer number generations but time can move in "jumps" whose size depending on the *density* of events around that particular time in the simulation. We then initialize time t at zero and set the maximum time (max_time) that we want the simulation to run. Finally we initialize the simulation to have the maximum number of monomers of A and B (n_A, n_B); in our example case we set it to 100, and no dimers (n_AB=0).

Now we are ready for the main simulation loop, shown in Listing 14-2, which we run for as long as the max_time that we specified earlier.

Listing 14-2. Main simulation loop of Gillespie algorithm

```
while t < max_time:
  A_counts.append(n_A)
  AB_counts.append(n_AB)
  time_points.append(t)
  dimer = k_D * n_A * n_B
  disso = k_U * n_AB
  rates = dimer + disso
  delta_t = exponential(1.0/rates)    # get time for next reaction
  type = uniform(rates)
  if type < dimer:  # do dimerization
     n_AB += 1
     n_A -= 1
     n_B -= 1
   else:             # do dissociation
      n_AB -= 1
      n_A  += 1
      n_B  += 1
  t = t + delta_t    # update the time
```

Note that the *system state* is completely defined by the current *time* (**t**) and the *number* of each of the three kinds of molecules (n_A, n_B, and n_AB). We start by appending t, n_A, and n_B to the three lists that we will use to plot the system state later. (Note that we don't have a list for n_B because in the particular model the number of molecules of B is always the same as the number of A molecules, so it's somewhat redundant to plot it.)

Getting Kinetic

Next we start getting into the actual biological kinetics of the model. The ***total rate*** of all possible events is just the *sum* of all the ***individual rates***. The individual rates are, in turn, made up of the ***rate constant***, multiplied by the ***number of molecular species*** involved. The rates also can be thought of representing the *probability* of the possible events. For example, the number of events dimerization is proportional to the number of individual copies of the individual monomers of A and B, multiplied by the rate constant (k_D) as shown in the code dimer = k_D * n_A * n_B. This should be fairly intuitive; the more monomers around, the more chance of a dimerization events. Likewise for dissociation, the chance of dissociation goes up the more dimers we have around, and we calculate this in the code disso = k_U * n_AB. So the total probability of *any kind of event* is the *sum* of these two.

Imagine we have a case where given the current number of molecules, there is a higher probability of dimerization than dissociation, we can visualize the rate calculation in Figure 14-2.

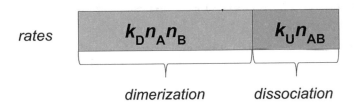

Figure 14-2. Visualizing rate calculation

Once we have this total rate calculation, we can then use that information to answer the first question that the Gillespie algorithm asks: *when* is the next event delta_t? We calculate this delta_t by drawing a random sample using NumPy's exponential function with 1.0/rates as the scale factor (see NumPy documentation[1] for more details). This means that the larger the rates, the shorter the time intervals drawn. Intuitively you can think of a larger rate, meaning a *higher density* of possible events, so we need to slow things down with shorter timesteps to simulate all those events accurately.

OK, all well and good, we've answered the first question. Now *what* event happens? This is actually pretty simple. We take the rates we already computed and sample uniformly from an interval of length rates (again remember this rates is made up of all the little *segments* of individual rates), and see in *which* individual segment rates it falls into. In the preceding code, we use NumPy's uniform function using rates as the interval we are sampling over to give us a random number type. Visually this looks like Figure 14-3, where the dotted line represents the location of type.

---

[1] http://docs.scipy.org/doc/numpy-1.10.1/reference/generated/numpy.random.exponential.html

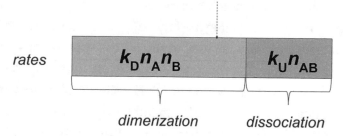

Figure 14-3. Selecting an event

In Figure 14-3 the random number type falls into the *left segment*, meaning that a *dimerization event* occurs, this is what the if type < dimer condition checks. Then, since we only have *two* possible events, anything *higher* than the dimer rate, by definition, falls into the *right segment*, meaning dissociation event occurs. We can then simply use an else statement, we don't need to explicitly check the rate.

Great, now we can actually *execute* the events in the next if conditional, this should be pretty clear. If a dimerization event occurs, we simply increment the number of dimers n_AB and decrement the number of A and B monomers, n_A and n_B (since we have one of each contributing to the dimer). We do the reverse for the dissociation case: decrement the number of dimers and increment the number of monomers. Lastly we update the current time by adding delta_t to the (now, old) current time, t.

And for the simulation at least, Robert is your paternal, fraternal relative! Now all that remains is to use matplotlib to print the output. Listing 14-3 shows the code.

Listing 14-3. Plotting the time series output

```
fig1 = plt.figure()
plt.xlim(0, max_time)
plt.ylim(0, max_molecules)
plt.xlabel('time')
plt.ylabel('# species')
plt.plot(time_points, A_counts,  label="A")  # A monomer
plt.plot(time_points, AB_counts, label="AB") # AB dimer
plt.legend()
plt.show()
```

We use time on the *x* axis and number of molecules on the *y* axis. This first part is kind of like setting up a figure in a paper: calling the `figure()` command. Next we set up the length of the axes we want to display, we want to run from *t*=0 to *t*=generations on the *x* axis and population size from zero (complete extinction) to 2*N* (maximum population size) on the *y* axis set using the `xlim`[2] and `ylim`[3] command. (This is slightly different to the way we did this in the previously chapters that we used matplotlib to plot curves such as Chapter 11 and Chapter 12. Here we specify the length of both axes, without `xlim` and `ylim` matplotlib will choose the axes itself, which may or may not be the region you want.) Thirdly, we label the plots using `xlabel` and `ylabel`. Then we plot two lines: the first is the list of time (`time_points`) against the number of monomers (`A_counts`) and the second is the list of time points against the number of dimers (`AB_counts`). We finish it off by plotting the legend and finally showing the figure. This should result in a figure like the one in Figure 14-4.

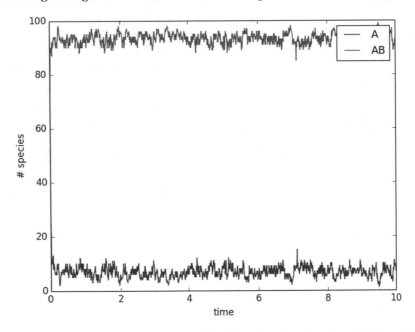

Figure 14-4. *Plot of time series output of Gillespie simulation of dimerization*

You can immediately see that although we start with no dimers, the simulation rapidly increases the number of dimers to an equilibrium value of about 90. But the randomness of the individual events continues to "wobble" around this mean; similarly the number of monomers drops to about 10.

---

[2]http://matplotlib.org/api/pyplot_api.html#matplotlib.pyplot.xlim
[3]http://matplotlib.org/api/pyplot_api.html#matplotlib.pyplot.ylim

Bring On the Noise!

Another nice thing we can do with our simulation is to see how **reducing the number of molecules** really **increases the amount of noise**, to the point where the equilibrium breaks down. Imagine we only have five molecules, we can do this by setting `max_molecules = 5`. Then, as you can see in Figure 14-5, the swings are really obvious and there's no real equilibrium. In some real-world cases within a cell, this might really make a difference to a biological process.

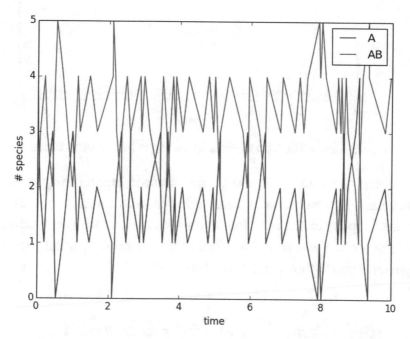

Figure 14-5. *Gillespie simulation with a very small number of molecules*

Or we can go the *other* way, by **increasing the number of molecules** to **reduce the amount of noise** and making the simulation closer to a continuous or deterministic model, by setting the number of molecules to a very high value, say `max_molecules = 1000`. As you can see in Figure 14-6, the numbers of the molecular species stabilize very quickly and the amount of noise is very small.

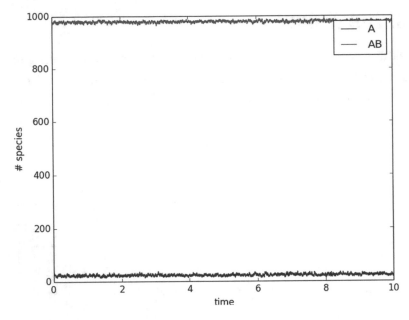

Figure 14-6. *Gillespie simulation with a large number of molecules*

OK, all well and good, but it still seems more *chemistry* than *biology* at this point. What about something closer to what happens inside cells containing all that molecular biology like transcription and translation, and which interact with each other to form gene networks of the sort we met in Chapter 12 on systems biology data mining. The Gillespie algorithm and Python can help us here too!

Getting more Realistic: A Toggle Switch

We're going to look at a very simple example of gene network: a ***toggle switch***. In fact using the word "network" might be a bit of a stretch, in that our switch contains just two genes. For consistency with the preceding dimer example, let's call them gene *A* and *B*. Let's say you take two genes and wire them up so that when gene *A* is *activated* it will tend to turn gene *B* off, and when gene *B* is *activated* it will tend to turn gene *A* off. This kind of genetic toggle has actually been created in *E. coli* (see Gardner (2000) for details).

As shown in Figure 14-7, it's a bit like a circular firing squad.

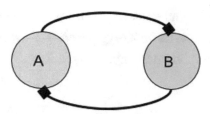

Figure 14-7. *Cartoon of a genetic toggle switch*

Of course this is just a very crude picture of what is going at the molecular level. In reality genes are turned on when enough transcription factors **bind** to the promoter regions of the DNA downstream of the actual coding region. The initiation of transcription itself is therefore somewhat random, but once it is initiated, the coding region is ***transcribed*** into an mRNA molecule.

This mRNA molecule will then be ***translated*** into a protein molecule. Each of these two molecules, the mRNA and protein, can also be ***degraded*** back into their constituent nucleotides or amino acids, respectively. All of these four processes, binding, transcription, translation, and degradation, can be modeled as individual *events* that happen at certain *rates*. Sound familiar? Inn Figure 14-8, we show a graphical snapshot of the processes involved.

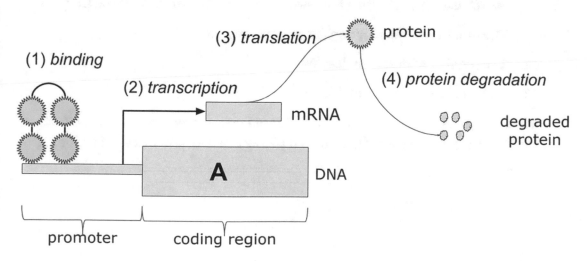

Figure 14-8. *Gene expression: binding, transcription, translation, and protein degradation*

By making each of the proteins ***transcription factors*** we can "wire up" the two genes *A* and *B* in a loop to create a ***gene circuit toggle switch*** showing the main molecular biology processes involved as shown in Figure 14-9.

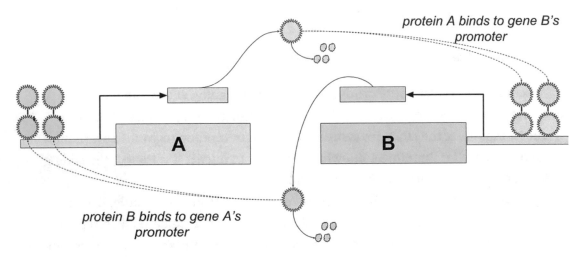

protein A binds to gene B's promoter

protein B binds to gene A's promoter

Figure 14-9. *Wiring two genes together to make a genetic toggle switch*

But this is already starting to look pretty complicated! Yes, indeed implementing the *full* toggle switch using the Gillespie framework would require us to keep track of

1. The number of transcription factors that are binding

2. The number of mRNA molecules

3. The number of protein molecules

for *each* of the genes. This would mean updating at least *six reactants* and many total *reactions*. That seems like a lot of bookkeeping. How can we make this a little easier for ourselves?

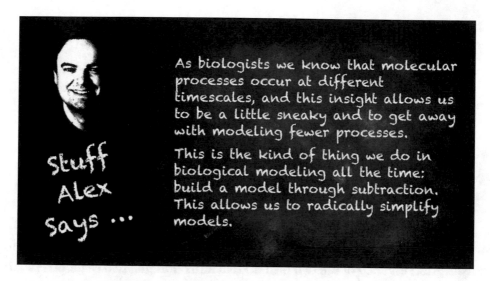

As biologists we know that molecular processes occur at different timescales, and this insight allows us to be a little sneaky and to get away with modeling fewer processes.

This is the kind of thing we do in biological modeling all the time: build a model through subtraction. This allows us to radically simplify models.

The answer: *simplify* the model using our knowledge of the underlying biological systems.

In our case we can reduce the model to just **two reactants** (representing the genes we started with, A and B) and only **four reactions**. How do we do that? Let's start by looking at turning genes "on."

Three Into One: Turning a Gene On

There are two important things to realize about transcription:

1. ***Transcription factor binding events are generally really fast*** relative to the timescale of *transcription initiation*. For example, in *E. coli,* transcription factor binding events occur on the order of milliseconds,[4] whereas transcription initiation occurs only every few seconds.[5] We can therefore "*lump*" binding and initiation of gene *A* into one reaction, driven by the number of protein molecules of the gene *B* (and vice versa).

---

[4]http://bionumbers.hms.harvard.edu/bionumber.aspx?s=n&id=102037&ver=4

[5]http://bionumbers.hms.harvard.edu/bionumber.aspx?&id=111997&ver=5&trm=transcript ion%20initiation

2. ***Translation happens in bursts***: Transcription and translation can be "*lumped*" together because although a single initiation event will produce a *single* mRNA, that mRNA will hang around long enough for the ribosomes to translate more several proteins. In *E. coli*, mRNA is synthesized at a rate of ~ a few nanomoles per minute, and translation happens at ~ a few mRNA per minute. This "*burstiness*" in the number of translation events can be modeled as a "jump" in the number of protein molecules for each transcription event, effectively combining the transcription and translation step into a *single reaction*.

For the purposes of the Gillespie algorithm, then, we can compress both binding and transcription for each of the two protein reactants into just two reactions (again in the code we will use n_A and n_B for the numbers of proteins of types A and B), and, like in the earlier case, we indicate the rate at which these reactions occur in brackets in Figure 14-10.

$$n_A \rightarrow n_A + p \qquad (\alpha_R \times s([B]))$$
$$n_B \rightarrow n_B + p \qquad (\alpha_R \times s([A]))$$

Figure 14-10. *Chemical reactions for binding and transcription*

The first reaction combines three lumped processes (binding, transcription, and translation) resulting in *p* new **p**rotein molecules of type *A* produced by this event. The rate of the event does the main business of capturing this overall process, so it will need a little bit more explanation. The rate of these protein "bursts" of type *A* is going to be proportional to two things:

1. The ***rate of activity of the promoter***: $s([B])$, that is, the rate at which transcription factor binding *s*ite events occur that ***initiate*** the mRNA synthesis

2. Once started, the rate of ***mRNA synthesis*** (α_R)

Let's start with the first thing: for $s([B])$ we need to calculate a rate as a *function* of the *concentration* of the protein of type *B*. Let's assume that the transcription factor *B* is active as a *dimer* (as in the original example, earlier) and that dimerization is *instantaneous* (so we don't model it). Let's also assume that the gene is turned on by the dual interacting repressor motif that we already saw in Chapter 12.

As a reminder, this consisted of *an operator* with *two binding sites* where dimers bind independently of each other, and that when the two dimers bind, they shut down (or "repress") transcription at a rate w. Also from Chapter 12, we define the rate of *dissociation* of the dimers from their respective DNA binding sites as K_D. If both of the transcription factors are the same, then both of their concentrations are $[B]$ and it is possible to derive the rate of activity as a function of the concentration, $s([B])$, as shown in Figure 14-11.

$$s([B]) = \frac{\left(1 + \frac{[B]/K_D}{w}\left(2 + [B]/K_D\right)\right)}{\left(1 + [B]/K_D\right)^2}$$

Figure 14-11. *Equation for the rate of activity of the B promoter*

As we saw in the visualization of the kinetics in Chapter 12, as concentration of the protein, $([B])$, *increases,* the rate at which transcription initiates (s) will *decrease.* Again this builds on the intuition from Chapter 12 that the more copies of the transcription factor protein are around, the more chances they will bind to the promoter on the DNA and therefore switch *off* the gene A and consequent production of protein A. The main difference with the treatment in Chapter 12 is that now we are using the formula to get the *probability* of the transcription event as a probabilistic event, rather to plot the rate as continuous function of concentration.

Phew! now that we've got the first reaction out of the way, the second reaction is a doddle. It's simply the same form as the first reaction except that the promoter activity $s([A])$ is now a function of the protein concentration of A, since B is regulated by the A protein.

All Proteins Eventually Die

It is a sad fact of biological life that all proteins eventually die. Luckily for us, loss of a protein molecule is a *lot* simpler to model. Here we are just dealing with simple biochemical degradation. Again, as shown in Figure 14-12, we have just two reactions, both proportional to their respective concentrations and a protein degradation rate, β_p:

$$n_A \rightarrow n_A - 1 \quad (\beta_p\,[A])$$
$$n_B \rightarrow n_B - 1 \quad (\beta_p\,[B])$$

Figure 14-12. *Two chemical equations for protein degradation*

Returning to our graphical picture in Figure 14-13, you can see how the "lumped" binding + transcription + translation process (in the gray box) "maps" on to the original biological mechanism, allowing us to just keep track of the protein concentrations. This gets us back to just *two reactants* (the two proteins) and *four events*, shown as solid lines (the broken lines of the original events are now implicit in the lumped event).

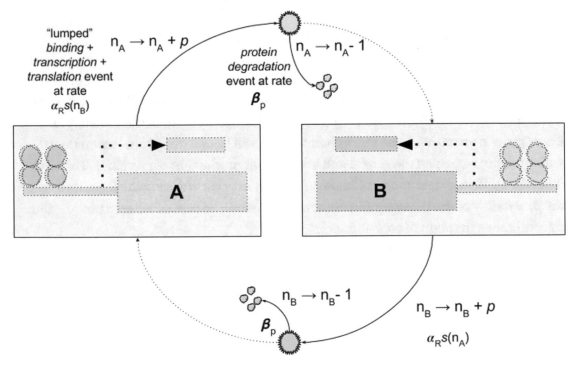

Figure 14-13. *Simplified model of gene toggle showing the primary modeled events*

Enough with the Biochemistry! Show me the Code!

"Enough with all the biochemistry already," I hear you saying, "and I'm about ready to see some Python code now." Well, we've presented enough of the biology and the model to start on the code, so without further ado... may I present, in Listing 14-4, the `calculate_reaction_rates` function (with associated global variables).

Listing 14-4. Calculating reaction rates for gene toggle switch

```
alpha = 1     # synthesis mRNA
p   = 10      # number of protein molecules per mRNA event
protein_degr_rate = 1/50.0   # degrading protein

w_fold  = 200     # fold repression
K_D = 25          # strength of the DNA binding creating repression

def calculate_reaction_rates(n_A, n_B):
  A_conc = n_A/scaling
  B_conc = n_B/scaling

  A_synthesis_rate = scaling*alpha*(1+(B_conc/K_D/2)/w_fold*(2+(B_conc/
  K_D/2)))/(1+(B_conc/K_D/2))**2
  B_synthesis_rate = scaling*alpha*(1+(A_conc/K_D/2)/w_fold*(2+(A_conc/
  K_D/2)))/(1+(A_conc/K_D/2))**2
  A_degradation_rate      = scaling*protein_degr_rate*A_conc
  B_degradation_rate      = scaling*protein_degr_rate*B_conc

  return [A_synthesis_rate, B_synthesis_rate, A_degradation_rate,
  B_degradation_rate]
```

The function takes the number of each type of protein as arguments and converts them to concentrations using the scaling factor `scaling`. This should be pretty self-explanatory at this point: we then implement the first two reactions which lead to a production of new proteins. The rate constants K_D and w are represented in the code by `K_D` and `w_fold`, respectively. The last two reactions which lead to a reduction of new proteins by a degradation rate of β_p (in code `protein_degr_rate`) are implemented in the second set of the four. At the end of the function, we return the rates as a list.

Molecular Accounting: Keeping Your Books Straight

With the calculation of the rates out of the way, much of the complexity of modeling the biology is actually done at this point. The next major part of the biology is way simpler, it's simply bookkeeping of the number of the molecules and, as in the dimer example, it flows very naturally from the chemical reactions shown earlier. But it's now sufficiently complicated that rather than have the code inline in the main function, we will give its own function in Listing 14-5.

Listing 14-5. Performing the chemical reaction

```
def do_reaction(n_A, n_B, next_reaction):
  if next_reaction == 0:
    n_A = n_A + p   # p copies of A are created
  elif next_reaction == 1:
    n_B = n_B + p   # p copies of B are created
  elif next_reaction == 2:
    n_A -= 1         # A is degraded
  elif next_reaction == 3:
    n_B -= 1         # B is degraded
  return n_A, n_B
```

Again we pass in the number of each of the protein molecules as well as the reaction type, next_reaction, and update the numbers according to the rules (note that the burst size is represented by the global variable, p).

We're Ready to Simulate!

We're now ready to introduce the main program in Listing 14-6, and we've retained the same basic data structures and names as in the dimer example, using lists to record the time points and protein counts (A_counts, B_counts, time_points) so it should be easy to follow (note that you'll need to execute the code in Listings 14-4 and 14-5 for this code to work).

Listing 14-6. Main simulation loop for genetic toggle switch

```
scaling = 1.0
max_time = 20000.0
time_points = []
A_counts  = []
B_counts  = []
n_A = round(11*scaling)
n_B = round(34*scaling)
```

```
seed(50)
t = 0.0
num_reactions = 4

while t <= max_time:
  time_points.append(t)
  A_counts.append(n_A)
  B_counts.append(n_B)
  rates = calculate_reaction_rates(n_A, n_B)
  total_rates = sum(rates)
  delta_t = exponential(1.0/total_rates)
  type = uniform()*total_rates
  # find the reaction
  for reaction in range(0, num_reactions):
   if (sum(rates[0:reaction+1]) >= type):
    next_reaction=reaction
    break
  n_A, n_B = do_reaction(n_A, n_B, next_reaction) # carry out reaction
  t = t + delta_t
```

The while loop structure of the program is almost the same as in the dimer example, except that here we fix the random number seed to 50 in the seed(50). The number 50 is just arbitrary, but it ensures that your figure will always look the same as the one we show next. We first calculate the total_rates, this time by calling the calculate_reaction_rates function, returning the list of rates and summing them. For this we introduce the built-in Python sum() function[6] which adds up all the elements in any supplied list. We then obtain the delta_t using exponential() and the type of reaction by sampling from a uniform() distribution of length total_rates. Another main difference is that finding the event to execute is a little more complicated, because we now have four types of reactions. So our interval now looks like Figure 14-14.

---

[6]https://docs.python.org/2/library/functions.html#sum

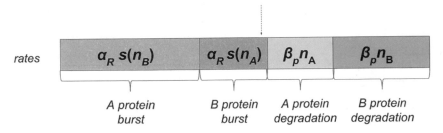

Figure 14-14. *Choosing chemical reactions (events) in Gillespie algorithm for genetic toggle switch*

To find out which reaction to run, we use a `for` loop that progressively sums the reaction rates, and once we have reached a sum that exceeds `type`, it will `break` the loop and use that reaction. So the loop will first sum the rates in the sublist `rates[0:1]`, then `rates[0:2]`, and so on, up to, in this case, `rates[0:4]`. If at any point this exceeds the `type`, we have found our reaction. It's worth bearing in mind that the list *order* returned from `calculate_reaction_rates` must be used *consistently* throughout, so that the zeroeth entry in the `rates` list always corresponds to the zeroeth reaction in the `do_reaction` function (a burst event for protein *A*), and the first entry corresponds to first reaction and so on. Although this is not an issue in this particular example, it could be a problem if you were to rewrite the code without realizing that the indices must keep the *same* original order.

After we've got the `next_reaction` index, we `do_reaction`, and update the protein numbers `n_A` and `n_B` returned by `do_reaction`, and update the timestamp, `t`. Now we're ready to plot in Listing 14-7, and the code is practically verbatim from the dimer example.

Listing 14-7. Plotting output of Gillespie simulation

```
fig1 = plt.figure()
plt.xlim(0, max_time)
plt.ylim(0, 1000)
plt.xlabel('time')
plt.ylabel('# species')
plt.plot(time_points, A_counts, label="A") # species A
plt.plot(time_points, B_counts, label="B") # species B
plt.legend()
plt.show()
```

Now let's look at the full, complete program in Listing 14-8 and run it using the default parameters.

Listing 14-8. Full program of Gillespie algorithm simulation of genetic toggle switch

```
from numpy.random import exponential, uniform, seed
import matplotlib.pyplot as plt

# Model 2: toggle switch: four reactions
alpha = 1      # synthesis mRNA
p    = 10       # number of protein molecules per mRNA event
protein_degr_rate = 1/50.0    # degrading protein
w_fold  = 200       # fold repression
K_D = 25                # strength of the DNA binding creating repression
def calculate_reaction_rates(n_A, n_B):
  A_conc = n_A/scaling
  B_conc = n_B/scaling
  A_synthesis_rate = scaling*alpha*(1+(B_conc/K_D/2)/w_fold*(2+(B_conc/
  K_D/2)))/(1+(B_conc/K_D/2))**2
  B_synthesis_rate = scaling*alpha*(1+(A_conc/K_D/2)/w_fold*(2+(A_conc/
  K_D/2)))/(1+(A_conc/K_D/2))**2
  A_degradation_rate     = scaling*protein_degr_rate*A_conc
  B_degradation_rate     = scaling*protein_degr_rate*B_conc

  return [A_synthesis_rate, B_synthesis_rate, A_degradation_rate,
  B_degradation_rate]

def do_reaction(n_A, n_B, next_reaction):
  if next_reaction == 0:
    n_A = n_A + p  # p copies of A are created
    elif next_reaction == 1:
    n_B = n_B + p  # p copies of B are created
    elif next_reaction == 2:
  n_A -= 1         # A is degraded
```

```
  elif next_reaction == 3:
    n_B -= 1          # B is degraded
    return n_A, n_B

scaling = 1.0
max_time = 20000.0
time_points = []
A_counts  = []
B_counts  = []
n_A = round(11*scaling)
n_B = round(34*scaling)
seed(100)
t = 0.0
num_reactions = 4

while t <= max_time:
  time_points.append(t)
  A_counts.append(n_A)
  B_counts.append(n_B)
  rates = calculate_reaction_rates(n_A, n_B)
  total_rates = sum(rates)
  delta_t = exponential(1.0/total_rates)
  type = uniform()*total_rates

  # find the reaction
  for reaction in range(0, num_reactions):
   if (sum(rates[0:reaction+1]) >= type):
     next_reaction=reaction
     break
  n_A, n_B = do_reaction(n_A, n_B, next_reaction) # carry out reaction
  t = t + delta_t

fig1 = plt.figure()
plt.xlim(0, max_time)
plt.ylim(0, 1000)
plt.xlabel('time')
plt.ylabel('# species')
```

```
plt.plot(time_points, A_counts, label="A") # species A
plt.plot(time_points, B_counts, label="B") # species B
plt.legend()
plt.show()
```

You'll notice that running the program will take a little longer than the rest, this is because it's doing many more computations to get to interesting events. You should see something resembling Figure 14-15.

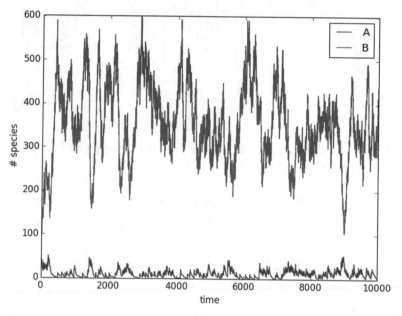

Figure 14-15. *Plotting output of Gillespie algorithm simulation of genetic toggle switch*

Note that the number of *A* molecules reaches a steady state of around 400 molecules fairly quickly (in about 100 timesteps or less), while the number of *B* molecules is very low (indicating that *A* is effectively ON and *B* is OFF). The switch seems to be doing its job and staying in a single ON state.

What happens if we reduce the total number of molecules by a quarter? We can do this simply by setting `scaling = 0.25` and re-running the simulation, and the output should look something like Figure 14-16.

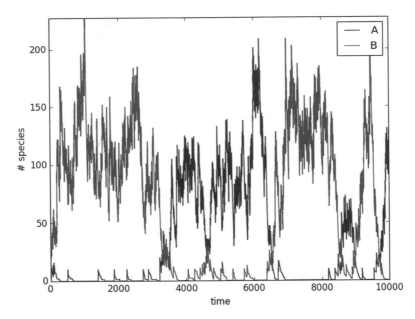

Figure 14-16. *Output of simulation with a smaller number of molecules shows the genetic switch being "toggled"*

Although we do see the A molecules reaching a steady state of around 80 molecules, this state is now *unstable*! We see several switching events from one state to the other during the same 10,000 timesteps. Note that this happens without any *external input* at all. It just switches ghost-like all on its own! Simple molecular "noise" is enough to occasionally switch the state. We leave it as an exercise to the reader to experiment a bit with the various parameters such as the scaling factor, the random number seed (which we set to 50 in the preceding runs), and number timesteps to see when and how often the switch becomes unstable.

Why Should we Care About Stochastic Switching?

So it's a neat simulation, but why should we care about stochastic switching of gene circuits in the first place? There are several reasons. One has practical biomedical significance: chance events that could switch state with no external inputs may underlie some aspects of diseases. For example, we normally think of cancer as being purely a result of external tweaks like mutations, but there is also evidence that internal cellular stochastic events could play a role in how cancer develops (Gupta et al. 2011). On longer timescales, Arkin (1999) and colleagues showed that stochastic switches in lambda phage lysis/lysogeny decision circuit can cause an otherwise *genetically identical* population of *E. coli* cells to differentiate into *subpopulations* with *different phenotypic* states. Similar processes have been observed using stochastic Petri net representations of plasmid replication in bacteria (Goss & Peccoud 1999). Over time these processes could lead to very different evolutionary outcomes. Noise matters!

We have now built a complete model in Python of a recognizably *biological* system, more than mere chemistry, but somehow less than a moving, growing, living thing. Let's fix that in Chapter 15, where we use Python to create a very simple of plant growth using a staple of artificial life research: L-systems.

References and Further Exploration

Books

- Uri Alon, *An Introduction to Systems Biology: Design Principles of Biological Circuits*[7] (CRC Press, 2006). Good general introduction to systems biology approaches in the context of microorganisms like *E. coli* and yeast

- Hamid Bolouri, *Computational Modeling of Gene Regulatory Networks: A Primer*[8] (World Scientific, 2008). Practical primer for getting started modeling gene networks

- Bower and Bolouri, eds., *Computational Modeling of Genetic and Biochemical Networks*[9] (MIT Press, 2001). Edited volume, although older, it's still a very good overview of techniques

- West-Eberhard, *Developmental Plasticity and Evolution*[10] (Oxford University Press, 2003). Chapters explore the important role of noise and stochasticity in organismal development

---

[7]www.crcpress.com/An-Introduction-to-Systems-Biology-Design-Principles-of-Biological-Circuits/Alon/p/book/9781584886426

[8]www.worldscientific.com/worldscibooks/10.1142/p567

[9]https://mitpress.mit.edu/books/computational-modeling-genetic-and-biochemical-networks

[10]www.oupcanada.com/catalog/9780195122350.html

- Darren Wilkinson, *Stochastic Modelling for Systems Biology*[11] (CRC Press, 2011). Book length treatment of stochastic models in systems biology

Articles

- Arkin *et al.* (1998). Stochastic Kinetic Analysis of Developmental Pathway Bifurcation in Phage λ-Infected Escherichia coli Cells.[12] *Genetics*, **149**, 1633–1648

- Bintu *et al.* (2005). Transcriptional regulation by the numbers: applications.[13] *Current Opinion in Genetics & Development*, **15**, 125–135

- Gardner *et al.* (2000). Construction of a genetic toggle switch in Escherichia coli.[14] *Nature*, **403**, 339–342

- Gillespie (1977). Exact stochastic simulation of coupled chemical reactions.[15] *The Journal of Physical Chemistry*, **81**, 2340–2361

- Goss and Peccoud (1998). Quantitative modeling of stochastic systems in molecular biology by using stochastic Petri nets.[16] *PNAS*, **95**, 6750–6755

- Gupta *et al.* (2011). Stochastic State Transitions Give Rise to Phenotypic Equilibrium in Populations of Cancer Cells.[17] *Cell*, **146**, 633–644

- Merlo *et al.* (2006). Cancer as an evolutionary and ecological process.[18] *Nat Rev Cancer*, **6**, 924–935

---

[11]www.crcpress.com/Stochastic-Modelling-for-Systems-Biology-Second-Edition/Wilkinson/p/book/9781439837726

[12]www.ncbi.nlm.nih.gov/pmc/articles/PMC1460268/

[13]www.ncbi.nlm.nih.gov/pmc/articles/PMC3462814/

[14]www.nature.com/nature/journal/v403/n6767/full/403339a0.html

[15]http://web.mit.edu/endy/www/scraps/dg/JPC(81)2340.pdf

[16]www.ncbi.nlm.nih.gov/pmc/articles/PMC22622/

[17]www.cell.com/abstract/S0092-8674(11)00824-5

[18]www.cs.unm.edu/~karlinjf/papers/merlo-NRC-AOL.pdf

- Thattai and van Oudenaarden (2001). Intrinsic noise in gene regulatory networks.[19] *PNAS*, **98**, 8614–8619

Other

- BioNumbers[20]: a database of useful biological values for use in models along with their derivation in the literature

- Python for Systems Biology[21] (**PySB**): a Python framework for Systems Biology

- Systems Biology Markup Language[22] (**SBML**): an open interchange format for sharing systems biology models between researchers. The site has a list of SBML-compatible software[23]

---

[19]www.ncbi.nlm.nih.gov/pmc/articles/PMC37484/
[20]http://bionumbers.hms.harvard.edu/
[21]http://pysb.org/
[22]http://sbml.org/
[23]http://sbml.org/SBML_Software_Guide

CHAPTER 15

Growing a Virtual Garden

Modeling Plant Development with L-Systems

Three cards were walking through a field carrying their pails of paint, when they came upon a most odd-looking structure protruding from the dirt.

"This thing must have been the result of all-powerful force," said the Five of Spades. "With so many twists and turns, it just boggles the mind – no natural process could have generated such a tangled beast."

"Yes, just look at all the different shapes at the end of the structure," exclaimed the Seven of Spades, "No two look exactly alike. Clearly this thing – whatever it is called – is of the finest hand-tooled artistry."

The Two of Spades, who up until now had been silent, shifted uncomfortably from foot to foot. "Hmm, well, you know, I've been counting the number of splits from the end of that thing that's in the ground. And I think I see a pattern…."

Five and Seven glanced at each other briefly, and then burst out laughing. "That's just so typical of you and your obsession with numbers. The next thing you'll be saying is that you are the difference between us."

turtle *graphics,* **+=** *operator, read-only, race condition*

Developmental biology, cell reproduction, filamentous growth, algae, plants, generative behavior, complex systems

A. Lancaster and G. Webster, *Python for the Life Sciences*, https://doi.org/10.1007/978-1-4842-4523-1_15

As we have seen so far in our travels, computational biology is about so much more than sequence analysis. Moving up the scale of biological systems, the amazingly fluid, yet highly robust process of organismal development has been source of interest for as long as there have been microscopes. Python is an excellent platform to explore the nature of development via the **generative** power of simple **rules or behavior**. This is a powerful idea, because even very simple rules, iterated over time, can generate complex and unpredictable patterns. From the *flocking behavior of birds* to the *swarming of bees*, biology is replete with examples where simple behaviors generate endlessly fascinating patterns – an area of study that has become known as complex adaptive systems (Chapter 16 and Chapter 18 explore these themes even further). You can even *grow* plants in your computer as Austrian biologist Aristid Lindenmayer did back in 1968 by modeling growth and development as found in filamentous organisms such as algae.

Lindenmayer began by imagining a single one-dimensional line of cells, with any individual cell receiving signals to either divide or grow only from their immediate left or right neighbor. He allowed that each individual algae cell existed in one of two possible states: *reproduction* or *growth*. A cell in the reproduction state would split into two cells: one that would start in the growth state, and the other that would stay in the reproduction state. In addition, a cell that started in the growth state would eventually become a reproduction cell. Putting these two rules together, Lindenmayer came up with a model of filamentous growth that captured some key features of real growth in plants such as constant apical growth[1] where the central "stem" (in the model this is a set of cells) remains the same in appearance even as cells divide and move away from this central set of cells.

Increasing Productivity: Algorithmic Production Rules

The heart of translating this idea into code is defining these biological intuitions as rigorous algorithmic **production rules**. You can take the preceding two intuitions and codify them into two simple rules. Call a cell in the reproduction state **A** and a cell in the growth state **B**. A production rule basically says, take a symbol on the *left-hand side* and replace it with another set of symbols on the *right-hand side*. Here's what it looks like:

---

[1]http://archive.bio.ed.ac.uk/jdeacon/microbes/apical.htm

B → A (rule #1: growth cell becomes a reproduction cell)

A → AB (rule #2: reproduction cell splits into another reproduction, plus a growth cell)

To complete the algorithm, we simply need to give the algorithm a cell to kick things off, say a reproduction cell **A**. We can run growth "by hand" (or perhaps we should really say "by head") by starting with A, then noticing that **A** is not a growth cell, so the first rule *doesn't apply*, but it *is* a reproduction cell, so we *do apply* the second rule. We now have a *reproduction* cell and *growth* cell, or **AB**.

Let's run the rules again, in this case the reproduction cell **A** will again become **AB** and the second growth cell **B** will become a growth cell again, resulting in **AB** + **A**, or **ABA**. Keep doing this and you get **ABA** -> **ABAAB** -> **ABAABABA** and so on.

So how do we build this algorithm in Python? The function `algae_growth` that implements this is surprisingly short, we simply supply the number of iterations of the rules we want to run, and the initial symbol (we default to **A**). The main code in Listing 15-1 consists of *two* nested for loops.

Listing 15-1. Simulating algae growth with an L-system rule

```
def algae_growth(number, output="A", show=False):
  for i in range(number):
    new_output = ""
    for letter in output:
      if letter == "A":          # rule #2
        new_output += "AB"
      elif letter == "B":        # rule #1
        new_output += "A"
    output = new_output    # only update state after all letters are read
    if show: print("n =", i+1, output, "[", len(output), "]")
  return output
print("n = 0", "A", "[ 1 ]")
algae_growth(6, output="A", show=True)
```

The outer loop runs through number iterations, storing the result in the variable output. At the beginning of each loop, we reinitialize our new_output to the empty string "". Then we take our existing output and use an inner for loop to go through it letter by letter. For the current `letter` in the loop, we check whether it is an **A** or **B**. If it is an **A**, we simply append the two new letters to our `new_output` string using the "+=" operator. Likewise if it is a **B**, we append an **A**. Once we have examined that letter, we now assign the `new_output` back to `output` to start the process all over again for the next iteration of growth and reproduction (the outer loop).

Note that we use two different variables here, not just the one `output`. Why is that? This is because we need to keep the `output` variable *read-only* during the application of the two rules; otherwise, we would be like the snake chasing its proverbial tail. (To convince yourself of this, try removing the `new_output` variable and replacing all instances of `new_output` with `output`, it will still work, but it will represent more of a death spiral.) So only once we have *applied* the rules, do we update the `output` variable with the contents of `new_output`.

The final step in Listing 15-1 calls the function and *grows* the algae (it runs six generations of the algorithm). The following output shows the growth of the cells in its full glory:

```
n = 0 A [ 1 ]
n = 1 AB [ 2 ]
n = 2 ABA [ 3 ]
n = 3 ABAAB [ 5 ]
n = 4 ABAABABA [ 8 ]
n = 5 ABAABABAABAAB [ 13 ]
n = 6 ABAABABAABAABABAABABA [ 21 ]
```

Note that after only six iterations, we already have very interesting patterns. We've also printed out the length of each of the iterations of the cycle. Alert readers will have noticed an interesting pattern: these represent the Fibonacci sequence. This is actually pretty incredible when you think about it: a set of two very simple rules iterated over and over can produce a sequence of cells, the number of which is deeply connected to one of the most fundamental mathematical sequences found in the arrangement of leaves on stem and the formation of pinecones. We can also see the constant apical growth mentioned at the beginning: the **ABA** pattern at the left-edge remains even as the growth continues.

Using Python Turtle Graphics to Grow Ferns

So you might be asking yourself at this point that as cool as it is, the patterns are kind of boring. After all, cells don't really live in a line and they don't look very plant-like. Can we do something better? Can we use these ideas to generate something that actually *looks* like a plant? Well, I'm very glad you asked that question, because the answer is yes, yes we can. To realize this requires a set of rules with a more complicated language, but still using the same basic simple logic.

We first imagine the "plant," let's imagine it as a "fern," is growing on a two-dimensional (2D) surface. Here the outputs of the L-system are actually instructions telling the plant where on this 2D surface to "grow" next. There are six basic symbols which can be thought of as representing a developmental "command":

F = *go forward*

X = *stay*

+ = turn *right* 25 degrees

- = turn *left* 25 degrees

[= *save* current (x, y) position

] = go *back* to saved (x, y) position

The production rules treat **F** and **X** as *variables* (meaning that only those two symbols are expanded into other symbols), and +, –, [,] are *constants* (they are *terminal* symbols: symbols that don't get expanded into anything else). So without further ado, here are the two rules:

F → FF

X → F−[[X]+X]+F[+FX]−X

OK, so these are *definitely* more complicated than the previous rules, but they work basically the same. Every time you see an "**F**", replace it with an "**FF**", every time you see an **X**, replace it with that monstrosity on the right! That long expression embeds within its commands for the plant to move forward, some commands to rotate left and right and to save and restore position. Think of it like a little genetic program playing out in real time.

Each of the saving ([) and restoring (]) of positions then represents the completion of the growth of an individual "frond" and start of a new "frond" from the position where the original frond was! This will become clearer when we implement the code to draw the resulting plant. Meanwhile, in Listing 15-2 we see how we actually implement the production rules in Python.

Listing 15-2. Plant growth using a two-dimensional L-system

```python
def plant_growth(number, output="X", show=False):
  for i in range(number):
    new_output = ""
    for letter in output:
      # rule #1
      if letter == "X":
        new_output += "F-[[X]+X]+F[+FX]-X"
      elif letter == "F":
        new_output += "FF"
      else:
        new_output += letter
    output = new_output
    if show: print("n =", i+1, output, "[", len(output), "]")
  return output
```

You'll notice that the structure of the code is identical to the algae growth code! The only difference in the new code is the right-hand side of the production rules in the new_output is different. Starting at the initial symbol of **X**, we can run the growth using this code:

```python
print("n = 0", "X", "[ 1 ]")
plant=plant_growth(2, output="X", show=True)
```

Because the fern grows very quickly, we only show two iterations of the growth (already at $n=2$, there are already 89 symbols!)

```
n = 0 X [ 1 ]
n = 1 F-[[X]+X]+F[+FX]-X [ 18 ]
n= 2 FF-[[F-[[X]+X]+F[+FX]-X]+F-[[X]+X]+F[+FX]-X]+FF[+FFF-[[X]+X]+F[+FX]-
X]-F-[[X]+X]+F[+FX]-X [ 89 ]
```

So, all well and good so far, but you might be asking yourself at this point that this doesn't look like a fern, I know: I want to see something that *looks* like a fern. For that, we're going to delve into the world of turtle graphics.

If you ever took computer classes in elementary or high school, chances are that you might have encountered a language called Logo, created back in the late 1960s by scientists working at Cambridge, Massachusetts-based company, BBN. It was used as a language to teach kids how to program the drawing of **graphics** by imagining they were programming **turtles** that could move *forward*, rotate *left* and *right,* and *jump* from place to place.

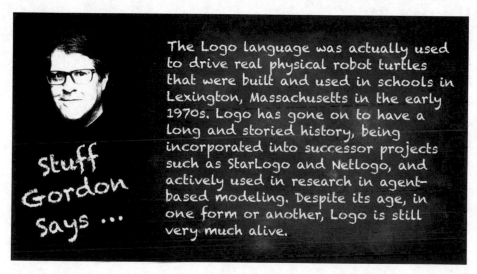

Python has taken the core concept of turtle graphics and implemented them in a module with the name, wait for, drum roll, please.... `turtle`. Turtle graphics can be used to control a turtle on a two-dimensional *"canvas."* The turtle will leave a "trail" of lines creating complex patterns, much as a series of cells or fronds leave their trail in real plant growth. Conceptually then, turtle graphics are an ideal match for drawing the output of L-system: the turtle moves, leaves a trail, moves somewhere else. Here's the code in Listing 15-3.

Listing 15-3. Implementing visualization of plant growth using Python turtle graphics

```
import turtle
def draw_plant(actions):
  stk = []
  for action in actions:
```

```python
    if action=='X':            # do nothing
      pass
    elif action== 'F':         # go forward
      turtle.forward(2)
    elif action=='+':          # rotate right by 25 degrees
      turtle.right(25)
    elif action=='-':          # rotate left by 25 degrees
      turtle.left(25)
    elif action=='[':
      # save the position and heading by "pushing" down on to the stack
      pos = turtle.position()
      head = turtle.heading()
      stk.append((pos, head))
    elif action==']':
      # restore position and heading: by "popping" the stack
      pos, head = stk.pop()
      turtle.penup()
      turtle.setposition(pos)
      turtle.setheading(head)
      turtle.pendown()
    else:
      raise ValueError("don't recognize action", action)
    turtle.update()
```

This code should look relatively straightforward to you by now: the function takes a series of actions (implemented as a string) and loops through the action (each character in the string) to tell the turtle to do things using the turtle language. The commands that the turtle obeys almost map one-to-one to the symbols:

1. turtle.forward() corresponds to **F**.

2. turtle.left() and turtle.right() correspond to the rotation commands "–" and "+".

3. Saving the turtle state [is a little bit more complex: as we need to get both the current (x, y) position using turtle.position() and the direction the turtle is facing using turtle.heading(). Both of

these positions can be *saved* by appending the tuple made up of
position and heading to a list. (This is like "pushing" onto a stack.)

4. Returning the turtle to the saved position reverses the preceding
    step, we first "pop()" the last element off the list (or stack).
    We also stop the turtle from leaving its trail by bringing its
    turtle.penup(), then plop it back down in the saved position
    using setposition() and setheading(), and put the pen down so
    the trail of cells can be continued.

And we're done with the draw function! In Listing 15-4 we connect the output of the
growth of the fern to the graphics (note that the code in Listings 15-2 and 15-3 needs to
be executed first for this to work).

Listing 15-4. Main program that grows the plant, then visualizes it

```
print("n = 0", "X", "[ 1 ]")
plant=plant_growth(6, output="X", show=False)

# get initial position
x = 0
y = -turtle.window_height() / 2

turtle.hideturtle()
turtle.left(90)
turtle.penup()
turtle.goto(x, y)
turtle.pendown()
draw_plant(plant)
```

Note that in order to actually draw the graphics, we do some initial setup of the turtle
position based on the size of the window and then move the turtle into position and put
its pendown() to start the visualization of the growth! If you run the program, you should
see something that looks rather like Figure 15-1.

Figure 15-1. *"Fern" grown using a two-dimensional L-system in Python*

Congratulations, you've grown your very first virtual plant! In the *next* chapter (Chapter 16), we'll extend these modeling approaches to look at a famous model of development initially created by the mathematician Alan Turing that has since been demonstrated to actually occur in real organisms.

References and Further Exploration

- Lindenmayer (1968). Mathematical models for cellular interactions in development I. Filaments with one-sided inputs.[2] *Journal of theoretical biology*, **18**, 280–299

- Philip Ball, *The Self-Made Tapestry: Pattern Formation in Nature*[3] (Oxford University Press, 1997) and its follow-up, a three-volume

---

[2]http://w0.cs.ucl.ac.uk/staff/p.bentley/teaching/L6_reading/lsystems.pdf
[3]https://global.oup.com/academic/product/the-self-made-tapestry-9780198502432

set *Nature's Patterns, a Tapestry in Three Parts*[4] (Oxford University Press, 2009) are excellent introductions to the science of pattern formation in biology and beyond. A coffee-table photographic version is available as well, *Patterns in Nature*[5] (University of Chicago, 2016). Ball really likes his books in threes!

- Kuma and Bentley, *On Growth, Form and Computers*[6] (Academic Press, 2003). An excellent book-length review of computational modeling of development

- Melanie Mitchell, *Complexity: A Guided Tour*[7] (Oxford University Press, 2009). A fantastic guided tour to the sciences of complexity

---

[4]https://global.oup.com/academic/product/shapes-9780199237968
[5]http://press.uchicago.edu/ucp/books/book/chicago/P/bo23519431.html
[6]www.sciencedirect.com/science/book/9780124287655
[7]https://global.oup.com/academic/product/complexity-9780195124415

CHAPTER 16

How the Leopard Got its Spots

Cellular Automata Models of Turing Patterns

Alice realized that she hated the silly game the King and Queen had made her play all day.

"What if we could use the same board, but didn't have to worry about somebody always having to win?"

"Yes," she murmured to herself, *"I would just have each square just change color depending on who its neighbors were. Then, I would just start them off all randomly, not in this silly battle formation,"* she started to speak out loud, throwing her scepter away.

"There would be an endless series of ever-changing games, not this obsession with checkmate," she exclaimed as she jumped up cast away the uncomfortable crown they had made her wear.

Then she heard the King and Queen stirring, so she quickly scooped up her crown and scepter and sat back down, sighing.

---

 numpy *two-dimensional arrays,* **zeros()**, *colormaps,* **matplotlib   pcolor()**, **pause()**

 Developmental biology, activator-inhibitor system, Turing patterns, morphogens, leopard spots, morphogenesis, cellular automata, zebrafish

---

A. Lancaster and G. Webster, *Python for the Life Sciences*, https://doi.org/10.1007/978-1-4842-4523-1_16

The quantitative study of the amazing process of organismal development has a long history. L-systems, which we saw in the previous chapter, date back to the late 1960s, but the history extends much further than that. D'Arcy Thompson wrote his classic *On Growth and Form* in 1917 well predating the discovery of the double-helix structure of DNA in 1953. In fact just 1 year prior – 1952 – the British computer scientist Alan Turing published a paper describing a mathematical model that attempted to answer the question: how does the leopard get its spots? Of course, Turing is most well-known for his work in breaking the code behind Germany's Enigma machine during World War II, and his untimely death due to the utterly reprehensible persecution of homosexuality during the 1950s, but his contributions to theoretical biology are no less significant.

Turing wondered if a simple **chemical mechanism** that operated at the level of *individual cells* could produce the *global multicellular patterns* observed in animals such as the intricate coat patterns of leopards and the stripes of zebras. This is very similar in conceptual spirit to the Lindenmayer systems we just described in the previous chapter. Turing first imagined a single **differentiated** cell that secreted just *two chemicals, or* **morphogens**, that would diffuse into the neighborhood of that cell, as in Figure 16-1.

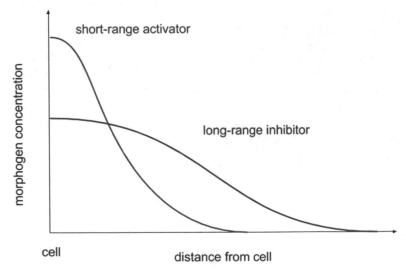

Figure 16-1. *Concentration gradients of the two morphogens underlying Turing patterns*

1. A **short-range activator** that diffused away from the source cell, but be eliminated very quickly (due to decay), so that there would be a high concentration of the activator very close to the cell, but much less further away

2.   A **long-range inhibitor** that would also diffuse from the source
     cell, but would be eliminated much more slowly, so that the
     concentration would be lower than the activator near the source
     cell, but would remain present much further away from the cell

He further imagined that the *relative amounts* of the activating and inhibiting
morphogens would determine whether neighboring cells would, in turn, *differentiate*
and initiate *their own* secretion of the two morphogens (this is the reason that they are
called activator and inhibitor in the first place). The interplay of the chemical diffusion
process in two dimensions produced patterns that were strikingly similar to animal
coats. Turing deployed some heavy-duty partial differential equations to model this
process, but luckily for us, there is a much simpler and more generative approach that
captures the essential dynamics that Turing described: that is the cellular automata.

A cellular automata (or **CA**) is a *two-dimensional lattice of objects*, normally known
as "cells," which have a state that is affected by its neighboring "cells" through a series of
update rules (we shall discuss more of these in Chapter 18 on agent-based modeling).
(Note that calling them "cells" is normally just a convenient metaphor, but in our
particular case, we are treating them as *actual cells* that are part of a multicellular matrix
of cells that make up a tissue.) At each timestep of the simulation, every cell in the
CA consults its immediate neighbors and updates its state as a function of the state of
those neighbors. These update rules form the heart of our implementation of Turing's
diffusion scheme.

Cellular Automata Initialize!

As usual, let's dive straight into the Python code in Listing 16-1, and we'll explain the
dynamics as we go.

Listing 16-1. Setting up the cellular automata

```
from numpy import zeros
from numpy.random import random, seed
seed()
probability_of_black = 0.5
width = 100
height = 100
```

```
# initialize cellular automata (CA)
CA = zeros([height, width])        # main CA
next_CA = zeros([height, width]) # CA next timestep
activator_radius = 1
activator_weight = 1
inhibitor_radius = 5
inhibitor_weight = -0.1
time = 0
```

We start by importing the needed numpy (zeros) and numpy.random (random and seed) libraries and then set the random seed. We then define the probability that any given cell in the two-dimensional (2D) array is **black** (i.e., *differentiated*) with probability_of_black. To keep with the leopard theme, we imagine all non-black cells (i.e., *undifferentiated* cells) as being **orange**. We then create *two* 2D cellular automata:

1. CA is the current cellular automata state: When we run the model, we will *read* from this array of cells when doing updates.

2. next_CA is the state of the cellular automata at the *next* timestep, during the updates we will *write* to this cellular automata.

Updates done in this way are sometimes referred to as *synchronous* because every cell CA is updated at a *single* time. Each CA is essentially a two-dimensional matrix (also called a two-dimensional array), and we use another NumPy library feature, zeros(),[1] to create these matrices. zeros() creates empty *matrices* with the dimensions specified in the list [height, width]. (This is a very useful function, because it can also be used to create a one-dimensional *array* which will come in handy when storing large numbers of points for plotting in later chapters.)

We next define the *radius* of the *activator* (this corresponds to maximum distance away that the activating chemical will diffuse, by default we set it at just 1, so only the nearest 9 neighbor cells are considered) and the *weight* of this activating chemical. Then we define the maximum *inhibitor radius* (note that this takes into account all cells that are within a 5x5 grid from the currently activated) and the *weight* of the inhibitor (we set it to be negative so it is clear down from the activator). Lastly, we set the time to zero.

---

[1]http://docs.scipy.org/doc/numpy/reference/generated/numpy.zeros.html

We next initialize the CA by looping through the dimensions and then assigning each cell to be randomly differentiated or undifferentiated using our old friend, the random() function. Here is the code fragment in Listing 16-2.

Listing 16-2. Initializing the cellular automata

```
# initialize the CA
for x in range(width):
  for y in range(height):
    if random() < probability_of_black:
     cell_state = 1
    else:
      cell_state = 0
  CA[y, x] = cell_state
```

By convention, we consider all cells with a state of **1** as **black** (and differentiated) and cells state with state **0** as **orange** (and *un*differentiated). In Figure 16-2 we show a randomly initialized cellular automata.

Figure 16-2. *Randomly initialized cellular automata*

Creating Update Rules

With everything set up now, we are ready to dive into the guts of the biology and start actually simulating development in the simulation_step function. The basic idea is that we loop through every cell in the lattice of the automata as we did earlier and decide whether each cell will differentiate or dedifferentiate. Listing 16-3 shows the function for the simulation step.

Listing 16-3. Simulation function to advance the cellular automata by one timestep

```
def simulation_step(CA, next_CA):

  for x in range(width):
    for y in range(height):
      cell_state = CA[y, x]  # get current state

      activating_cells = 0
      inhibiting_cells = 0
      # count the number of inhibiting cells within the radius
      for xpos in range(- inhibitor_radius, inhibitor_radius + 1):
       for ypos in range(- inhibitor_radius, inhibitor_radius + 1):
                inhibiting_cells += CA[(y+ypos)%height, (x+xpos)%width]
      # count the number of activating cells within the radius
      for xpos in range(- activator_radius, activator_radius + 1):
        for ypos in range(- activator_radius, activator_radius + 1):
                activating_cells += CA[(y+ypos)%height, (x+xpos)%width]
      # if weighted sum of activating cells is greater than inhibiting
      # cells in neighbourhood we induce differentiation in the current cell
    if (activating_cells * activator_weight) + (inhibiting_cells *
    inhibitor_weight) > 0:
          cell_state = 1
        else:
          cell_state = 0
      # now update the state
      next_CA[y, x] = cell_state
    return next_CA
```

The first part is pretty straightforward, we loop through the **x** and **y** coordinates of the cellular automaton lattice and retrieve the current cell_state at x and y. The next two (inner) for loop is where the two inhibition and activation *act* on that current cell. Let's break this down:

1. ***Inhibition loop***: The first loop examines all the cells within a radius of inhibition_radius of the current cell. This loop counts the cells that appear **black** – that is, those cells that currently have the chemical inhibitor close enough to the current cell to affect it. The more cells that are black within that neighborhood, the more inhibition will affect the current cell (tending to switch it off to the **orange** state). Let's take our original CA as shown in Figure 16-2 and highlight the cells that can potentially contribute to inhibition by a light blue overlay for the case when inhibition_radius is 5 as shown in Figure 16-3.

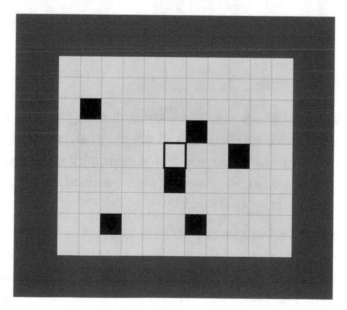

Figure 16-3. *Inhibition range*

In this particular example, there are *six* cells that will affect the state of the current cell, and thus inhibiting_cells will be set to 6 at this timestep.

2. ***Activator loop***: Similarly, the second loop examines all the cells within a radius of `activator_radius` of the current cell, shown in Figure 16-4 in light red.

Figure 16-4. *Activator range*

Again, the more cells that are black within that neighborhood, the more the activating chemical will affect the current cell, but in contrast to the previous case, it will tend to switch the cell on and thus become **black**. In the preceding case, we have two cells, and therefore `activating_cells = 2`.

3. ***The decision***: The last step after the two loops is to make the decision as to whether cell should become orange or black. We do this in code by weighting the sum of activating the cells and adding it to the weighted sum of the inhibiting cells. In our code example, this sum is

$$(2 \times 1) + (-0.1 \times 6) = 2 - 0.6 = 1.4 > 0$$

Because this sum is positive in this example, then there is enough activator to cause the cell to become **black** and thus set `cell_state` to 1. If this sum was negative, it would be set to 0. Biologically this implements the main feature of Turing's morphogenesis model that if there is, on balance, more activating than inhibiting chemicals in the neighborhood, then the cell will differentiate, or dedifferentiate if not.

4. **The update**: OK, we're almost (but not quite!) done. We have to *write* the output to the appropriate location in the next_CA cellular automata. This is a crucial point: we can't write to the original CA lattice until every cell has been updated, otherwise we have what computer scientists like to call a "*race condition.*"

5. **Returning the new CA**: Once every cell has been updated, and we have our freshly written next_CA, the last thing that simulation_step does is to return this next_CA to the main program. We leave the actual update to the next section.

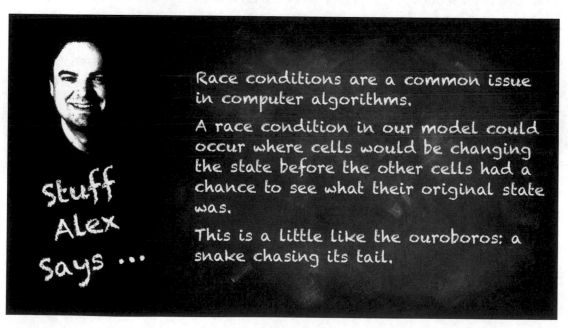

Stuff Alex Says ...

Race conditions are a common issue in computer algorithms.

A race condition in our model could occur where cells would be changing the state before the other cells had a chance to see what their original state was.

This is a little like the ouroboros: a snake chasing its tail.

Generating the Cellular Automata Coat Patterns

Now we are ready to plot the output of our simulation and run some morphogenesis! We can use our matplotlib skills in Listing 16-4.

Listing 16-4. Visualizing morphogenesis using matplotlib

```
# create plot
fig1 = plt.figure()
# loop through times
for time in range(10):
    plt.pcolor(CA, vmin = 0, vmax = 1, cmap = "copper_r")  # plot current CA
    plt.axis('image')
    plt.title('time: ' + str(time))
    plt.draw()
    plt.pause(0.5)
    CA = simulation_step(CA, next_CA)  # advance the simulation
```

As usual we set up the plot using the figure() function, then we loop through ten timesteps of the model, plotting new figure each time. For the plot itself, we use the pcolor[2] matplotlib function; this takes a NumPy array and a particular colormap (cmap) to plot a heat map of the cellular automata states. The particular colormap we use is "copper_r" which ranges over colors from orange to black, giving, you guessed it, a leopard skin pattern. And since our CA only has two states: when the cell state is 0 it shows up as **orange**, and when it is 1 it displays **black**.

This is followed by calls to axis(), title(), draw(), and pause(). Note that we use the draw() command followed by the pause() command rather show() as we did in previous examples because it will cause the code to stop. This way the current **CA** at each timestep of the simulation is displayed for 0.5 seconds before the next timestep.

At the end of the for loop, before we move to the next timestep, we call the simulation_step(). Here we give as function parameters the current CA and the next_CA. Crucially, we assign the result of the simulation_step back to CA. *This* is the synchronous update step we mentioned earlier, passing the baton to the next timestep: the *written* now becomes the *read*.

---

[2]http://matplotlib.org/examples/pylab_examples/pcolor_demo.html

Morphogenesis in Action

Let's see this in action.... We start with a random grid of an equal number of blacks and oranges at *t=0*. You can see in Figure 16-5 that even in the first *t=1* timestep that structure is beginning to emerge.

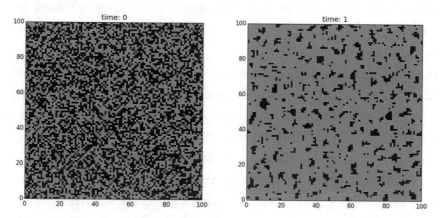

Figure 16-5. *First two timesteps of morphogenesis simulation*

As you see in Figure 16-6, by *t=2*, we are already seeing those leopard skin pants! And by *t=5* the pattern has already stabilized.

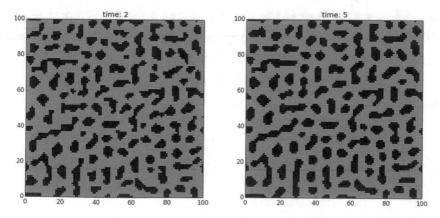

Figure 16-6. *Later timesteps of morphogenesis simulation*

We encourage you to play around with grid size and the relative radii and weights of the activator and inhibitor strength to generate your own coat patterns. You will find the full code that concatenates Listings 16-1 to 16-4 into a single file in either the code download provided with this book or our GitHub site (as described in Chapter 1).

By about now the died-in-the-wool bench biologist might be wondering, well this all seems a little *abstract*. Real embryos don't develop in these discrete timesteps and are there any examples in actual nature where real cells secrete chemicals that interact in any kind of way like this?

In a twist of history, in 2012, exactly 60 years later, a research team published a paper (Müller, 2012) that experimentally verified Turing's mechanism in zebrafish embryos. They were able to identify and quantify two morphogens in the generation of embryonic patterns in the zebrafish that corresponded to Turing's proposed mechanism and measure the rate constants that mapped back to the original equations. They also built a model (a little more complicated than that presented here) that recapitulated the patterns found in the experimental organism, closing the loop between theoretical prediction and experimental verification. Although the CA model here is still an approximation of the original Turing equations, and at the risk of banging you over the head again, it's an indication that even simple models implemented in just a few lines of Python can be powerful tools for building intuitions into fundamental processes in developmental biology. Computational developmental biology has become an active areas of research; see the references in this chapter, as well as in Chapter 15.

We now move on from looking at biological processes such as development which occur *within individual organisms*. The next few chapters (Chapters 17–19) will be devoted to using Python to computationally explore the dynamics of *population of multiple organisms*.

References and Further Exploration

- James D. Murray (1988). How the leopard gets its spots.[3] *Scientific American*, **258**, 80–87

- Turing (1952). The chemical basis of morphogenesis.[4] *Philosophical Transactions of the Royal Society of London B: Biological Sciences*, **237**, 37–72

- Forgacs and Newman, *Biological physics of the developing embryo*[5] (Cambridge University Press, 2005)

- Müller *et al.* (2012). Differential Diffusivity of Nodal and Lefty Underlies a Reaction-Diffusion Patterning System.[6] *Science*, **336**, 721–724

---

[3]www.math.ttu.edu/~lallen/murray_SciAm.pdf
[4]http://rstb.royalsocietypublishing.org/content/237/641/37
[5]www.cambridge.org/catalogue/catalogue.asp?isbn=9780521783378
[6]www.ncbi.nlm.nih.gov/pmc/articles/PMC3525670/

CHAPTER 17

Foxes Guarding Henhouses

Ecological Modeling with Predator-Prey Dynamics

"Why are you crying Mock Turtle?" asked Alice.

"Do you have any idea what it's like to be a combination of different animals that get preyed upon?" sniffed the Mock Turtle forlornly. *"I have people who'd like to eat me for my pork, and giant hungry seabirds who would snatch me from the water's edge and make a snack of me if I didn't watch my back."*

"That sounds simply horrid," said Alice sympathetically.

"Well speaking as one mythical, hybrid organism to another, I can't say that I've ever really been bothered about being a mashup," pontificated the Griffin in his most dismissive and condescending tone.

"Well that's easy for you to say," retorted the Mock Turtle, *"You're a combination of the kind of predators that don't have to worry about whose lunch they're going to be!"*

"Well excuse me for not being a basement dweller on the food chain!" said the Griffin huffily.

"Bloodthirsty beast!" snapped the Mock Turtle.

"Walking salad bar!" retorted the Griffin.

`max()`, `matplotlib.animation`, *tuple unpacking*, `numpy`

Ecology, ecosystems, population dynamics, boom-bust, discrete model, predator-prey, carrying capacity, state space, Lotka-Volterra model

---

© Alexander Lancaster and Gordon Webster 2019
A. Lancaster and G. Webster, *Python for the Life Sciences*, https://doi.org/10.1007/978-1-4842-4523-1_17

The next level "up" from the individual organism is the ecosystem: organisms interacting with each other and their environment. In any real ecosystem, the number of individuals of any species is constantly changing as individuals give birth, and die. Obviously the growth of any population of organisms is also limited by the amount of resources available, and ultimately by a theoretical upper limit beyond which there be dragons, known as the "carrying capacity." And if those "resources" are in turn another species, then more's the pity for that species. While the old aphorism of "nature, red in tooth and claw" is an oversimplification, in many cases, the increase in the number of a "prey" species may mean more dinner for a "predator." It works both ways, however: if the predators start to eat all the prey, then it might be time for the predators to go on a diet, lest they start starving themselves.

Ecological population dynamics is the field that studies the interactions of species and the growth and change in populations. The modeling of population dynamics is growing in relevance beyond its origins in organismal ecology (although it is still very important there too!) into the study of population dynamics at the cellular or molecular level in diseases such as cancer and infectious diseases such as viruses. So biologists of all stripes are well-advised to learn more about population dynamics. There are also many other applications of population dynamics outside biology, from the growth and bust of economic bubbles to the rise (and fall) of social networks. When you start looking around and seeing how things rise and fall (from your favorite band), and maybe rise again, in popularity you can be sure that some form of population dynamics is driving it.

Python is again well-placed to help you model and visualize population dynamics with an elegant sufficiency of code. The staple of ecological models is the concept of a "predator-prey": a single species of **predator** and a single species of **prey**. While this may be a gross oversimplification of a full ecosystem with many species, the basic structure of predator-prey model can be viewed as a nice conceptual "building block" for more complex models. Many of the dynamics in full ecosystems are recapitulated in-the-small in the predator-prey model.

So let's just dive in by imagining a population of **chickens** in a backyard that are being preyed on by a nearby population of **foxes** which are camping out nearby in the woods. We set up the model in Listing 17-1 by keeping track of the number of both species over a specified number of generations using a Python NumPy array. For brevity in the code, we use "Ch" for chickens and "Fx" for foxes. Here we use the NumPy zeros() function (which we first met in Chapter 16) to create arrays that store the number of species at each time point. The main difference between the previous use of zeros is we are creating *one-dimensional arrays* rather than *two-dimensional arrays* which only require a *single* integer argument rather than a *list* of dimensions.

Listing 17-1. Initializing and running the chicken and foxes ecological model

```python
import numpy as np
generations = 5000
# setup empty arrays
Ch = np.zeros(generations+1)
Fx = np.zeros(generations+1)
# initialize the population
Ch[0] = 100.0
Fx[0] = 10.0

b_Ch = 0.5    # prey birth rate
d_Ch = 0.015 # predation rate (death rate of prey)
b_Fx = 0.015    # predator birth rate
d_Fx = 0.5      # predator death rate

# set parameters
dt = 0.01    # scale parameters so that timestep doesn't "jump"

for t in range(0, generations):
  Ch[t+1] = Ch[t]        + dt * (b_Ch * Ch[t]  - d_Ch * Fx[t] * Ch[t])
  Fx[t+1] = Fx[t]        + dt * (-d_Fx * Fx[t]   + b_Fx * Fx[t] * Ch[t])
```

We first create the arrays and initialize the population sizes. Next, we set up the rest of model parameters. To start with, we define a number of parameters to control the rate at which both the predators and prey are **born** (indicated by the prefix "b_") or **die** (prefix "d_"). This model uses discrete timesteps that we first introduced in Chapter 13. This is in keeping with our philosophy of introducing problems using direct simulation approaches. We therefore need to introduce a timestep size – dt –the reasons for which will be explained shortly.

Toward the end of Listing 17-1, we run the model, the code for which, you'll note, is just ***three lines!*** And that's the whole model. We then simply loop through the number of generations, each new generation (t+1) updating based on the value of the generation before (t). For both chickens and foxes, we start with the current number of each species and **add** to that number (through births) and **subtract** (through deaths) for each species.

The number of chickens ***born*** (the first term in the equation b_Ch * Ch[t]) is only dependent on the number of *current* chickens (this assumes an infinite amount of food). However, the number of chickens that ***die*** depends on the number of foxes: more predators means more chicken deaths... oh the horror, the horror! This means that for chicken deaths, there will be an *interaction term* between the number of each species; we therefore multiply the death rate (d_Ch) by both the current number of foxes (Fx[t]) and the current number of chickens (Ch[t]).

The situation is exactly reversed for the foxes. Foxes will ***die*** at their natural rate (nothing keeping these foxes alive other than those pesky chickens!); hence, we multiply d_Fx by Fx[t]. But the rate at which new foxes are ***born*** will depend on the number of prey around, so in that case, we multiply the birth rate of foxes (b_Fx) by both the number of foxes (Fx[t]) and the number of chickens (Ch[t]).

To make it 100% clear what part of the sum means what, we add comments to the code:

```
for t in range(0, generations):
              # old prey    +    newly born prey    -   killed prey
   Ch[t+1] = Ch[t]          + dt * (b_Ch * Ch[t]   - d_Ch * Fx[t] * Ch[t])
              # old predators    -   predator death    +   births of predators
   Fx[t+1] = Fx[t]          + dt * (-d_Fx * Fx[t]      +  b_Fx * Fx[t] * Ch[t])
```

stuff
Alex
Says ...

Commenting your code is an excellent practice to get into when doing any kind of programming.

If you ever plan on sharing your code with other programmers, or having somebody else maintain it in the future, you need to make it readable and understandable.

And as we've said before in this book, always remember that this future programmer might even be you!

As alluded to earlier, the one final wrinkle is that because we are doing **discrete** time intervals, we introduce a timestep size: dt. This scales the number of both new births and deaths by the timescale in question (each generation may represent a smaller timestep), hence the reason it is outside the brackets in the preceding code, and ensures the simulation numbers change smoothly.

Seeing the Boom and Bust

Now the hard work of the simulation is done, as in previous chapters, in Listing 17-2, we turn to **matplotlib** to plot the output.

Listing 17-2. Plotting simulation output using matplotlib

```
# do the plotting
# get the maximum of the population so we can scale window properly
popMax = max(max(Fx), max(Ch))
fig1 = plt.figure()
plt.xlim(0, generations)
plt.ylim(0, popMax)
plt.xlabel('time')
plt.ylabel('population count')
time_points = list(range(generations + 1))
plt.plot(time_points, Fx, label="Foxes")
plt.plot(time_points, Ch, label="Chickens")
plt.legend()
plt.draw()
plt.show()
```

Altogether the code is shown in Listing 17-3.

Listing 17-3. Complete code for model and visualization

```
import numpy as np
from matplotlib import pylab as plt
import matplotlib.animation as animation
```

```
generations = 5000
# setup empty arrays
Fx = np.zeros(generations+1)
Ch = np.zeros(generations+1)

# initialize the population
Ch[0] = 100.0
Fx[0] = 10.0

# set the parameters
dt = 0.01      # scale parameters so that each timestep doesn't "jump"

b_Ch = 0.5      # prey birth rate
d_Ch = 0.015    # predation rate (death rate of prey)
b_Fx = 0.015    # predator birth rate
d_Fx = 0.5      # predator death rate

# run predator-prey!
for t in range(0, generations):
            # old prey + newly born prey - killed prey
   Ch[t+1] = Ch[t] + dt * (b_Ch * Ch[t] - d_Ch * Fx[t] * Ch[t])
            # old predators - predator death + births of predators
   Fx[t+1] = Fx[t] + dt * (-d_Fx * Fx[t] + b_Fx * Fx[t] * Ch[t])

# do the plotting
# get the maximum of the population so we can scale window properly
popMax = max(max(Fx), max(Ch))
fig1 = plt.figure()
plt.xlim(0, generations)
plt.ylim(0, popMax)
plt.xlabel('time')
plt.ylabel('population count')
time_points = list(range(generations + 1))
plt.plot(time_points, Fx, label="Foxes")
plt.plot(time_points, Ch, label="Chickens")
plt.legend()
plt.draw()
plt.show()
```

Running the code in Listing 17-3 should produce something that looks like Figure 17-1, showing a number of cycles as the populations of the chickens and foxes begin to interact. Note that as the number of chickens increases from its initial number of 100, the number of foxes rapidly catches up as there is more yummy prey around! This halts the growth of the chickens at around 120, and the number of chickens starts to fall. But now, as there are not as many delicious chickens running around, the foxes start to have a hard time, this gives time for the chicken population to recover, and the cycle starts again.

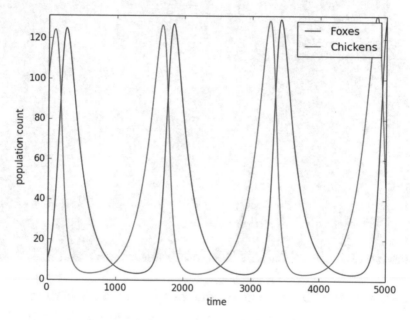

Figure 17-1. *Visualization of predator-prey model*

Figure 17-1 shows the classic cyclic pattern of boom and bust that occurs in most predator-prey models, where two species are involved in an ongoing "dance". It has been widely applied to many other biological entities such as virus populations and has applications outside biology. The cyclic nature of the pattern makes one wonder if there might be an even better way to visualize what is going on than two rising and falling time series.

Animating Predator-Prey

It turns out there is! This is because it is an example of a dynamical system that can be viewed as a point that moves around in a two-dimensional state space. The path that the system follows over time through this space is known as a **trajectory**. Depending on where the system starts, it will follow a different trajectory.

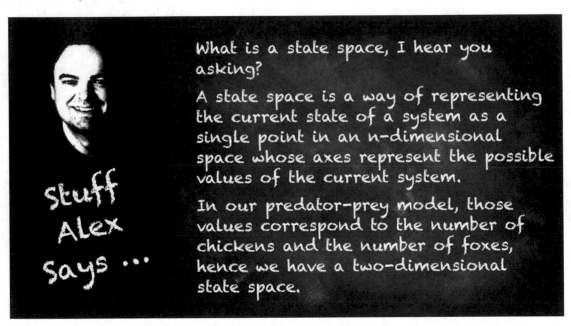

Again, the **matplotlib** library comes to the rescue, via the use of the animation subpackage (we somewhat gave this away by showing the import in Listing 17-3). More details on the animation package are available in the matplotlib documentation.[1]

Listing 17-4. Animating the state space

```
fig2 = plt.figure()

plt.plot(Ch, Fx, 'g-', alpha=0.2)  # state space
plt.xlabel('Chickens (prey population size)')
plt.ylabel('Foxes (predator population size)')
line, = plt.plot(Ch[0], Fx[0], 'r.', markersize=10) # draw point as red
```

---

[1]http://matplotlib.org/api/animation_api.html

```
def init():
  line.set_data([], [])  # set empty data
  return line,

def animate(i):
  line.set_xdata(Ch[i])
  line.set_ydata(Fx[i])
  return line,

ani = animation.FuncAnimation(fig2, animate, range(0, len(time_points)),
init_func=init, interval=25, blit=False)
plt.show()
```

Let's go through this step by step. We first set up the overall figure as before and then plot the state space. This is fairly simple, we simply plot the number of chickens (Ch) against the number of foxes (Fx), rather than as a function of time. 'g-' indicates a solid (-) green (g) line, and alpha sets the transparency of the line, so that it appears as slightly faded. Labels for the axes are then added. To add the initial point in the trajectory on the state space plot, we plot the first time point, which is the x-y position: Ch[0], Fx[0], like so:

```
line, = plt.plot(Ch[0], Fx[0], 'r.', markersize=10)
```

But the assignment to the variable points requires a little more explanation. The plot command always returns a tuple (see Chapter 3 for more on tuples) containing a list of all the lines in the plot. Because this particular plot only has *one* line, we do something called **tuple unpacking** on the line to get the *first* element in the list (for more details, see the tutorial in the matplotlib documentation[2]).

We then set up two helper functions for doing the animation:

1. init() creates the base frame that animation will "rest" upon by returning a line object that can be updated by the next function.

2. animate() takes as input an integer **i** with the current timestep of the simulation. This function updates the line frame created in the init() function which has the effect of moving the red dot using the functions set_xdata and set_ydata, thus updating the position of the system in the overall state space.

---

[2]http://matplotlib.org/users/pyplot_tutorial.html#controlling-line-properties

The final piece actually *runs* the animation by calling the `animation.FuncAnimation` and passing in the parameters: `fig2`, the range of `time_points` over which the animation will run (effectively move the red dot through the state space), and the two functions described in the preceding text to initialize and then update the animation. A final invocation of `plt.show()` shows the graph.

If you take the full code in Listing 17-3 and append in the code in Listing 17-4, then run it. It should generate a plot that looks like the one shown in Figure 17-2, except the red dot will start in the bottom middle and start spiraling outward. We can now see clearly the cyclic nature of the system in one glance, taking in the complete trajectory.

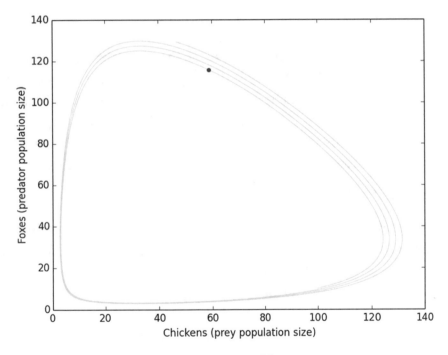

Figure 17-2. *Visualization of the chickens and foxes state space*

The astute reader will have noticed that the trajectory is unstable, that is, it doesn't converge to a stable circle, but starts to spiral slightly outward in each iteration. If you increase the number of generations, you will start to see the spiral go out even further (with corresponding increases in amplitude in the time-series plots). This instability is due to the fact that we are dealing in *discrete* timesteps, which implicitly introduces a *time lag* in the simulation. This lag can be reduced by making the dt parameter even smaller, reducing the time lag and making the simulation more smooth. But to do this requires moving to the *continuous* version of the model using the Lotka-Volterra differential equations, we link to an example that uses the SciPy library to solve the equations in the reference section.

The next chapter builds upon the notion of modeling population dynamics using integer numbers of individuals, but goes one step further: modeling *the individuals themselves* as discrete, unique, agents.

References and Further Exploration

- Roughgarden, *Primer of Ecological Theory*[3] (Prentice Hall, 1997). Good primer on ecological and population genetics with coding examples. We'll forgive Roughgarden's use of SPlus, given that Python (or R) didn't yet exist at the time of writing.

- Edelstein-Keshet, *Mathematical Models in Biology*[4] (Siam, 2004). Classic text on traditional mathematical modeling in biology and ecology, short on the stochastic models

- Example Python code solving the Lotka-Volterra equations using SciPy[5]

---

[3]www.pearsonhighered.com/program/Roughgarden-Primer-of-Ecological-Theory/PGM148871.html
[4]http://epubs.siam.org/doi/book/10.1137/1.9780898719147
[5]www.gribblelab.org/compneuro/2_Modelling_Dynamical_Systems.html#orgheadline6

CHAPTER 18

A Virtual Flu Epidemic

Exploring Epidemiology with Agent-Based Models

In time the Mock Turtle and the Griffin resolved their differences. The Mock Turtle apologized for calling the Griffin a bloodthirsty beast, and the Griffin apologized for calling the Mock Turtle a walking salad bar.

"I think we can both agree that it's no picnic being a hybrid organism," said the Griffin. "Er – no pun intended there," he added hastily for fear that he might have upset the Mock Turtle again with his poor choice of words.

"Many a true word spoken on a desolate rocky shore my cat-bird friend," said the Mock Turtle sagely.

"Well you guys do have one big advantage!" said Alice suddenly. "Hybrid vigor."

"What's that?" asked the Mock Turtle.

"Organisms with a richer and more diverse genetic repertoire like hybrids," said Alice, "are often less susceptible to diseases that can run rampant through a genetically homogeneous population."

"What a nerd!" exclaimed the Griffin, clumsily disguising his words with a fake sneeze.

"Are you coming down with something?" asked Alice.

 pop(), *Python classes,* **numpy.random** *module*

 Epidemiology, influenza, SIR model, agent-based model, epidemic, pandemic

© Alexander Lancaster and Gordon Webster 2019
A. Lancaster and G. Webster, *Python for the Life Sciences*, https://doi.org/10.1007/978-1-4842-4523-1_18

The flu appears every year, and it would be nice if there was some way of modeling the dynamics of what happens in broad outlines. Well, never fear, dear reader, we have just the model. **SIR**! In this chapter we will introduce the SIR model, which stands for susceptible–infectious–recovered, a basic conceptual model in the fields of epidemiology, public health, and virology, among others. It will also allow us to introduce the idea of an agent-based model or **ABM** *in which individual entities have their own unique identity within the model.* This is distinct from simply modeling *the aggregate number of individuals* as we did in the previous chapter on predator-prey dynamics (Chapter 17).

Agent-based models are a powerful methodology that have been used to model complex phenomena across science from the stock market to sociology, but have deep roots in biology, particularly in ecology (where they are sometimes referred to as **individual based models**). Many presentations of agent-based models emphasize the complexity, or use of existing ABM packages, but our approach in this chapter is to start with a very simple all-Python agent-based model as jumping off point for adding the richer dynamics that ABM allows.

SIR Model: Susceptible–Infectious–Recovered

The basic idea behind the SIR model of infectious disease is that we have a population of individuals, each of which can exist in one of several possible states: **susceptible–infectious–recovered**. At any given time, an individual will be in **one** of those three states and will progress from an initial *susceptible* state through to being *infectious* and then will eventually die, or *recover*. Typically, it is assumed that a disease is introduced into a population in just *one* individual (the infamous ***patient zero***) and that the population is "well mixed," that is, there is a random chance of any particular susceptible individual being infected by patient zero. Once all these conditions are set up, we want to know what's the overall disease progression. In other words, how will the numbers of each kind of patient rise and fall over the course of the "flu season"? As mentioned earlier, this model can be built with deterministic mathematics, but as we have seen before, nature is often not built that way...

Not-So-Secret Agents

Okay, so this is cool, but what's *agent-based modeling* got to do with it? Well, as we have seen before, many kinds of biological systems are fundamentally *noisy*, because outcomes are sometimes dependent on just a few copies of a gene, or few individual organisms. Agent-based models build on this insight of keeping track of the discrete number of individuals, but take it one step further by allowing each agent to have its own *internal* unique properties. Normally we refer to this property as the **agent state**, and we also allow these states to be affected by other aspects of the world they live in, that is, they have **agent behaviors**.

Perhaps the best thing to do then is to just jump straight in by rolling up our virtual Python sleeves and see what this looks like in code. Let's start by looking at the lowest level of the model, the individual patient. Without further ado, in Listing 18-1 we present the Patient class.

Listing 18-1. Patient: a simple agent class in Python

```python
class Patient():
  # default state is susceptible
  def __init__(self, state = 'susceptible'): self.state = state
  def infect(self): self.state = 'infected'
  def recover(self): self.state = 'recovered'
```

You'll notice straight away by the use of the class keyword that we are using our object-oriented programming skills we developed back in Chapter 7. Here we have just one instance variable "state," which is, surprise surprise, used to keep track of how the patient is feeling. Let's break down these *agent behaviors*:

1. We initialize each instance of the patient object in the
   __init__ method by passing in a string representing the state.
   We also provide the default keyword for state as susceptible,
   because in most cases that's what we'll be wanting to create at the
   beginning of the simulation (but note that it can be overridden).

2. Next we have a method infect that changes the state to infected.
   Yep, never would have predicted that.

3. Last, we have the method recover, which, you guessed, makes
   the agent recover!

Yes, it's as simple as it looks, and although it might seem a little more than a wrapper, it sets up the ability to make complicated agents further down the track, and it makes the important cognitive leap in the modeler's mind that we are firmly focused on modeling *individual* agents.

Agent Lists: Keeping Agents on the Straight and Narrow

The next thing we need to do when managing a population of patients is to be able to manage them as a collection. This is the purpose of the `PatientList` class shown in Listing 18-2. It serves the purpose of managing all the individual agents, as well as keeping up to date *global properties* of the collection of agents, such as how many of each agent type are there at any given moment.

Listing 18-2. PatientList: a class to manage a collection of agents

```python
class PatientList():
  # create lists for each type of agents
  def __init__(self):
   self.susceptible_agents = []
   self.infected_agents = []
   self.recovered_agents = []

  def append(self, agent):
    if agent.state == 'susceptible': self.susceptible_agents.append(agent)
    elif agent.state == 'infected': self.infected_agents.append(agent)
    elif agent.state == 'recovered': self.recovered_agents.append(agent)
    else: print("error: must be one of the three valid states")

  def infect(self):
    shuffle(self.susceptible_agents) # shuffle list to random order
    patient = self.susceptible_agents.pop() # remove patient from list
    patient.infect()
    self.append(patient) # move to the appropriate list
```

```python
def recover(self):
  shuffle(self.infected_agents)
  patient = self.infected_agents.pop()
  patient.recover()
  self.append(patient)

def get_num_susceptible(self):
    return len(self.susceptible_agents)

def get_num_infected(self):
  return len(self.infected_agents)

def get_num_recovered(self):
  return len(self.recovered_agents)

def get_num_total(self):
    return len(self.susceptible_agents)+len(self.infected_agents)+ \
    len(self.recovered_agents)
```

The basic idea here is that this class functions similar to a native Python list (e.g., it also has an append method), but has extra functions specific to our model such as infect and recover. (Note the code for this class is actually longer than it needs to be in principle, because we include extra error checking: this is very important and is in line with our earlier stated principles of building in robustness.) Let's break down the class:

- __init__ creates an instance of this class, with *instance variables* within the class with sublists of the three kinds of individuals (susceptible_agents, infected_agents, recovered_agents).

- append adds the already-created agents to the appropriate list type (the work of creating the agents is done in the main code). This includes some error checking to make sure that the state is valid. Note that we could simply have a single list with all agent types, but we would potentially need to scan the full list to find an agent of the appropriate type, by having separate lists we speed up the search.

- `infect` this method first shuffles the existing `susceptible_agents` list. We then use the `pop()`[1] method to get the individual agent to infect. Note that `pop()` both *returns* the agent beginning of the list and *removes* that agent from the list. We then `infect()` that individual agent and transfer it to the list of infected agents.

- `recover` has exactly the same structure as infect, except that it shuffles the infected agents and chooses a random infected agent, which is then instructed to recover itself, and again we transfer it to the list of recovered agents.

- `get_num_susceptible`, `get_num_infected`, `get_num_recovered`, `get_num_total`: These are pretty self-explanatory methods that return the different counts (as well as the total). It might seem like a little bit of overkill, but it's a generally good habit to get into when you're doing object-oriented programming: provide get functions for any internal states that can change over time. In addition, it saves us from having to use a bunch of `len()` functions all over the place.

Phew! So in 40 or so lines of Python (less if you exclude comments and spaces), we've set up the key data structures for our actual model. This setup will pay off when we write down the model itself, because we can express it in a very straightforward and intuitive manner. But before we do that, let's start with the initialization of the model, including all of the basic parameters and creation of the agents in Listing 18-3 (requires execution of the class definitions in Listings 18-1 and 18-2 prior to running this code).

Listing 18-3. Setting up the agent-based SIR model

```
beta = 0.09   # susceptibility rate
gamma = 0.05 # recovery rate
susceptible_count = 1000
infected_count = 1
recovered_count = 0
# lists to record output
S = []
I = []
```

---

[1]`https://docs.python.org/2/tutorial/datastructures.html`

```
R = []
t = []
time = 0.0
patients = PatientList()

# create the individuals patients
for indiv in range(susceptible_count):
    agent = Patient()       # by default all new patients are susceptible
    patients.append(agent) # add to list
for indiv in range(infected_count):
    agent = Patient(state='infected')
    patients.append(agent)
for indiv in range(recovered_count):
    agent = Patient(state='recovered')
    patients.append(agent)
```

We start with defining the key parameters of the SIR model: the **susceptibility rate** (β, represented in code by beta) – this is the rate at which susceptible patients can be infected by the disease – and the **recovery rate** (γ, gamma in code) – the rate at which an infected patient will recover. These are key parameters and also appear in the mathematical version of the model. The ratio between these values known as R_0 ($=\beta/\gamma$) can be thought of as the probability of the virus or disease spreading through the population. Fans of the 2011 movie *Contagion*[2] will remember that R_0 plays a key part of the plot. When $R_0 > 1$, a disease will spread through the population and become an epidemic, rather than die out, which makes sense intuitively: when the patients are infected at a higher rate than they can recover, then it is highly likely that the *whole* population will become infected. (In *Contagion*, the concern is that the epidemic becomes a pandemic, which is an epidemic that has crossed international borders.)

Next we initialize the number of susceptible individuals as being 2000, and one single individual infected individual (and at this point, there are no recovered individuals). We next add four empty lists S, I, R and t to record the number of individuals of each kind as well as the time points and then create the initial instance of PatientList, patients. Lastly, we then loop through each of the numbers and create individual agents representing each of the three agent types using the state = '<type-of-agent>' keyword and add them to patients.

---

[2]www.imdb.com/title/tt1598778/

Note that because we set up `Patient` and `PatientList` classes to be robust to the order of addition of agents, these can be done in any order, and even theoretically on the fly.

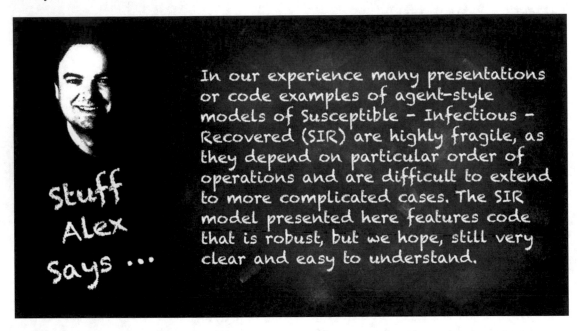

In our experience many presentations or code examples of agent-style models of Susceptible – Infectious – Recovered (SIR) are highly fragile, as they depend on particular order of operations and are difficult to extend to more complicated cases. The SIR model presented here features code that is robust, but we hope, still very clear and easy to understand.

Running the Epidemic

OK, now we're at the point where we can actually write down the model dynamics fairly compactly in Listing 18-4.

Listing 18-4. SIR model dynamics

```python
from random import shuffle
from numpy.random import random

while len(patients.infected_agents) > 0:
  for susc in range(patients.get_num_susceptible()):
    if random() < beta * (patients.get_num_infected()/  float(patients.
get_num_total())):
      patients.infect()  # infect patient
```

```
for infected in range(patients.get_num_infected()):
  if random() < gamma:
    patients.recover() # recover patient

# record values for plotting
t.append(time)
S.append(patients.get_num_susceptible())
I.append(patients.get_num_infected())
R.append(patients.get_num_recovered())

# update time
time += 1
```

With all of our hard work earlier, writing down model is fairly simple: as long as we have infected agents (the while conditional), we do a step of the simulation. The first item in the simulation is to *loop through all the patient agents that are still susceptible* and ask whether they should be infected or not. This decision is based on the ratio of the number of infected individuals *I* to the total population size *N* multiplied by the previously mentioned susceptibility parameter β. If the randomly chosen number is less than $\beta \times I/N$, then we infect the agent; otherwise we leave it alone. This effectively assumes that any susceptible individual agent is equally likely to bump into an infected agent or not. (If we wanted to explore other assumptions about the probability of infection of a given agent, this is where we could intervene to test other possibilities.) We then ask the list of agents to infect() a random patient.

The second item in the simulation *loops through all the patients that are infected* and asks whether one will recover. Similar to the infection step, we recover an agent with the probability γ and similarly call the list to recover() a random patient.

Astute observers will have noticed that all this looping can be inefficient and there are "better" ways to choose agents that don't depend on looping through these lists; in particular we could "jump" time forward in a way similar to the Gillespie algorithm we presented in Chapter 14. We are aware of this; however, we believe that in the interests of presenting a simple model, we gloss over these issues for the time being.

The last thing we do in the loop is to update the recorded numbers and time and increment the timestep. All of this recording of data should be very familiar to you now, as should be the following matplotlib commands which plot the final time courses in Listing 18-5.

Listing 18-5. Plotting the output of the SIR model

```
# plot output
import matplotlib.pyplot as plt

fig1 = plt.figure()
plt.xlim(0, max(t))
plt.ylim(0, susceptible_count+infected_count+recovered_count)
plt.xlabel('time')
plt.ylabel('# patients')
plt.plot(t, S,  label="S")
plt.plot(t, I,  label="I")
plt.plot(t, R,  label="R")
plt.legend()
plt.show()
```

If you run the final model, you should see something resembling Figure 18-1.

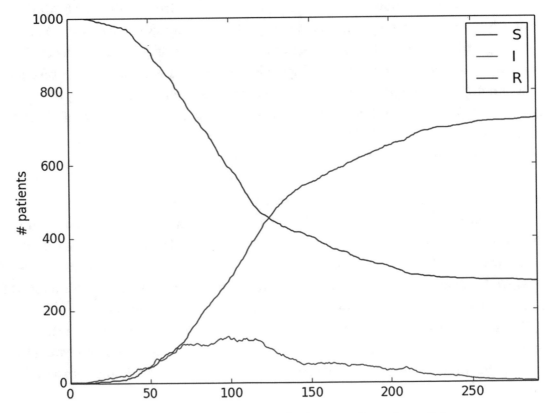

Figure 18-1. *Representative output run of SIR agent-based model*

Here you see the susceptible agents (**blue** line) becoming infected (**green** line), and in this particular run, they start to recover fairly quickly with the peak of the infection around about 100 timesteps. After about that time, all the agents becoming infected are recovering fairly rapidly (the **red** line). The infection then starts to run its course, with the number of new cases declining until around 300 timesteps, the infection has completely died out. In other runs you will see that the exact time that infection plateaus or dies out varies considerably. This reflects the reality of true epidemics, especially in smaller populations where the random nature of encounters can shift the duration of the epidemic. We saw this random nature in both the systems biology and ecological models we introduced earlier.

Note also that in some runs you may not see curves at all and the population may immediately crash. This is to be expected, because this is a stochastic simulation, there will always be some cases where the initially infected individual manages to recover *before* it spreads its infection to another.

Beefing up Your Agents

So far the agent-ness of the patients in the model hasn't played a very prominent role, largely they are a placeholder for the type of agent, in this sense they are very "thin" agents. However, with our setup, we can very easily add more biological wrinkles, and this is where the fun starts. We can ask very direct questions and implement them directly into code in a very intuitive way. Let's say we idly wonder what will happen if some of the time the recovered agents immediately become susceptible again.

One could go back to the mathematical formulations of alternative epidemiological models and re-derive an agent-based model from that, but there's nothing to stop us doing some modifications of the original SIR model directly. Think of it like an aftermarket car modification – shush – we won't tell the manufacturer if you don't. The Python modification is trivial; in Listing 18-6, we simply modify the agent class `Patient` and *nothing else.*

Listing 18-6. Modified Patient agent class

```python
class Patient():
  # default state is susceptible
  def __init__(self, state = 'susceptible'): self.state = state
  def infect(self): self.state = 'infected'
```

```
def recover(self):
  self.state = 'recovered'
  if random() < 0.8:
   print("switch back to susceptible")
   self.state = 'susceptible'
```

Once the state has been switched to recovered, we simply switch the state back to susceptible 80% of the time (0.8). As you might guess, this makes the infection persist a lot longer, with those "apparently" recovered patients, keep flipping back to becoming susceptible again. A typical run is shown in Figure 18-2.

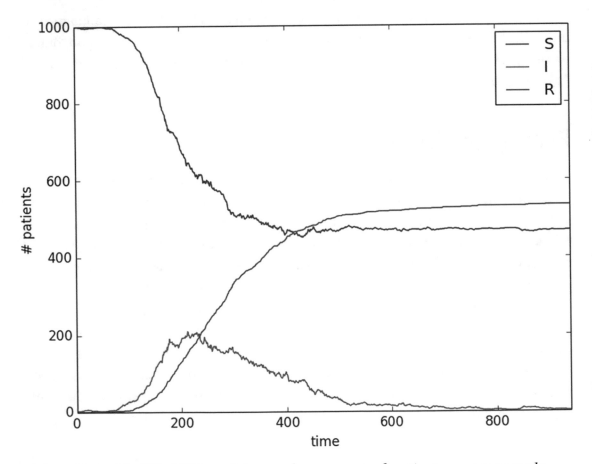

Figure 18-2. *Modified SIR model run where recovered patients spontaneously become susceptible again*

You'll notice that infection persists a *lot longer*, and the susceptible individuals line has a lot more noise, and wobbles around a lot more as recovered individuals become susceptible once more, rather than the smoothly decreasing line that we saw earlier. It's possible to make this change very easily in code, because we are using the object-oriented programming principle of ***information hiding***, the Patient class is fully self-contained with the state and behaviors, any change in behavior will propagate through the rest of the model requiring no other changes in code. Object-oriented programming is just made for the agent-based style of modeling.

In Listing 18-7 we show the full code for the model including the extra agent behavior.

Listing 18-7. Full code of modified SIR model

```python
from random import shuffle
from numpy.random import random
import matplotlib.pyplot as plt

class Patient():
  # default state is susceptible
  def __init__(self, state = 'susceptible'): self.state = state
  def infect(self): self.state = 'infected'
  def recover(self):
   self.state = 'recovered'
   if False:  # set to true to explore alternative model
     if random() < 0.8:
       self.state = 'susceptible'

class PatientList():
  # create lists for each type of agent
  def __init__(self):
    self.susceptible_agents = []
    self.infected_agents = []
    self.recovered_agents = []

  def append(self, agent):
    if agent.state == 'susceptible': self.susceptible_agents.append(agent)
    elif agent.state == 'infected': self.infected_agents.append(agent)
    elif agent.state == 'recovered': self.recovered_agents.append(agent)
    else: print("error: must be one of the three valid states")
```

```python
  def infect(self):
    shuffle(self.susceptible_agents)  # shuffle list to random order
    patient = self.susceptible_agents.pop() # remove patient from list
    patient.infect()
    self.append(patient)  # handle appropriate list

  def recover(self):
    shuffle(self.infected_agents)
    patient = self.infected_agents.pop()
    patient.recover()
    self.append(patient)

  def get_num_susceptible(self): return len(self.susceptible_agents)
  def get_num_infected(self): return len(self.infected_agents)
  def get_num_recovered(self): return len(self.recovered_agents)
  def get_num_total(self): return len(self.susceptible_agents)+len(self.
    infected_agents)+len(self.recovered_agents)

beta = 0.09  # susceptibility rate
gamma = 0.05 # recovery rate
susceptible_count = 1000
infected_count = 1
recovered_count = 0
S = [] # lists to record output
I = []
R = []
t = []
time = 0.0
patients = PatientList()

# create the individual patients
for indiv in range(susceptible_count):
  agent = Patient()       # by default all new patients are susceptible
  patients.append(agent) # add to list
for indiv in range(infected_count):
  agent = Patient(state='infected')
  patients.append(agent)
```

```python
for indiv in range(recovered_count):
    agent = Patient(state='recovered')
    patients.append(agent)

while patients.get_num_infected() > 0:
    for susc in range(patients.get_num_susceptible()):
        if random() < beta * (patients.get_num_infected() / \
                              float(patients.get_num_total())):
            patients.infect()  # infect patient
    for infected in range(patients.get_num_infected()):
        if random() < gamma:
            patients.recover() # recover patient

    t.append(time)# record values for plotting
    S.append(patients.get_num_susceptible())
    I.append(patients.get_num_infected())
    R.append(patients.get_num_recovered())

    time += 1 # update time

fig1 = plt.figure() # plot output
plt.xlim(0, max(t))
plt.ylim(0, susceptible_count+infected_count+recovered_count)
plt.xlabel('time')
plt.ylabel('# patients')
plt.plot(t, S,  label="S")
plt.plot(t, I,  label="I")
plt.plot(t, R,  label="R")
plt.legend()
plt.show()
```

In our example we show a simple tweak of a single method, but it illustrates a powerful point that agent-based models provide a very simple direct way of exploring your intuitions of how variation in individual biological entities within a system can affect global properties. And all with a fairly minimal amount of Python code. The last 20 years has produced an explosion of tools and frameworks to produce a wealth of highly sophisticated agent-based models, as well as research using those tools, which we encourage you to explore. But remember that the fundamentals of agent-based approaches can be grasped very easily in compact Python programs.

343

In the next and final chapter, we kick up the timescale a notch again: moving from **ecological** to **evolutionary** timescales. We'll move from using Python to model populations of individuals in which we don't include reproduction to modeling populations which change their genetic composition.

References and Further Exploration

- Grimm and Railsback, *Individual Based Modeling and Ecology*[3] (Princeton University Press, 2005)

- Railsback and Grimm, *Agent-based and Individual-based Modeling: A Practical Introduction*[4] (Princeton University Press, 2011)

- Project Mesa[5]: Python-based agent-based modeling environment

- pyAbm[6]: another Python-based agent-based modeling framework (in hibernation as of this writing)

- Swarm Development Group[7]: home to the original agent-based modeling toolkit, **Swarm**. One of the authors of this current book (AKL) was part of the original development team. The SDG is currently the custodian of the annual SwarmFest meeting that brings together modelers from all disciplines as well as tool developers including Swarm, NetLogo, RePast, and others.

- NetLogo[8]: descended from the original Logo system developed by Seymour Papert, NetLogo is an agent-based modeling toolkit with a large model library and active community.

- OpenABM (Open Agent Based Modeling) Consortium[9]: web site with details to theory, software, and models

---

[3]http://press.princeton.edu/titles/8108.html
[4]www.railsback-grimm-abm-book.com/
[5]https://github.com/projectmesa
[6]https://pypi.python.org/pypi/pyabm
[7]www.swarm.org/
[8]https://ccl.northwestern.edu/netlogo/
[9]www.openabm.org/

CHAPTER 19

Retracing Life's Footsteps

Evolutionary Dynamics with the Wright-Fisher Model

All the creatures gathered around the rat to hear his tale of adventure. Alice having seen it all by now was happy to just sit down and listen.

"There were thousands of us to begin with," Rat began, sagely. "We all believed we would get to the other side of the river. Some just couldn't swim that well, but even really good swimmers just got caught by really strong currents. It was horrible." Rat paused briefly and then brightened, "but at least a few hundred of us survived."

Just then the Dodo spoke up. "Yes it happened to me too. I'm the last one of my kind." The rest of the circle fell quiet and looked down at their feet, paws, or pincers.

Alice was anxious to break the heavy mood, "How about that Tea Party!" she exclaimed.

numpy.random library, `binomial()`

Population genetics, evolutionary biology, Hardy-Weinberg equilibrium, allele frequency, fixation, genetic drift, natural selection, heterozygote advantage, sickle cell anemia

A. Lancaster and G. Webster, *Python for the Life Sciences*, https://doi.org/10.1007/978-1-4842-4523-1_19

In this final chapter we move our Python lens from modeling *ecological dynamics* to modeling *evolution*. Various scientists will quibble about how to exactly define evolution, but most agree that evolution at its heart is **a change in allele frequencies over time**. And the primary theory that undergirds these changes is population genetics.

Population genetics has a long and storied history (see Provine (2001)), and it predates many of the mechanistic biological life sciences such as molecular biology. The backbones of the discipline were laid down back in the 1930s by a number of luminaries of the era. Two names in particular stand out: English statistician Sir Ronald Fisher and American mathematician Sewall Wright. The theories they built were, for many years, like beautiful engines: glistening chrome cylinders and carburetors of abstruse mathematics, but with little fuel (i.e., data) to make them truly sing. The gargantuan amounts of data generated from sequencing projects such as human genome project have completely changed that and made population genetics even more relevant than ever.

Luckily for you, though, the basics of population genetics are easily accessible with only a modicum of mathematics. With just a small amount of Python, you can start building your own explorations of evolution by looking at two fundamental mechanisms: **genetic drift** and **natural selection**. We will start our explorations by building a simple version of the model that bears their name: the Wright-Fisher model, and, as in previous chapters, we use a simulation-based approach.

So let's imagine that we have finite population containing individuals that have either one variant of gene (called on allele), call it allele A, or another, call it allele B. At any time t, therefore the entire population is defined by just *two* numbers: the number of alleles of A (call it n_A) and of B (call it n_B). To store the *results* of the simulation that runs for generations, we create a two-dimensional matrix that stores **generations rows** and uses *two* **columns** (one for each of the alleles) in Listing 19-1.

Listing 19-1. Creating two-dimensional matrix for storing allele counts

```
from numpy import zeros
num_alleles = [10, 10]
twoN = sum(num_alleles)
allele_counts = zeros((generations + 1, 2))
allele_counts[0, :] = num_alleles
```

Let's unpack this:

1. We first calculate the total population size, 2N, which is always the number of alleles of each type defined as Python array of just two numbers: $[n_A \; n_B]$ (in Listing 19-1 we set these to 10 and 10). We then sum() all the elements in the array (just two in this case) and return a single number: $2N = n_A + n_B$.

2. We then initialize the NumPy array of zeros where the *first column* (index 0) stores n_A and the *second column* (index 1) stores n_B. This is similar to how we stored values in the two-dimensional cellular automata in Chapter 16.

3. Lastly we initialize the generation zero (t=0) to the initial number of alleles using the slice ":" operator to initialize that first row using the $[n_A, n_B]$ as a column.

(Technically we only need to store *one* number, because the population remains constant size (2N), we could always compute the number of alleles of B, from the number of alleles of A and vice versa: using the formula $2N = n_A + n_B$, but it is useful for later plotting purposes to store *both* numbers simultaneously.)

Get my (Genetic) Drift?

Now, let's try and figure out the number of alleles of each kind at the next generation, t+1. How do we do this? Conceptually what we are simulating is the process of the alleles **randomly mating** with each other in the population and generating the *next generation* of offspring. We can think of this as putting all the 2N individuals into a bag, letting them mate and reproduce and then pulling out the same original number of individuals (because the population remains constant) to get the number of alleles of each type in the *next generation* of the population.

Now if only there was a piece of mathematics that could do that for us. Hmm. Luckily there is, it is the binomial distribution. The *probability* that there will be exactly k A alleles after 2N draws from the bag *given* the current frequency of the A allele ($f_A = n_A/2N$) is $p(k)$, is given by Figure 19-1.

$$p(k) = \frac{(2N)!}{k!(2N-k)!} f_A{}^k f_B{}^{2N-k}$$

Figure 19-1. *Equations for binomial distribution*

That looks kind of messy, luckily the **NumPy** package again comes to the rescue here, it has a nice built-in function: `binomial()`[1] which *returns* a new number of A alleles, k, from the preceding probability distribution given 2N draws. Therefore, we give the function just two parameters: the original frequency A allele (f_A) and the number of "draws" from the bag, in this case, 2N, and the function will *return* the new number of counts of A. So let's take look at the code in Listing 19-2 (which continues from Listing 19-1).

Listing 19-2. Calculating the new allele counts assuming genetic drift

```
from numpy.random binomial
f_A = allele_counts[t,0] / twoN  # current frequency of A
f_B = (twoN - allele_counts[t,0]) / twoN # current frequency of A
allele_counts[t+1,0] = binomial(twoN, f_A) # new A allele count
allele_counts[t+1,1] = twoN - allele_counts[t+1,0] # new B allele count
```

The code first calculates the frequency of the A allele and then the frequency of the B allele (note that we can always calculate f_B from f_A because the total of the frequencies must always sum to one, i.e., $f_A + f_B = 1$). The next thing it does is get the new counts, by using the NumPy binomial formula to get the allele count for A, and then calculate the new allele count for B (again n_B is always $2N - n_A$).

And that's the heart of it! We have successfully implemented one generation of genetic drift in Python! To calculate this over **multiple generations**, we simply use the old generation counts (at time t) to calculate the new generation (at time t+1) by creating a loop and wrapping the whole thing in a function for good measure as in Listing 19-3.

Listing 19-3. Function for simulating population over a specified number of generations

```
def simulate_population(generations, num_alleles):
  twoN = sum(num_alleles)
  allele_counts = zeros((generations + 1, 2)) # create array
```

---

[1]http://docs.scipy.org/doc/numpy/reference/generated/numpy.random.binomial.html

```
allele_counts[0, :] = num_alleles                # initialize t=0
for t in range(generations):
  f_A = allele_counts[t,0] / twoN # current frequency of A
  f_B = (twoN - allele_counts[t,0]) / twoN # current frequency of A
  allele_counts[t+1,0] = binomial(twoN, f_A) # new A count
  allele_counts[t+1,1] = twoN - allele_counts[t+1,0] # new B count
  print(allele_counts[t+1, 0], allele_counts[t+1,1])
return allele_counts
```

We have a complete self-contained function that given just two numbers (allele counts of *A* and *B*) will calculate the number of alleles for up to *t*=generations. Woo-hoo! As in previous chapters, the function range generates the list of time integer points for which we will run the simulation forward in time. We show the code in Listing 19-4 for the main program that runs evolution for just three generations with an initial setup of 10 *A* and 10 *B* alleles (Listings 19-1 through 19-3 need to be executed first).

Listing 19-4. Main program for simulating evolution for three generations

```
if __name__ == "__main__":
  generations = 3 # generations
  num_alleles = [10, 10] # initial number of alleles [A, B]
  print(num_alleles[0], num_alleles[1]) # print first generation
  allele_counts = simulate_population(generations, num_alleles)
```

The output should look something like this:

10 10
8.0 12.0
8.0 12.0
5.0 15.0

but *not exactly*, because the binomial function draws ***at random***, so your numbers will likely look a bit different, but if you run the function several times, you'll begin to see how they vary. We are now ready to see ***evolution in action***: a change in ***allele frequencies via genetic drift***! Let's use our old friend, matplotlib, to plot the output.

Plotting Genetic Drift

To start out, we set up drawing a simple time plot for our allele count data. Using matplotlib should be second nature by now, so we dive straight into the code setting up the ranges to plot and the labels:

```
fig1 = plt.figure()
plt.xlim(0, generations)
plt.ylim(0, twoN)
plt.xlabel('time')
plt.ylabel('allele count')
```

Plotting should be easy, for the *y* axis we've already stored our data in nice NumPy arrays; we can simply pass this to the main `plot()` command as we did in previous chapters. Note that we use `[:,0]` and `[:,1]` (see the NumPy documentation for more information on advanced indexing[2]) to pass all the rows that are in column 0 or 1 of the original array, respectively. Also as in the previous chapters, we create a `time_points` list using the `range` and the `list` commands to create the legend and draw the plot:

```
time_points = list(range(generations + 1))
plt.plot(time_points, allele_counts[:,0], label="A") # print A count
plt.plot(time_points, allele_counts[:,1], label="B") # print B count
plt.legend()
plt.draw()
```

We use `draw()` not immediately followed by `show()`, because `show()` will cause the code to stop at that point and the user will have to close the figure before continuing. As we saw in Chapter 16 on Turing patterns, `draw()` gets around this by preparing the figures in the background and allowing execution to continue. We can then wait until we're ready to display all the graphics before issuing the `show()` command. Let's again wrap this all up in a function that can be easily reused for different kinds of plots in Listing 19-5.

---

[2]http://docs.scipy.org/doc/numpy/reference/arrays.indexing.html

Listing 19-5. Function to plot allele counts over specified number of generations

```python
def plot_population(allele_counts, generations):
    twoN = sum(num_alleles)    # total number of alleles (2N)
    fig1 = plt.figure()
    plt.xlim(0, generations)
    plt.ylim(0, twoN)
    plt.xlabel('time')
    plt.ylabel('allele count')
    time_points = list(range(generations + 1))
    plt.plot(time_points, allele_counts[:,0], label="A") # allele A
    plt.plot(time_points, allele_counts[:,1], label="B") # allele B
    plt.legend()
    plt.draw()
    return
```

Putting these two functions together, we can now do the simulation and generate the plot in the main program in Listing 19-6, but let's run for a bit longer this time, say 30 generations. Note the final plt.show() that actually displays the graphs.

Listing 19-6. Simulating evolution for 30 generations

```python
if __name__ == "__main__":
    generations = 30           # generations
    num_alleles = [10, 10]    # initial number of alleles [A, B]
    print(num_alleles[0], num_alleles[1])
    allele_counts = simulate_population(generations, num_alleles)
    plot_population(allele_counts, generations)
    plt.show()
```

Running the preceding programs, you should now be able to generate a plot that looks something like Figure 19-2.

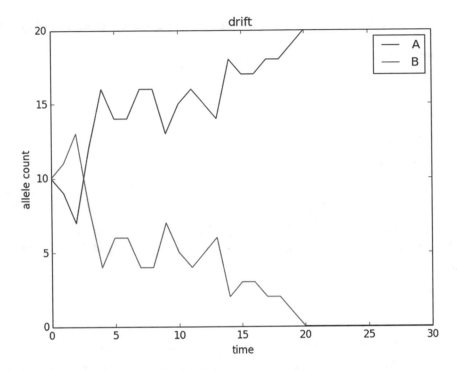

Figure 19-2. *Simulating genetic drift for 30 generations*

You can now really go to town with exploring the evolutionary simulation. Try increasing the number of generations and see how long the population can go before one of the alleles ends up dominating the population. This is the point where we say the allele has "***gone to fixation,***" meaning without any other changes, such as a new **mutation**, the population is now fixed for that particular allele (whether *A* or *B*). Try running the simulation many times and count the number of times the *A* allele goes to fixation. Noticing a pattern?

You should see that any given allele goes to fixation in about 50% of the cases. This can be understood from the original mathematical solutions, which says that the probability of fixation of a given allele is equal to its original frequency in the population, which in our case is $f_A = n_A/2N = 10 / 20 = 0.5$. But having run the simulations, you should now have an even more intuitive feeling for how this works in the real world where any given individual population may fix for either of the two alleles. But here you can, to use the late great evolutionary biologist's Stephen Jay Gould metaphor, "replay life's tape" many times and start seeing this overall statistical pattern emerge from each of the individual special cases, and Python provides you the tools!

Adding Natural Selection to the Mix

But populations don't always just "drift" around like this. Sometimes a particular combination of alleles will be more favored than others. We can easily extend the existing Wright-Fisher code by just *"dropping in"* a selection function to capture the fact that sometimes some **genotypes** have a relative advantage over than others.

We'll pause here for a quick detour into some very basic genetics, feel free to skip ahead if talk of alleles and genotypes starts sending you to sleep. Most of you will remember that diploid organisms (such as humans) have two copies of any given gene (one on each chromosome). Any given gene (or **locus**) consists of two alleles, one from each chromosome; the particular combination of alleles is called the **genotype** of that locus. In the case we're describing here, the two possible alleles A and B can be arranged in one of four possible genotypes:

AA AB BA BB

$f_{AA} + f_{AB} + f_{BA} + f_{BB} = 1$

AA and BB are the two **homozygous** genotypes, where AB and BA are the **heterozygous** genotypes (since AB and BA are normally functionally indistinguishable, we normally abbreviate this to just AB, but note that the fact that there are two ways to get the AB heterozygote will become important later!) As shown in the preceding equation, each of these genotypes also has a corresponding **genotype frequency** in the population (note that like allele frequencies, these always *sum to one!*).

OK, so all well and good, so how do we go from the allele frequencies f_A and f_B to the frequencies of the genotype in the population? Here we can turn to another important principle of population genetics, the **Hardy-Weinberg principle**. You can look up the Wikipedia article for a detailed explanation, but the intuitive idea is that the frequency of genotypes in randomly mating population is just proportional to the *product* of the frequency of the alleles that make up those genotypes. This leads to the following for the genotype frequencies:

$f_{AA} = f_A \times f_A = f_A^2$

$f_{AB} = f_A \times f_B + f_B \times f_A = 2f_A f_B$

$f_{BB} = f_B \times f_B = f_B^2$

(Note that there are *two* ways of getting the *AB* genotype, so we sum the product of the frequencies of *AB* and *BA*.) Here's a snippet of Python code (note that we use the built-in x**y power operator[3] which is Python's version of the superscript x^y):

```
# calculate current genotype frequencies from the allele frequencies
f_AA = f_A**2
f_AB = 2 * f_A * f_B
f_BB = f_B**2
```

Because selection operates at the level of the genotype, calculating the proportion of genotypes in the *current* generation, *t*, of the population is the first step to calculate the proportion of the genotypes in the *next* generation, *t*+1. We can represent the *strength* of selection on each of the three possible genotypes by using three different weights: w_{AA}, w_{AB}, and w_{BB}. These are just *relative weights*, so they could be anything, but by convention they are typically all numbers between 0 and 1. For example, when $w_{AA} = w_{AB} = w_{BB}$, it means that all genotypes are equally advantageous (or disadvantageous) and is equivalent to saying that there is no selection acting on the population.

To get to the next generation, we just apply these weights to the existing genotype frequencies to get the new *absolute fitnesses (note these do not sum to one!)*:

```
g_AA = f_AA * w_AA
g_AB = f_AB * w_AB
g_BB = f_BB * w_BB
```

We aren't yet done, because these new numbers are not yet true genotype frequencies in the population. We need to *normalize* these frequencies by the *mean fitness of the population*, by convention known as w (put bar mark here), which is simply the sum of the absolute fitnesses:

```
w_bar = g_AA +  g_AB  + g_BB
```

Then divide the fitnesses to get the *new* genotype frequencies (they *do* sum to one!)

```
f_AA = g_AA / w_bar
f_AB = g_AB / w_bar
f_BB = g_BB / w_bar
```

---

[3]https://docs.python.org/2/reference/expressions.html#the-power-operator

Almost done! Lastly to get back to the allele frequencies (which we need for the drift step), we notice that each AB genotype contains one A allele, so we add *half* the frequency of the AB genotype (f_{AB}) to the frequency of the AA genotype (f_{AA}). This gives us back the allele A frequency (f_A). From here it's simple to calculate the frequency of the B allele, as $1 - f_B$. In Python:

```
f_A = f_AA + f_AB/2
f_B = 1 - f_A
```

So let's put it all together in a function in Listing 19-7 that takes as input allele frequencies at generation t and returns new allele frequencies for the next generation $t+1$.

Listing 19-7. Function to perform selection on input allele frequencies

```
def do_selection(f_A, f_B):
  # calculate current genotype frequencies from allele frequencies
  f_AA = f_A**2
  f_AB = 2 * f_A * f_B
  f_BB = f_B**2

  # now apply selection to get absolute fitnesses of genotypes
  # note these DO NOT sum to 1!
  g_AA = f_AA * w_AA
  g_AB = f_AB * w_AB
  g_BB = f_BB * w_BB

  # calculate the mean fitness, the weighted sum of the above
  w_bar = g_AA +  g_AB  + g_BB

  # now use mean fitness to get *new* genotype frequencies
  # note that these DO sum to 1!
  f_AA = g_AA / w_bar
  f_AB = g_AB / w_bar
  f_BB = g_BB / w_bar

  # get find new frequency of A:
  # AA genotype + half of all AB genotypes contain A
  # so add them together:
  f_A = f_AA + f_AB/2
```

```
# frequency of B is just 1 - frequency of A
# frequencies must sum to 1!
f_B = 1 - f_A

return f_A, f_B
```

We can now drop this do_selection function into our original simulate_population in Listing 19-8, placing it just *after* computing the allele frequencies from the current allele count, but *before* simulating the random mating and drift using the binomial draw. You can see how nice this is conceptually: selection is just a step where the allele frequencies are *transformed* into a *new* set of allele frequencies. We also use this opportunity to add a new keyword argument selection (set to False by default) so that we can selectively "toggle" selection on and off.

Listing 19-8. New simulation function with optional selection (keyword argument)

```
def simulate_population(generations, num_alleles, selection=False):
  twoN = sum(num_alleles)
  allele_counts = zeros((generations + 1, 2)) # create array
  allele_counts[0, :] = num_alleles # initialize t=0
  for t in range(generations):
    f_A = allele_counts[t,0] / twoN # current frequency of A
    f_B = (twoN - allele_counts[t,0]) / twoN # current frequency of A
    if selection:
      f_A, f_B = do_selection(f_A, f_B)
    allele_counts[t+1,0] = binomial(twoN, f_A) # new A count
    allele_counts[t+1,1] = twoN - allele_counts[t+1,0] # new B count
    print(allele_counts[t+1, 0], allele_counts[t+1,1])
  return allele_counts
```

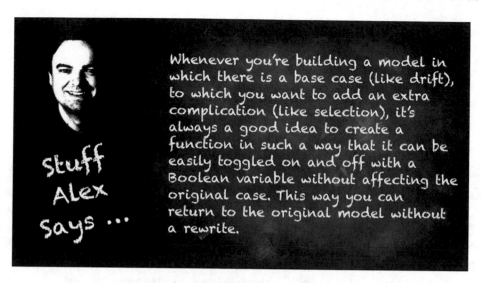

Whenever you're building a model in which there is a base case (like drift), to which you want to add an extra complication (like selection), it's always a good idea to create a function in such a way that it can be easily toggled on and off with a Boolean variable without affecting the original case. This way you can return to the original model without a rewrite.

So let's imagine a real-world example where selection is known to act and start seeing if we can simulate the effects using our Python code. One of the more interesting cases is where the heterozygote (*AB*) is fitter than each of the homozygotes (*AA* and *BB*). This is known as **heterozygote advantage**, or **overdominance**. One of the best documented cases of heterozygote advantage is that in areas with persistent outbreaks of malaria, those with just one copy of the recessive allele for sickle cell anemia have a fitness advantage over those with either *two* copies of the allele (recessive homozygote: in our nomenclature, *AB*), or those *neither* (homozygous for the dominant allele: *AA*). This is because the recessive homozygote is almost uniformly deleterious (leading to the sickle cell disease), but the dominant homozygous (AA) lacks the resistance to malaria that individuals containing just one copy of the sickle cell allele (B) have.

In a finite population being subjected to heterozygote advantage, over time the population keeps a higher degree of diversity (often referred to as **polymorphism**) by keeping both copies of an allele around for longer than in a population that is only subject to genetic drift (where an allele can be more easily lost). We can qualitatively observe this in our model by setting the fitness weights, adding in selection, and then running for 10 generations with the code in Listing 19-9 (depends on first running the code for the functions in Listings 19-7 and 19-8).

Listing 19-9. Simulating heterozygote advantage for 10 generations

```
w_AA = 0.33
w_AB = 0.95
w_BB = 0.33
if __name__ == "__main__":
  generations = 10        # generations
  num_alleles = [10, 10]  # initial number of alleles [A, B]
  print(num_alleles[0], num_alleles[1])

  # drift + selection
  allele_counts = simulate_population(generations, num_alleles,
  selection=True)
  plot_population(allele_counts, generations, selection=True)
  plt.show()
```

Now take a look at the output in Figure 19-3.

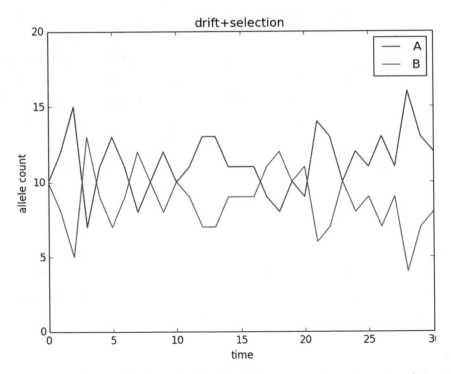

Figure 19-3. *Simulating drift and selection (heterozygote advantage) for 30 generations*

If you run this model a few times, you'll also start to see a pattern: that the number of alleles of each type of *A* or *B* will be retained longer in the population. Heterozygote advantage indeed. Congratulations, in this final chapter you have begun to start on the pathway toward exploring the longest timescale of all in biology: evolution. We are a long way from where we started on three-dimensional protein structures that change on a nanosecond timescale, way back in the early chapters. Yet all these biological timescales are available for you to explore via Python.

References and Further Exploration

- simuPop[4]: Python-based scripting environment for doing forward-in-time population genetics simulations

- popRange[5]: although it's in R, this is an interesting package for population genetics simulations (it has a package on CRAN[6])

- **PyPop**[7]: a Python-based population genetics framework that analyzes genotype data for, among other things, deviation from Hardy-Weinberg equilibrium developed by one of the authors (AKL)

- Stephen Jay Gould, *Wonderful Life: the Burgess Shale and the nature of history* (WW Norton & Company, 1990)

- William Provine, *The Origins of Theoretical Population Genetics*[8] (University of Chicago Press, 2001)

---

[4]http://simupop.sourceforge.net
[5]www.ncbi.nlm.nih.gov/pmc/articles/PMC4399400/
[6]https://cran.r-project.org/web/packages/popRange/index.html
[7]http://pypop.org/
[8]http://press.uchicago.edu/ucp/books/book/chicago/O/bo3618372.html

Epilogue

Because Breaking Up is Hard to DO

And as quickly as they had appeared, the strange effects of drinking from the small bottle faded and Alice found herself once more standing at the little table at which she had originally taken the drink, with the now empty bottle still in her hand.

"Wow!" she said. "That was quite a trip. Where am I?"

"You're in the epilogue," said a mysterious, disembodied voice.

"What's an epilogue?" asked Alice, still a little groggy from her experience.

"It's like the concluding chapter of a book," said the voice. "Everybody takes stock of where they are, talks about what they learned, and generally gets all gushy and emotional about 'the journey being over' and stuff like that."

"Sounds a lot like daytime TV," quipped Alice.

© Alexander Lancaster and Gordon Webster 2019
A. Lancaster and G. Webster, *Python for the Life Sciences*, https://doi.org/10.1007/978-1-4842-4523-1

Where to Go From Here

Well gentle reader, we have come to the end of our book, and this is the point at which we're probably supposed to say something like "This is not an end, but just the beginning...," or "We hope you have enjoyed reading this book as much as we enjoyed writing it...," etc. etc. But since you've probably got a million-and-one things waiting to be done in the lab, we'll try to keep it brief (and not too gushy).

Beyond this book, there is a wealth of fantastic resources for anybody wanting to learn or improve their Python skills, thanks in no small part to the large and enthusiastic community of programmers that has nucleated around the success of the Python language in many fields. One valuable human resource that we highly recommend is your local Python meetup group. We are fortunate enough to live in the metropolitan area of Boston, USA, which has one of the largest Python meetup groups in the country. Chances are, if you live in or near a city of any size, there's a Python meetup group near you.

The formats for these groups undoubtedly vary somewhat from place to place, but if you join your local group (and it's free), you'll be able to enjoy a mix of lectures, seminars, code workshops, and even social activities with other Pythonistas, as well as having access to a pool of experienced Pythonistas who can provide expertise to help you out with your own projects. So do yourself a real favor find your local Python meetup group, and sign up!

Every year, there's also PyCon,[1] a huge gathering of Pythonistas from all over, who get together to talk not only about the Python language and its future but also to showcase all of the incredibly cool stuff that people are doing with Python. The Python community, like the language itself, is all about connection, collaboration, and sharing, so these kinds of community events are really a big deal in Python land.

How You the Reader can Help us

We have worked hard to make this book as good as we can – even a book that we ourselves would want to have read when we were starting out learning Python. We are aware however that no amount of work can guarantee that this book does not contain errors or omissions both in the text and in the Python code that it contains. In fact, we are pretty certain that you, our readers, will find plenty of flaws in this book once you

---

[1]`https://us.pycon.org/`

start using it. With this in mind, we would be grateful to get your feedback on the book – good or bad – just so long as it's constructive. If you do notice an error or omission in the book, please let us know via e-mail at

info@amberbiology.com

We can then incorporate the fixes into the next edition. For obvious reasons, any updates to printed versions of the book will take a little while (it's hard to find good scribes these days and there's no expedited delivery on those goose feather quills). From time to time, we also post updates related to the book at the book's very own web site:

http://pythonforthelifesciences.com

Consulting and Teaching

We couldn't really finish this book without giving ourselves a modest plug. We are both partners at our digital biology research firm Amber Biology,[2] based in Cambridge, Massachusetts. Working at the intersection of biology and computer science, we provide specialized skills and expertise in support of life science R&D and life science software and product development. Python turns out to be our weapon of choice for the great majority of the client projects that we take on, and in addition to the software development component, most of our projects have a strong life science research flavor. We are both trained scientists with years of collective experience solving real-world research problems both in industry and in academia, so we are just as comfortable wearing our scientific researcher hats as we are wearing our coder and software developer hats.

---
[2]www.amberbiology.com/

In addition to our consulting work, we provide Python training to organizations, groups, and individuals that need it, again – with an emphasis on the life sciences. If you would like us to import any of the material from this book into a classroom setting for your group or organization, please contact us at info@amberbiology.com or visit our web site http://amberbiology.com and we would be happy to tailor a Python and/or biocomputing training program to suit your needs.

And One Last Thing…

We felt that this book needed a little something at the very end to tie it all together nicely, and there's nothing that ties a room together so well as a good rug,[3] so we thought that it just might work for a book as well – so here you go. :-)

Our very best wishes to you all.

---

[3]http://thebiglebowski.wikia.com/wiki/The_Rug

Index

A

Agent-based model (ABM), 330
    behaviors, 331, 332
    state, 331
Alignment, 123, 125
Allele frequency, 346, 347, 355
Append method, 333
apt, 6, *See also* Debian
Arduino, 206
argparse library
    ArgumentParser(), 136
    arguments, 138
    option-style arguments, 136
    parse_args, 138
    positional arguments, 136
Arithmetic operators, 24
Arrays, *see* NumPy
"as" keyword, 202, *See also* import
    statement
Avogadro's constant, 218

B

BAI (BAM index) file, 126
BAM (Binary Alignment/Map) file
    indexing, 126
    SAM to BAM, conversion, 126
    sorting, 126
Bayesian biomarker function, 56–58
Bayesian function

return statement, 58
    string formatting within function, 59, 60
Bayes' theorem, 52
    biomarker, 53
    CA-125 biomarker, 55
    equations, 56
    hypothetical disease, 55
Bayes, Thomas, 52
Binomial distribution, equation for, 348
Biochemistry, 21, 278
Biological kinetics, 230
    chemical reactants, 275
    cooperative binding, 236
    dissociation constant, 231
    rate calculation, 268
Biopython package, 70
Bond rotation, 213, *See also* 3D molecular
    structures
Boolean type, 36
    false, 36
    true, 36
bowtie algorithm, 125, 145
Built-in values, 36, 65
bwa algorithm, 125, 140
Bytecodes, 85

C

CamelCase, 99
Carrying capacity, 318
Casting, 65

A. Lancaster and G. Webster, *Python for the Life Sciences*, https://doi.org/10.1007/978-1-4842-4523-1

H

I

J

K

L

M

Printed in the United States
By Bookmasters